YO-DLG-868

THE MIDDLE EAST REMEMBERED

THE MIDDLE EAST REMEMBERED

JOHN S. BADEAU

WASHINGTON, D.C.

1983

THE MIDDLE EAST INSTITUTE

Copyright © 1983. The Middle East Institute.
All rights reserved.
Library of Congress Catalog Card Number 83-61202
ISBN 0-916808-21-1

Designed by Maria Josephy Schoolman
Manufactured in the United States of America

PREFACE

This is a very personal memoir. It is taken from an oral history which was recorded by Dr. Leon Carl Brown of Princeton University in 1978 and early 1979. The tapes were then transcribed at Columbia University and this transcription is the basis of the present volume. Colleagues at Columbia, Georgetown University, the Near East Foundation and the Middle East Institute, together with some of Dr. Badeau's former students, raised the funds for this work.

Editing of this transcription was done by William Sands, the former editor of *The Middle East Journal*, Jeanne Badeau Barnett, Patricia Dockham, John Dockham, and members of the Middle East Institute's Department of Publications. The footnotes throughout are ours, not Ambassador Badeau's.

Like most such narratives based on personal recollections (over a period of 75 years in this case) this is a collection of illuminating observations, anecdotes and reflections, picking out those events which seem particularly relevant in perspective. It is not a day-to-day, comprehensive account. It is a broad sweep of the brush, touching here and there, covering some things in considerable depth, and leaving others unmarked. As such, it is pleasurable reading. Those who know Ambassador Badeau's incisive wit and skill as a raconteur will find them reflected fully here. They will also find his views instructive and thought-provoking, covering as they do a period during which the American role in the Middle East changed from one of passive spectator to major actor. John Badeau was a distinguished player in this drama, and he had an unusually close association with the events of the period.

—Richard B. Parker
Director of Publications

JOHN S. BADEAU

PARTICULARS

Born February 24, 1903, Pittsburgh, Pennsylvania, to Mary Lyle and Charles Stothoff Badeau

B.S. Union College, 1924, Schenectady, New York

Married 1924, Margaret Louise Hathaway, Schenectady, New York

B.D. New Brunswick Seminary, 1928, New Brunswick, New Jersey

Missionary 1928-1935, Iraq, United Mission in Mesopotamia, Reformed Church in America. Mosul, 1928-1930. Baghdad, 1930-1935

S.T.M. Union Theological Seminary, 1936, New York, New York

Educator, American University in Cairo, Egypt
    Associate Professor of Religion and Philosophy, 1936-1938
    Dean, Faculty of Arts and Sciences, 1938-1944
    President, 1945-1953

Regional Specialist, Middle East, Office of War Information, 1943-1945, Washington, D.C.

President, Near East Foundation, 1953-1961, New York, New York

Ambassador, 1961-1964, Cairo, Egypt

Educator, Columbia University, 1964-1971, New York, New York
  Director, Middle East Institute
  Professor, Middle East Studies
  Professor Emeritus, 1971-

Professorial Lecturer, Georgetown University, 1971-1974, Washington, D.C.

Children: Jeanne Hathaway, born Iraq, 1930
  Roger Carroll, born Lebanon, 1934
  Peter Weekes, born Egypt, 1938

Publications:
East and West of Suez, Foreign Policy Association Headline Book, 1943
The Emergence of Modern Egypt, FPA, 1953
The Lands Between, Friendship Press, 1958
Bread from Stones, Prentiss Hall, 1966
The American Approach to the Middle East, Council on Foreign Relations, Harper & Row, 1968
Genius of Arab Civilization, New York University Press, 1975, introduction "The Arab Role in Islamic Culture"
Numerous articles

CONTENTS

FOREWORD		1
Chapter 1	The Prelude	5
Chapter 2	Meeting the Middle East in Iraq	13
Chapter 3	Decision in Baghdad	39
Chapter 4	Cairo Before the War	49
Chapter 5	Egyptian Friends and Associates	85
Chapter 6	Egypt After the War	101
Chapter 7	The Egyptian Revolution	131
Chapter 8	New Horizons: The Near East Foundation	147
Chapter 9	Returning to Egypt Under Kennedy	171
Chapter 10	The Yemen Adventure	201
Chapter 11	Leadership Under the Egyptian Revolution	217
Chapter 12	Postscript in America	247
Index		261

FOREWORD

To succeed John Badeau in anything requires more courage than one should have to muster in a lifetime. To succeed him on his own ground where you were an utter stranger required not only courage but a degree of foolhardiness. Nevertheless, I succeeded John Badeau as Ambassador to Egypt in 1964 and came very quickly to recognize that he had been and would continue to be one of the great Middle East students of our time. While my own involvement with Egypt had been very superficial prior to my assignment there, his had been in depth. He had been President of the American University in Cairo for many years. He was fluent in Arabic. He had written and lectured widely on deep subjects of interest to Egyptians and Americans. He had painted the Egyptian scene in charming oils, was known by every *bawwab* and *suffragi* in town, as well as every dealer in antiquities.

I remembered well how he was selected to be Ambassador to Egypt. Chester Bowles in the beginning of the Kennedy administration was responsible for lining up for presidential approval a list of ambassadorial candidates. Although he made wide use of the career service, Mr. Bowles made some extremely imaginative appointments to ambassadorial and other foreign affairs assignments which brought a special kind of flair to American representation in numerous capitals and posts. I have in mind such appointments as Edwin Reischauer to Japan and Edward R. Murrow to USIA. John

Badeau was one of these.

Chester Bowles, with whom I was regularly in touch at this time, sought out individuals who had a special tie and relationship to a specific country. It was Chet himself who thought of John Badeau, at that time unknown to me. From the beginning I considered it a brilliant stroke. John, who had left AUC and was President of the Near East Foundation, returned to Cairo with pleasure and served there brilliantly for three years.

John was a most effective Ambassador, bringing a kind of educational and cultural proficiency that made him an ideal choice for the period of his service. In some ways it was a difficult period; in others it was not. A new effort was underway by President Kennedy to maintain a meaningful dialogue with President Nasser. Aid to Egypt reached new heights. Many serious problems were postponed or "put in the icebox" to use the popular phrase of the day—including the Arab-Israeli issue. Perhaps John Badeau kept some of the built-in strains between the United States and Egypt from showing or bursting out at the seams. Many came popping out later during my period of service.

After his tour of diplomatic service, John Badeau resumed his profession as teacher and taught a whole generation of students what life was like in Egypt under Nasser and what Nasser's regime and revolution had done to that country just then emerging as a major political force in the world. His course at Georgetown, entitled "Egypt under Nasser," became one of the most famous courses in American Middle East studies. This book, as did that course, will provide an opportunity for students of the scene to learn from the master. It is a valuable book and an account of a valuable life spent in scholarship, learning, diplomacy.

It is a cliché of corporate hierarchical life that one always dislikes his predecessor, particularly if he was a hard act to follow. But in the case of John Badeau I have no feeling but gratitude for having known him, and pleasure in his company, a guiding light to be followed. I am privileged to have known him, and to have attempted to replace him. I will continue my association through this volume.

—Lucius D. Battle

CHAPTER 1

THE PRELUDE

The Egyptians have a folk saying, *"Rabbuna byidabbir,"* which means "The Lord has a way of doing it," or *"Allah yudabbir,"* "God has a plan for it." As a good Calvinist and therefore a predestinarian, I should really say, first of all, *Allah yudabbir*. It has been a very strange thing in my life. Throughout, doors have somehow opened to me when I have needed them, and I am never quite sure who put the key in the lock. I do not know.

* * *

I was brought up in New Brunswick, although I was not born there. My mother had come from an old New Jersey family, with a farm near Middlebush. When I was a boy, my father died, Mother brought us home and we settled in New Brunswick.

I went to New Brunswick High School, then went away to Union College in Schenectady to become a civil engineer. All my brothers are engineers, and my father and all his brothers were engineers. The profession was thoroughly in the family blood, and at Union I took civil engineering.

In the midst of the course, however, I became interested in the possibilities of going abroad in missionary service under the auspices of the Dutch Reformed Church, to which I belonged. As I look back, I think there really were two reasons for what was a very drastic change of outlook. One was the fact that I was brought up in a religious home—what I would call a good, normal, religious home. When my grandfather said grace, God sat next to him at the table and they talked to each other—that kind of religious piety. When I got away from home, I think I passed into the period when I appropriated for myself this particular heritage that had come down to me. And it was a very liberal one indeed.

The second reason was that while I was interested in engineering—and indeed have continued to be, doing quite a good deal of building, design and construction in the Middle East—I came to the conviction in college that I did not want to invest my life primarily in dealing with things, big buildings, objects.

All this was just after World War I. There was idealism in the air; we had fought the war to make the world safe for democracy. I was a boy in New Brunswick High School when Armistice Day occurred, and this idealism translated itself for me into the feeling that I wanted to put my life into something other than mechanical construction. In those days there was really very little one could do with a humanitarian sense outside the church. So these things together, as well as the fact that a group of young associates at Union College, some of whom had quite brilliant careers later, were all interested in the same sort of life, shifted me from a desire to be an engineer to a desire to give service in this kind of humanitarian and religious endeavor.

I went to Union College in Schenectady partly because I didn't want to go to Rutgers—Rutgers being the old home-town school—and partly because my father as a young man had been an engineer in the General Electric Company at Schenectady. When he and my mother were first married, this is where they originally settled. And the connection of Union College with that past suggested itself to me.

Moreover, my father had an associate whom I never knew very well, a Mr. Smith, and through circumstances that I am unaware of, Smith felt that somehow he was beholden to my father—I think it had something to do with a business deal. When I got ready for college, he wrote to my mother—we were not in affluent circumstances—suggesting that he would be willing to be of some assistance in my college education; he proposed Union College since he was living in central New York State. Those circumstances brought me to Union.

I did not really know very much about the college. Of course, Union was well known as a college training for electrical engineering, because of its relationship with General Electric, and at that time I had set electrical engineering as my goal. However, I had only been in college about a year when I shifted from electrical to civil engineering. Somehow, electrical engineering had very little charm for me.

The great Charles P. Steinmetz, the wizard of electricity, was still alive then, and he used to come to Union to lecture to us. After listening to one lecture so erudite it was completely incomprehensible to everybody I decided that it was not electrical engineering that I really wanted to do. So I got into civil engineering, and particularly into the option that was called sanitary engineering—water supply, sewage disposal and such.

My college years were in many ways very uneventful. I had to work, and I did. There were the usual rounds of waiting on table and other jobs, working in the summer at the American Locomotive Works, for instance. I did not join a fraternity. Partly, I did not have the money, and I was not particularly interested. I was active in the debating society. I played football for a while, although not very successfully, and I was quite active in the college, or campus, YMCA, because in those days the student "Y" was quite an institution. Out of that came some of the friendships that turned me toward the Middle East.

There were other engineers that moved the same way. George Carpenter, who graduated a year before me, was a civil engineer, and he went under the Baptist Board to the Congo, spent much of his life there, came back to be General Secretary of the interchurch missionary movement, and was a distinguished linguist and administrator in that field. It was really the association with that group of people that I remember best. Also, I suppose I ought to say that very early on in college I met a girl, and after that I was pretty well occupied.

Union was a small institution. In spite of the fact that General Electric was there, Schenectady was essentially a small town. I was a small-town boy, and I simply did the things that one enjoyed doing, quite different from the more sophisticated things that go on today.

There was then a movement called the Student Volunteer Movement. It was associated with the "Y", with John R. Mott, and represented a student organization interested, in general, in humanitarian work. It was active at Union College, and brought a number of people like the famous missionary to India, Stanley Jones, and John R. Mott himself, to speak at the college. Those were days when there still was a response to a liberal, religious movement on the campus, and I was greatly involved in it.

In broader and later retrospect, one has to say that essentially I came to the conclusion that my real interest was dealing with people. If I were to counsel a young man now about a career, I would say, decide first what you want to deal with. If you want to deal with things, be an engineer or a scientist. If you want to deal fundamentally with ideas, be a scholar. If you want to deal with people, then become an administrator, or join one of those professions, now called the social sciences, which bring you into certain kinds of interested, humanitarian work.

I think that all of my interests in the Middle East and in education have, in the end, involved a very strong interest in people as such. I suppose it was perhaps the unconscious discovery of that as being the most satisfying focus of what I wanted to do that moved me over. However, I have always been fascinated by engineering; I've always built things; I build now. When I was in Cairo as Ambassador I scandalized the servants by having a workshop down in the basement of the Embassy. When we wanted to have the garden of the Embassy floodlighted, we got in an electrician who did a bad job, so I got a ladder and did it myself, and the next time I went out to see President Nasser, he said, "Is it true that you put up the lights in your own garden?" I was sure some of my servants were in the pay of Egyptian intelligence, and I said, "Yes, Mr. President, it's true, because your men couldn't do it right."

My interest is in dealing with people and the situations that people find themselves in, and a good many of my concerns and interpretations of Middle East events are mediated by the fact that they are of concern to people. They spring from human values, human situations, and not merely a disembodied political process.

At Union, I did not know anything about the Middle East at all; I had never heard of the place. I got shunted over to the Middle East because, coming out of my experience at Union, I decided to enter the ministry. I had grown up, as I said, in New Brunswick. My mother was of Dutch extraction. Her family was Stothoff from the old Stothoff farm, out near Middlebush, and the Dutch church was the church of her family.

What did one do in those days? There was no Peace Corps, and very few other opportunities for what we would now call humanitarian social service. So I decided to enter the ministry. Also, I got married; I was teaching in high school all week away from my girl, who wanted to get married, so we got married. She went to work and I went to work and paid off college debts, and I taught biology for a year at Lindenhurst, Long Island. Then I entered the New Brunswick Theological Seminary, and while I was in the seminary the Church Board came to me and wanted to know if I was interested in going to the Middle East.

The Dutch Reformed Church has a particular history of interest in the Arab world. Dr. Samuel M. Zwemer and Dr. James Cantine had gone out as early missionaries to the Middle East, toward the end of the 19th century. There were stations all down the Persian Gulf, and old Dr. Cornelius Van Dyke had come out of the Dutch Church and was at the American University of Beirut, then the Syrian Protestant College. He was the great translator of the Bible into modern Arabic.

Thus, the Dutch Reformed Church had a long established tradition of interest in the Islamic world. After World I it was beginning a new venture in connection with the Presbyterians and what we used to call the German Reformed Church, made up of

Pennsylvania people, in Iraq, which had emerged as an independent nation after the war. These three denominations were staffing the missions, and the Reformed Church came to me and wanted to know if I would be interested. I knew as little about it as I did about any place else, so I said I was. So, in a sense, it was purely fortuitous that I went to the Middle East. There was no previous knowledge or any great sense of yearning to be there.

This was in the course of my theological training—as a matter of fact, in the second year of my three-year course. I had studied Hebrew, because the Dutch Reformed Church believes that you can't be godly without speaking Hebrew. I remember a history of the Dutch Reformation, written about 1710, that cast great aspersions on the Baptists, because the Baptist ministers of the Reformation knew not their Hebrew.

I did know my Hebrew, and my Hebrew professor knew Arabic, so I started to study Arabic with him, as soon as the church had indicated there might be an opening there. I studied about a year and a half of Arabic at New Brunswick Seminary. My professor knew classical Arabic, but as a matter of fact he knew it only as a cognate language to Hebrew. All that I learned was the structure of the language, for which Hebrew was very useful.

I discovered how little I really had learned when in 1928 we went out to the Middle East by boat. We stopped at Alexandria en route, and while the boat was discharging cargo we went to a hotel on shore. Since I knew Arabic I was going to use it. I went down to the docks, and I found a little Egyptian boy who had a fish on the end of his line. I pointed to it and said in my best classical Hebrew-Arabic, *"Ma ism hadha?"* which I suppose you might roughly translate by saying, "What is the appellation of yonder thing?"

Not colloquial, of course, at all. And he looked at me and shook his head, puzzled, and I repeated it, and he said, "Sir, no English." That sent me back to the drawing board.

So I came out of seminary knowing that I was going to the Middle East. My wife was equally involved in the interest and the decision of what we were going to do. She was a Schenectady girl named Margaret Louise Hathaway. She was not at Union College but studying music at Skidmore. Mine was an old Dutch and

Huguenot family—the Badeaus were Huguenots and the Stothoffs were Dutch—while hers was a very old New England English family, the Hathaways, who had migrated to Schenectady from Massachusetts.

Again the church plays so great a role. I met her at the Second Reformed Church in Schenectady. I went there because the pastor of the church in which I grew up in Highland Park had an uncle who was pastor of the Second Reformed Church in Schenectady. And he said, when you go to Schenectady, go and see my uncle. I did, not knowing that through him I would meet my future wife.

She was at Skidmore, and as I say, I was at Union, and we formed a young people's group. Furthermore, she was friendly with some of the professors' families. One in particular was a professor of civil engineering, and that reinforced the opportunities that threw us together.

I graduated from Union in June 1924 and started teaching in Lindenhurst in September. As I mentioned, the year after I started teaching I left it. I was fortunate in getting to New Brunswick Seminary. It is the oldest seminary of continuous teaching in the United States, going back to the early Dutch settlers, but always very small. In those days, there were seven in my seminary class and about 30 in the seminary. In my second and third years, for instance, we met for our theology seminar around the dining room table of our teacher, which is the way to study theology.

A couple of years before I went to seminary, there had been quite a refreshing introduction of a lot of new blood and better teachers, so that academically it was really much more respectable than formerly. I found those years at seminary a pure delight, because they answered some of the need that had not been met by sines, cosines, trigonometry, and the design of wire and truss bridges. They dealt with other things. I had good teachers, of liberal view, and very intimate associations.

In those days it was still a very traditional curriculum—Hebrew, Greek, and so forth. I had no Greek as an engineer, so I had to go to Rutgers and acquire enough Greek to use the New Testament. This turned out to be a very fortunate turn of events; I often thought of it when I got into educational work later. My

Greek instructor was just a young man—I suppose he was probably an assistant professor, maybe in his late 20's or something like that—but he was a great teacher. Like all beginning Greek students, we read Xenophon's *Anabasis*, and *Katabasis*, and he taught us so well that we would stay in class after the bell rang, to go on and read some more to see what happened. This was good teaching. (To digress a moment, the one thing that seems to be unrecognized in the area of academic preferment is good teaching. Good writing and good research, yes. Good teaching, no.)

I learned Greek and Hebrew, and exegesis, and church history with some good church historians. There had been an attempt to introduce psychology and sociology into religion, but these were very new subjects and not very well taught. They were the weakest part of the program. There was some teaching about the church abroad, but I would say that what I really got out of seminary was the necessary tools of language and of diagnosis and of theology, with which to think my way into my own religious position. But as a preparation for going to a people of another culture and another religion, practically nothing.

Most momentous decisions seem more so in retrospect than they did at the time. I had talked things over carefully with people that I knew in the Reformed Church, especially the Secretary of the Board, Dr. Chamberlain, a Rutgers graduate, and a man for whom I had great respect, who was quite an able scholar. My wife and I talked it over together. But we had already made what was for us a commitment that we would seek some kind of service abroad. We had talked at one time about Africa, for no particular reason, but it was in the offing.

When the offer came, it was in connection with the organization that I was associated with, the Dutch Reformed Church. And that was that. I really don't remember any very great agonizing about it. I was the oldest son in the family. My father, as I said, had died. I talked with my mother, but even that was not a very agonizing experience, because once I had left engineering and started to go into the ministry it was quite clear to her that my future would lie along those lines.

I do not recall any great sense of momentous decision at the time. It indeed turned out to be momentous; the decision not only took us into another physical and geographical setting, but it introduced me to a people, and especially to a culture, which I have found fascinating all the rest of my life.

CHAPTER 2

MEETING THE MIDDLE EAST IN IRAQ

I had not been in the Middle East dealing with things Arabic and Islamic very long before I began to feel that interest and response which so many Arabists and Islamicists feel. Whether I would have felt these equally had I gone some place else, who knows? It has become so associated with my life experience that when I go to India, I say: I am never going to spend my life in India. Or I've been in Africa and listened to the drums—well, Africa is not for me. But who knows how one would have responded?

There were a number of books on the Middle East at the seminary, and I read a few. Not many, because my studies there were fairly demanding, and they were not books of great significance. It was true then and I suppose it is still true now, that when one went abroad under such auspices the first two or three years were exclusively devoted to study.

As soon as I got out in the field, I settled down to study—not only language study, but a broad course of reading. I had read some books in this country. In a course that we had in the history of religion, there was Hume's book,* and he touched on Islam, and I did some cognate reading on the Islamic side. And there was a very well known book in those days by Sell, who I think was an Anglican bishop in India, called *The Faith of Islam*.† As I look back now, it must have been pretty awful, but at the time it was all that I had.

But I was not encouraged to do a great deal of specialized study—aside from the Arabic, which I was glad to have started—partly because of the demands of other education and partly because the whole scholarly approach to service abroad had not grown to the extent it did in later years. That was done in the field. My salary was paid and I had teachers, but it was much more self-study than specialized study in this country.

I graduated from the seminary in May 1928 and in mid-August we sailed from New York; the intervening time was taken up in getting ready, which was quite a job in those days, getting things put together. We left on one of the first ships to be operated by the American Export Line, which had just then come into being. They started their service to the Middle East, their principal ports of call, by buying a group of freighters from World War I, known as Hog Island freighters, from the shipyard where they were built. They were small boats that carried about eight passengers. We sailed on one of these, *The Clontarf*, from Brooklyn.

We went through all the wrenching that comes with long-distance separation. My wife's father was very upset about it, because he was sure he would never see us again. As a matter of fact, he lived to be 93 and we had 30 years of continued contact with each other.

We started out on this little Hog Island freighter. There were eight all together: my wife and myself, and six others who were also missionaries who were going out, in this case to Persia, under the Reformed Church in America. We made a nice little group and had the kind of fun that one has in a like-minded group on a small ship. It was our first time out of the country, and we saw everything, we enjoyed everything. It was a three-week trip from New York to

*Hume, David (1711-1776) *The Natural History of Religion*.
†Rev. Edward Sell's book was published in London in 1880.

Alexandria, because the Hog Island boats were very slow, and the screw didn't stop turning for three weeks. Then we put into Alexandria and had a layover while the ship was discharging cargo.

Being young and energetic, we wanted to see everything, so we decided to go to Cairo for a day, partly to see the city, and partly because I wanted to talk to Dr. S. M. Zwemer, one of the early missionaries who had taken a great interest in Islam and had written a lot about it. My wife and I took a train to Cairo; young and impecunious, we rode third-class in the last car of a dusty Egyptian train, which made no difference to us.

On that trip I had the first experience that begins to raise the kind of questions that are always raised when one goes into another culture. A young university student on the train spoke quite good English, and we talked—it was a two or three-hour ride from Alexandria to Cairo. We talked about what we were doing, and he said, "But have you ever considered that my religion, Islam, is also a good religion? Because it comforts me when I am sick, it helps me when I am in difficulty. It is my experience of God."

Nobody had ever said that to me before. At this time, most of the apologia that dealt with the missionary movement presented an idealized Christianity against the crass reality of some other faith. I mentioned Sell's book above. Sell goes through all the arguments for the superiority of Christianity, or rather for the weakness of Islam. But here was a living human being, a very nice person indeed, who simply said, don't count us out. This meant something to me, and I thought about it for a long time.

We did all the usual things in Cairo, such as going to the pyramids. Dr. Zwemer was not there, but Mrs. Zwemer took us around, and we came back at night to the ship feeling exhilarated with our first taste of what was much later to become our home.

Some 50 years have intervened. In 50 years, many of these things get to be so much a matter of habit that you do not remember your first adjustment to them. I am not particularly conscious of what I would call deep cultural shock. I was fascinated, and I was interested in learning everything I could. I've always been intrigued by knowledge *per se*. I think those years were much harder on my wife than on myself. Like myself, she had come from a small-town background, and she was concerned with kitchens, and kitchens in the Middle East are not clean. And the first night we spent at the hotel in Damascus, before starting out across the desert to get to Mosul, there were bedbugs in the bed; she had heard about these but never seen them. I think, generally speaking, this sort of encounter is more difficult for a woman than for men. She did not have problems adjusting to a strange culture, and she was a better Arabic scholar than I in many ways, because she had a much better accent, having a musical ear. But she did find it difficult to adjust to a different standard of living under very primitive circumstances.

In my own case, as I look back, I really was not as conscious of what I would call cultural shock, and I cannot say that I really was ever homesick. I think this may partly go back to the fact that I always found a great interest and satisfaction in people, and when one looks at them, rather than at the scene in which they are set, there is much less shock than one would expect.

Six or seven years later, when I left the Iraq mission and came to join the American University in Cairo, the then-president, Dr. Charles Watson, a great man, wrapped it up very neatly in a nutshell: the first morning I was to start teaching he called me into his office and said to me, "Badeau, you're going to face your first class of Egyptians this morning. It will probably seem strange to you. I know you've been in Iraq, but they're not Iraqis, they're Egyptians." He said, "Let me tell you something. Start out by remembering that these young people are 85 percent boys and girls and 15 percent Egyptians. Start dealing with the 85 percent and the 15 percent will take care of itself." I really think he stated what unconsciously one learns—that human reactions, while different, are sufficiently of a piece that there is much less strangeness in people than in the external scene.

The *Clontarf* went on to Beirut, and we disembarked there. This is where I really had my first experience not so much of the Orient as of the colonial system. All of our household goods were in transit to Mosul in northern Iraq, where we were going to live. I had several cases and boxes and trunks, and they should have gone in bond from Beirut by lorry, across the desert into Mosul—but I simply could not get them moved.

It happened that one of the professors of the American University of Beirut had a son who was fluent in French, and he volunteered to act as my interpreter, a 16-year-old boy. We went down and I found presently that the real problem was the French Director of Customs of the Port of Beirut—not some slavey but the French Director of Customs—who wanted a 20-dollar bribe to send those things through. As soon as I found that out, everything went along very well indeed.

From that time on, I will be perfectly frank to say that I have not had a high opinion of the French colonial service. Maybe the British did the same kind of thing, but they never did it to me.

We stayed in Beirut for just a short period. It has changed a great deal: no high-rise buildings then, a city much smaller, still very much the Mediterranean seaside town. When I think back to Beirut then, I think of the small, pastel-colored houses, of the traditional Lebanese structure with a large central hall, which is really a covered courtyard, and the other rooms around it, and a little garden in front, where the wonderful red hibiscus were blooming. Little outdoor cafes above the harbor, very Turkish in many ways.

We stayed at a hotel in Beirut that I would say was a real 19th century German pension. Inexpensive, clean, plain fare. And of course the French were everywhere. It was still only seven years or so after the French occupation, and the French were very much in evidence. But the town itself was charming and unsophisticated, the exact opposite of what it is today.

The last time I was in Beirut, in the late 1960's, I was in one of the grand hotels, and spoke Arabic to the boy who operated the elevator. He was absolutely insulted. He would speak French, Spanish, Italian. He would not speak Arabic, although it was his own language.

From Beirut we went across the mountains to Damascus and stayed there for the night, and as I said, in a hotel that was not notable for cleanliness. To get there we took, as one still does, a seat in a car, and went over the mountains and down into Damascus. In

Damascus, we hired a touring car; it probably was not a Ford, but in memory it looked like a Ford, with a canvas top and open sides. There were four of us. My wife and I had been joined in Beirut by Mrs. Roger Cumberland, who was going to Iraq to join her missionary husband—he was later assassinated by the Kurds there—and by Miss Ruth Woodsmall of the YWCA, a maiden lady of indeterminate years.

I remember Miss Woodsmall particularly because she was terrified by the way the Lebanese driver drove, which shows he was just a normal Lebanese. She assumed that I knew some Arabic, and she kept saying to me, "Tell him to go slow. Tell him to stop. Tell him not to hit that rock." And of course, I couldn't tell him anything very well. So I was caught between her and the driver.

I don't think she then knew much of the Middle East, but she was interested in women's conditions, and, as I remember, a book came out of this trip about the position of women in the Middle East. Years later, after the Second World War, she wrote another book,* with a grant from the Ford Foundation.

We filled the bottom of the back seat with watermelons, to give us something cool and refreshing to eat, and drove the first day from Damascus to Deir ez Zor on the Euphrates, where there was a mission hospital in which we spent the night. The drive that day had been through partially irrigated country.

The next day we drove from Deir ez Zor on to Mosul, which is really desert driving. Dry, dusty, hot. Some place in this journey, we picked up a fifth passenger, an Eastern woman, I think an Assyrian, who was returning to Mosul after years of residence in the United States. September is pretty hot, and she was terribly hot, and she would explode every once in a while and say, "This is hell. There is no hell but this. After I die, I do not want to go to hell."

The watermelons saw us through, and we finally rolled into Mosul some time in the latter part of September, when it was still very warm, but the end of the warm season was near.

Once we got to Mosul, we found that the British colonial

---

*Women and the New East. Washington, D.C.: Middle East Institute. 1960.

system had some problems of its own. We got to know many of the British colonial advisers, and on the whole they were very good and competent people. But, of course, as simple, democratic Americans, we did have to adjust to the sense of privilege and position that a British administrator has.

I recall an incident concerning my friend Roger Cumberland, whose wife had accompanied us over the desert. His chief interest was the Kurds, and he spoke Kurdish very well, one of the few Americans who did. In the wintertime he liked to wear an astrakhan lamb hat, which is very warm and comfortable. A new British administrator came to Mosul, collector of customs or something like that, and one day he saw Roger down at the bazaar wearing this hat. Later he sent him a note and asked him to drop around to the office. And when Roger did the official said, "I'd just like to talk to you, Mr. Cumberland. You realize that all we white people have to stick together, and when you wear native headgear you demean our position—it's all right for them to wear it, but I really must ask you not to wear it yourself."

But Roger was extremely irreverent, as well as very American, and of course the little talk didn't do any good. Attitudes like this were much more of a cultural shock than the Arab world was.

We made good friends with many British people and grew to like them very much, always within that system. I must say they were always very kind to us, and in their own way they had an interest in, and certainly a sympathy with, the local people. They were good administrators and, I think, had the interests of the people at heart. But it was always in terms of this imperial relationship, which I suppose is to be expected.

The cooperation between the British and us was in general good. However, I was not operating in any critical areas. Now, my friend Roger Cumberland went up into Kurdistan. At times he was not exactly restrained by the British—that would be quite unfair to say—but they were concerned to point out to him what the dangers were. I don't know of any case in which they tried to inhibit his work, however.

I think you have to say, on the other hand, that sometimes

missionaries and others are not very sensible and cooperative people. There was a well-known British woman, Freya Stark. According to the British, Stark was an absolute pain in the neck to the British consuls, because she was quite daring. When an Englishwoman really takes it up, there's nothing quite like her. She went places and did things that they thought she shouldn't do and had no business doing, and they would fulminate about her. But I personally had no experience of difficulty of restraint that I can recall after all these years.

* * *

We were sent to Mosul partly because it was a good Arabic city. There was a lot of English spoken in Baghdad, among other things, and I think quite rightly it was assumed that we might just as well drop into the heart of the country and into the heart of its language.

There had previously been two missionaries resident there: Roger Cumberland of whom I spoke, and his colleague, Jim Willoughby, who is still alive and retired in Worcester, Ohio, and these two for a while shared a bachelor house there.

The Assyrian people, who fled during the First World War from up around Lake Urumiyeh in Iran, had come down and settled around Mosul. Before the United Mission to Mesopotamia, there was missionary work done by the Congregationalists, who had followed the Assyrians, with whom they had been in contact, down to Mosul. So there was an Assyrian Protestant Church in existence, and there were five or six clergymen, *qasha*, as they were called. They operated out of Mosul and were generally supported and helped and given literature and so forth by Cumberland and Willoughby. But we were not sent there to do any work. We settled down to a regular program of study eight hours a day.

I confess that my deepest interests in the Middle East were always with the Muslims. Not on a religious basis particularly, that would be unfair to say. But I simply was interested in them. So I didn't feel, as some Christians have felt, a special call to this particular Assyrian group. However, since I was there during the

Assyrian revolt of 1932, they became important, because that was quite a political happening.

We were a group of, I think, eight young people who had come out to staff what was called the United Mission in Mesopotamia, united because it drew together the Presbyterian Church and the Dutch Reformed Church and the so-called German Reformed Church. To direct our study, an older missionary came out with us, Dr. James Cantine. Cantine had been a pioneer in the Middle East; it was around 1885 that he and Zwemer went there and, in a certain sense, they were pioneers of Arab interests in the American Christian community. Zwemer became very well known because he was a very dynamic person and wrote a number of books of a semischolarly standard. Some of his work is still very useful. Cantine had been with him during that period. He was at that time a man of 70 or more, and it was quite rightly felt that he would be an ideal guide to lead us into the mysteries of the Middle East.

A schedule was set up in which we had a variety of studies. We studied classical Arabic, using as our introduction a curious book called *Classical Arabic Made Easy*, and it was actually a most excellent book. It was written by an English missionary in Cairo, whose real name I don't know because he always lived by his Arab name of Abd al-Hadi. I knew him later, when I moved to Cairo.

Along with that, when we had gotten into the language, we used, I think, Wright's *Standard Grammar*. Then we studied colloquial, spoken Arabic, and for that we had the pastor of the local Protestant church, a Christian Arab, a so-called *mardinli* Christian. And he would come every day to give us colloquial.

We also studied theological works on Islam. One was a book by a Jesuit scholar in Beirut, Henri Lammens.* It's still the most excellent work. Alfred Guillaume had a book entitled *Islam*, and there were two or three books like that, and also a general history of the Islamic world and of Iraq in particular. That meant a schedule from about eight in the morning till four in the afternoon, either being actually under someone's guidance or studying on the side.

The mission already had inherited from the Congregational-

*Islam: Belief and Institutions, tran. from French by E.D. Ross.

ists, who had operated in Mosul as part of Turkey before World War I, a girls school and also a kind of hostel. There was a local Christian-Arab congregation, with services which we attended on Sunday, and where I must say we learned a great deal of Arabic.

Our days were pretty well spent in study, with roving around Mosul on the side. Mosul was an interesting city. It is the third of the large cities in Iraq—Basra in the south, Baghdad in the middle, and Mosul in the north, and down through history Mosul has always had a certain autonomous character. I have here in the house a copper coin I got in Mosul that dates back to maybe 1300. It carries the inscription of the *atabegs* of Mosul, when Mosul was a quasi-autonomous principality under whoever happened to be the Caliph at the time.

We went to Mosul only 10 years after the war, and the city still bore strong marks of the war years. There had been fighting in and around the area, and after the British mandate was set up following World War I Mosul was the base for operations against the Kurds. The memory of this was still fairly strong.

Mosul had been a real medieval walled city. After the war, as I recall, in connection with some of the political rebellions that followed the establishment of the mandate, the British bulldozed two large streets in two directions, right through the city, beginning with one wall and going right through houses and coming out of the other, in a great cross. You could still go down the street and see half a house facing the street where the bulldozing had gone on.

Very little modern reconstruction had at that time taken place. Generally, there was a good deal of ruin. Mosul, in a certain sense, justified its name because Mosul means the "place of meeting," and all kinds of influences in northern Iraq came together in the city.

In the first place, it was the nexus of the Arab-Kurdish population. The Kurds had been included in the Iraqi mandate, over their very strong protest. They never got along well with the Arabs and, of course, have not to this day. One saw a great many Kurds in Mosul, and the local military and political establishment had a responsibility for them.

Then there was the Assyrian group. It's a curious name, because they really had nothing whatever to do with the ancient

Assyrians, and I have never been able to find why the name was applied to them. They were Christian Syriac Nestorians, tribal people, who had lived intermixed among other hill people, principally the Kurds, and who had come down from Lake Urumiyeh during World War I, in a long, very bitter march, fleeing the German pressures in the area, and had settled either in Mosul or in the hill country around Mosul. They spoke Syriac and maintained both their identity with and their opposition to their Kurdish mountain brethren.

There was a third group in Mosul, the *mardinli* Christians that I mentioned. The term comes from the city of Mardin, in Turkey, which had an Arabic-speaking Christian population. These were original Christian groups that were never Islamicized. They too were strongly represented in Mosul, and one could quite easily spot them because they had certain pecularities in their use of the Arabic language. One peculiarity was that on the end of their pronouns they put the ending *zi*. Instead of saying *ana* (I), they would say *anazi*. Instead of *inta* (you), *intazi*. Instead of *huwa* (he), *huwazi*. A little investigation has shown that the "z" was really a contraction of the word *aydan*—meaning also or likewise. Therefore, even linguistically, they stood out quite distinctly and strongly.

I couldn't say for certain how large the pre-war population of *mardinli* Christians was, but I have the feeling that it was not very large and that, in part, their presence stemmed from an exodus due to the fighting. When the English began to progress up through Iraq during World War I, I think there was a general exodus of people who feared the Turks into the land held by the English.

There was also the Yazidi group. The Yazidis were an Arabic-speaking group, identified in the West as "devil worshippers." The principal site of their group was in a mountain that lay perhaps 50 miles distant from Mosul in the direction of Damascus, called Jebel Sinjar—Sinjar Mountain. There their leaders held forth, and one saw them very frequently; many of them lived in Mosul. And again, you could spot these people, because by tradition they always wore a checkered red *kaffiyeh* on their heads. Other people might also wear red *kaffiyehs*, but Yazidis *never* wore a *kaffiyeh* of another color.

They also had a peculiar linguistic habit—always avoiding any

Arabic letter that began with "s" or "sh." That is, with *sin* or *shin*. They would go to all lengths to put together a sentence without *sin* or *shin* in it. The reason for this is that their religion was based not upon the worship of but upon the placation of the devil, *Shaytan*. But he didn't like to be called *Shaytan*. He liked to be called *Malik Taus*, the King Peacock. And if you said an Arabic word that began with *sin* or *shin* and he overheard you, he might think that you were saying *Shaytan*, and he would be very angry with you. So you didn't pronounce these words. You could therefore spot these people rather quickly.

Then, of course, there were the desert—the real desert—tribal people. As I recall, not many of them lived permanently around Mosul, but Mosul was at the other end of the track from Damascus across the Jazirah and almost at the same time every year, the Shammar bedouin would stop off at Mosul. Shaykh Ajil was their ruling shaykh. As the Arabs said, "*Wallahi, huwa rajal*" (By God, he was a man). He was about six feet tall and six feet wide, and when he dashed around Mosul in his little open Chevrolet, he just flowed over the sides into the streets. The Shammar would come and camp outside of Mosul, come into town to buy things, and the shaykhs would come in with them. I learned to know some of these people quite well and found them very interesting indeed.

All these groups made Mosul truly a "place of meeting" and a very good place to learn some of the ramifications of the Arab world.

Mosul had quite extensive, but very traditional, bazaars, selling the products of the country—for instance, pistachio nuts, licorice, and almonds grown in the Kurdish mountains. One interesting commercial activity which still went on when I was there—one that goes all the way back to the time of the Assyrian monuments—was the floating of timber down the Tigris to Baghdad on rafts made out of skins. When the raft reached Baghdad, the lumber was sold, the skins were deflated and were carried by donkey back to Mosul. These rafts were called *kalaks*, and they came with the spring freshet. The Tigris, fed by nearby tributaries, rose sometimes to dangerous heights in the spring. I have often seen these rafts made, and from recollection I would say they were perhaps a hundred feet long. A gridwork of timbers would be lashed together, the inflated goatskins put in place, lumber from the mountains loaded on, and off they would go down the river to Baghdad. Perhaps six weeks later, the skins would come back again, ready for another year.

One did not find in Mosul, as I recall, very much evidence of wistful remembrance of or loyalty to things Turkish. Not nearly as much Turkish influence in this way as I saw in Egypt.

Mosul had suffered very heavily at the hands of the Turks during the war. When I first went to Mosul, I saw photographs taken by local inhabitants of two or three butcher shops in Mosul where human flesh had been sold at the height of the famine of the war, as a measure of survival. The butchers were apprehended and executed, but this was fresh in people's memory, and it was ascribed to the Turkish presence and Turkish brutality.

There were, practically speaking, no trees, because the Turkish soldiery quartered there had simply cut them all down with the exception of a very few palms in sheltered areas. There was no tree more than five or six feet tall. It was a terribly barren scene. As a matter of fact, the first summer that we left Mosul and went over to Lebanon, my wife said when she got to Lebanon she was going to kiss the first tree she saw because in Mosul she had learned what their absence really meant.

Thus one did not feel any very great pro-Turkish sentiment. Furthermore, the various groups that I mentioned were all groups who had suffered at the hands of the Turks. The Kurds, the Assyrians, the *mardinli* Christians had suffered. The poor inoffensive Yazidis had suffered from everybody, because they were neither Jew, Christian nor Muslim, and so fair sport for everybody.

If you turn this around and ask about Iraqi national feeling, this was really very nascent in the period I was there. I would say that to a degree it was the rise of the Assyrian problem, as Iraq approached the end of the mandate and the gaining of independence in 1931, that brought forth the most obvious national feelings, and then they were expressed in opposition to the Assyrians and their political claims.

One of the things that I later realized was significant was

difficulty in trying to decide really who an Iraqi is. One evidence of this was the information that had to be put down by a child who entered school. Either in Baghdad or in Mosul, I had occasion to look at a series of these forms. For instance, one year a set of questions for the registration of a child in a school would ask, "Are you a Christian or are you a Muslim?" Then another year they wouldn't ask that. Another would ask, "Where was your father born? Your mother born? Born in what is now Mesopotamia or somewhere else?" All this I took as an attempt to discover by what standards you decided the person was an Iraqi. Did he have to be a Muslim? Did he have to be born under the Turks in Mesopotamia?

During the two years I was in Mosul at the beginning, I wouldn't say there was a great sense of surface strain, but there was always Kurdish-Arab tension. This was not religious, because of course the Kurds were certainly Muslims, but it was ethnic and it was historic, and there was constant trouble up in the Kurdish mountains, of one kind or another. Either a challenge to British rule or a challenge to Iraqi rule, or since the two were synonymous at this time, a challenge to both.

The Christian community got along fairly well, although when the so-called Assyrian revolution broke out in 1933, it backfired especially on these *mardinli* Christians. If I recall correctly, two or three of them were actually executed for alleged complicity in this movement. In general there was an attempt, when there was political turmoil, either genuinely or as an excuse, to find some involvement by these foreign Christians. Nevertheless, in one's daily contacts, there was very little sense of that.

One of the incidents—it goes back long before this period, but it does show, I think, something of attitudes—was that of the minaret with the Trinity on it. When we went to Mosul, a group of four couples including ourselves ended up by renting a large Arab house which had been the British Officers' Mess—officers who led the Assyrian Levies. It was situated on the outskirts of town, and directly across the street was the Mosque of Seth, the son of Adam, with a beautiful minaret on it. Many a morning, when I slept on the roof, as we did in the hot weather, I was awakened early by the call to prayer from the minaret, the Muslim bid to rise and pray, "for prayer is better than sleep." Contentedly, not being a Muslim, I would turn over and go back to sleep again.

That minaret had three balconies on it, the only one in Mosul that had three balconies. I do not remember the exact period of construction, whether it was after or before the war, but it had been built by the time we reached there. Since it was the only minaret with three balconies, it was a landmark. At the time it was built, many of the stonemasons were Christians, as by tradition they were in Mosul, and the bazaar crowd of Muslims came to believe that these Christian masons had built the three balconies on the minaret to put the Christian Trinity on a Muslim mosque. A very ugly riot erupted, led by the butchers, who generally were in the forefront of trouble, and it could have resulted in a massacre had it not been that leading Muslim notables stepped into the fray and calmed their people down.

I think, as is often the case in the Muslim world, there was this curious mixture of Mosul authorities attempting to give the non-Muslim communities their rightful place as prescribed by law, and yet at the same time harboring certain suspicions and hatreds toward them. Another example of this same attitude was an occurrence in Basra, where a Muslim had been arrested and given a fairly heavy penalty, either a fine or prison sentence, because in conversation with a Christian, he cursed the Virgin Mary and said she was nothing but a prostitute. You can't do that with another man's religion. One had this mixture of respecting the formal exercise of religion, and yet being quite willing to put blame on a non-Muslim community for things that went on.

* * *

Dr. Cantine was a lovely man. Like myself, he started life as a civil engineer at Union College in Schenectady. I suppose that gave us a certain common bond across the years. As Zwemer was all heat and fire, Cantine was all quiet and coolness and sympathy. He was of a very mystical turn of mind, of sweetness and character. I learned that the Muslim responds to this. The Muslim, even if he is not a *Sufi*, respects the attributes of the "man of God," if you will. And

Dr. Cantine won a great many friends simply by being what he was.

One of my most vivid early memories was going out calling with him. He would take many of us along while he made his rounds, or went to call on people—quite an exercise in Arabic. At the beginning of Ramadan, in the first or second year that I was in Mosul, he took me with him to visit one of the senior shaykhs of the religious community, a man whose name was Abd al-Rahman. He had been the leader of the Muslim group that had brought to an end the threatened riot over the minaret with three balconies. He was a white-haired man, as was Dr. Cantine, and these two old men sat down and talked very quietly, very agreeably, very politely to each other, and in the course of the conversation about the marvels of the world and the wisdom of Allah in creating them, the old shaykh said to Dr. Cantine, "I suppose now in America passage is very rapid indeed?"

"Oh, yes," said Dr. Cantine. "Automobile, cars, go back and forth very quickly."

"So?" said the shaykh. "I suppose with the summer coming and it is hot, you simply go to the North Pole and the Arctic regions and spend a cool summer there, and come back again?"

"No," said Dr. Cantine. "Not yet, but some day, *Inshallah* (God willing)."

While speaking of that Muslim leader, I think of quite a different kind of religious leader in Mosul, the patriarch of the Jacobite Church—that is, the old Syrian Orthodox Church. Although he was called the Patriarch of Antioch, he had his residence in Mosul, and the traditional Cathedral of the Patriarchy was in Mosul. His name was Mar Ignatius, Saint Ignatius, and he was a bull of a man. Husky, large, broad, vigorous, deep-voiced. The first or second year that I was in Mosul, he invited me to attend the Easter service at the Cathedral, on the Eastern Christian date, not the Western Christian date.

The service began at 12 midnight and went from midnight to dawn, which was about half-past six in the morning. The church was very ancient and very dirty, and it was crowded with people. I sat up in the front of the church, stuffed among the deacons and the archimandrites. And Mar Ignatius, the Patriarch, preached on the occasion. He used a very interesting technique that I commend to American clergymen. He preached a very long time; he started out with, "*Abuna Adam,*" our Father Adam. Then he came all the way down, prophet by prophet, from Adam to Christ.

He would be preaching away and the congregation would get restless. Mothers had babies who had to be suckled and changed. When he saw that the congregation was bored and restless, he would nudge the deacon standing next to him, who carried a long pole on the end of which was a cymbal, the only music used in the church. The deacon would hit the cymbal and start up a hymn. And they would sing interminably, eight, ten, twelve verses of the hymn, until everybody was worn out singing and quiet. Then the Patriarch would pick up again and go on with his sermon.

This went on, as I say, from about midnight until almost dawn. In the center of the church was a large basket, about six feet across, lined with mud and filled with brush. When dawn came, a candle was taken from the altar and thrust into the pile of brush, which immediately took fire and a great flame leapt up in this ancient church—the church was all stone, so it couldn't burn. And this was the end of the progression from Adam down to Christ, because this was the light of the world.

The people then went out, and I went in and had breakfast with the Patriarch. I was learning enough Arabic so I could talk and understand a little bit, and while we were having breakfast the Patriarch expounded greatly upon the need for church unity, and for all churches getting together. He couldn't understand why Rome had not answered the invitation to come and join the Syrian Orthodox Church, since he was the direct follower of Peter, whose Seat was Antioch, and he would gladly welcome the Pope with his family into the Church.

Then he went on to say that in God's providence every church had its own special gift, and all we needed was to put all the gifts together. He said, for instance, "We churches of the East, we have the gift of spirituality, and you churches of the West, you have the gift of money. Now, if our spirituality and your money were put together, how wonderful it would be." He was very different from the old shaykh Dr. Cantine talked to, but an interesting character.

* * *

The Yazidis are a very small and restricted community who really represent an amalgam of all kinds of religious bits and pieces that were lying around the landscape. They were put together and forged into a religious group traditionally by a man called Shaykh Abi, and up in the Kurdish mountains, a couple of hours from Mosul, is the shrine of Shaykh Abi, their holy shrine.

The basis of their belief is that God is supreme, the ruler of creation, who created the stars and all the worlds. But there are so many worlds that God is far too busy to give his attention to every one of them and so He parcels out His worlds to His angels to take care of. And with a surprising amount of realism the Yazidis said, God has put the devil in charge of this world, and at the end of time, the devil will hand the world back to God and give a report on everybody.

They did not think the devil was good, but if the devil gave a bad report about them to God, they might be in trouble. So a large part of their religion was built on avoiding the giving of offense to *Shaytan*. One of the Yazidi practices was to deny literacy to the common people, and only the elite could read or write.

In our hospice in Mosul there was the daughter of one of the leading Yazidi chieftains, from Jebel Sinjar, a little girl who was brought to us because her father, in a drunken rage, struck the child and she had lost the sight of one eye. The family brought the little girl to us to be out of the father's way, so we took care of her. But every month her father would come into town and visit her, and I got to know him and listen to him. He was a rascal. We tried to work with him to keep him sober, and I remember his coming to town one time and coming over to see his daughter. He had dinner in our menage, and then he went off, and sure enough, the next morning he was picked up dead drunk somewhere in the middle of Mosul. And when he was confronted with this fact, he said, "Well, what could I do? I met some British officers down in a teahouse, and they said 'Cheerio' and I said 'Cheerio.' I woke up and here I was."

I went up to visit the shrine of Shaykh Abi, and the shrine itself gives evidence of these mixed beliefs. There is a well in the shrine—a cave built into the side of the mountain—and this well is supposedly connected with the Well Zam Zam in Mecca. There is clear evidence here of certain Muslim beliefs. On the lintel of the door that goes into the shrine is carved in marble a black snake, maybe five or six feet long, a representation of the devil. But if the devil had not come along and tempted Adam and Eve, we never would have learned the pleasures of reproduction. So we ought to be very grateful to *Malik Taus*, as they call him, for taking care of this.

* * *

The Assyrians were an interesting group; as I have indicated, the name is entirely fortuitous. What it refers to are the followers of the ancient Nestorian Church, a church that had been indigenous in what is now Iraq, from before Muslim times. During the Sassanian Empire, the ruling prelate of the Nestorian Church, as I recall it, had his headquarters at Ctesiphon, below Baghdad, and from Ctesiphon missionary effort went out from the Nestorian Church at least as far as China, and for a time Nestorian Christian influence in China was very great.

So the Nestorians represented an old, indigenous, religious group within the area where modern Iraq was created. In general, I think the theologies of the Middle East are expressions of political loyalties, and what the Assyrians in their Nestorianism were doing was asserting their own ethnic political entity. This entity still existed, and in it lay the center and the seed of the Assyrian problem. The Assyrians called themselves a nation—referred to themselves as such. Their spiritual leader was the patriarch, Saint Simon (Mar Shimun), who was always celibate and who, when I lived in Mosul, was a very young man. I do not think he was more than 18, and behind him stood a very awesome aunt, Lady Surma Hanim, the power behind the throne, and senior Assyrian tribal leaders.

As I said earlier, this group had trekked down from northern Iran, settling in and around the Tigris valley. There was a considerable community in Baghdad and a much larger community in Mosul and the adjacent hills.

At the time of the World War I peace settlement, the Assyrians, like the Kurds, had sought recognition from the peacemakers and from the League of Nations for their own autonomous state. They claimed they were promised such a state by the British, which very well may have been true, because in wartime, as T.E. Lawrence reminds us, no promises are sacred and all promises are made. They had fought with the British against the Turks—this is one reason why they fled. So they came to Iraq with a grievance against Britain and the world; as things were going, they were to be placed under the control of the Muslim community, against which they had maintained their religious and their quasi-political identity from the very rise of Islam.

When I first went there, the question was not serious, because Iraq was still almost completely under British control, even to the district officers, and these, on the whole, handled themselves well. The Assyrians felt a degree of security, because the British had raised a special force of Assyrian troops, called the Assyrian Levies, and they were very good soldiers indeed. They came from generations of fighting their fellow mountaineers and were officered by the British, giving the British an independent police force that they could use against the Kurds on one hand and against any Iraqi Arab nationalist insurgents on the other hand.

We saw these levies in Mosul. They were numerous; they gave employment to people. The fact that they existed gave the Assyrian community a feeling that they had their own protection.

As Iraq moved in the direction of ending the mandate, the speed with which it was terminated took everybody by surprise. After the first Labour government came in England under Ramsay MacDonald, there was a sudden, quite unheralded decision to cut commitments abroad and to cut commitments in Iraq. Iraq had been an awful headache—there had been continuous uprisings among the Kurds, and the Shia in the south had made difficulties. Faisal had been sufficiently accepted by the populace so that the British felt that they had a friend and ally they could work with.

Rather precipitously, in the view of many people, Great Britain decided to turn the mandate back to the League of Nations, and the League of Nations was prepared to give the Iraqis their independence.

This raised two different sets of questions. One was, what guarantees would be given to the various political and religious minorities in Iraq? Could the League of Nations trust the emerging Iraqi government to deal fairly with them? There were debates on that matter, but I was very far away from all that at the time.

The other aspect was the resentment on the part of both Kurds and Assyrians, and perhaps of some other groups. The *mardinli* Christians were accused of sharing this feeling. Whether they did or not, I am not sure. But certainly it was felt by the Assyrians and by the Kurds that the final hour had come; they had either to obtain some kind of autonomy and recognition now, or be submerged under the majority, both Muslim and Arab, that would form the government of Iraq. So there was a great deal of restlessness.

Among the Assyrians, it took the form of seeking recognition by the Iraqi government of the nationhood of the Assyrian peoples, giving them not only a certain political autonomy but also recognizing their traditional political structure—headed by Mar Shimun, the Patriarch—as being a responsible government. Responsible, to be sure, to the Iraqi government, but standing between the Iraqi government and the common Assyrian.

The Iraqis were not at all prepared to do this, and one can understand why. Iraq in a certain sense was a country of minorities, and if you did this for the Assyrians, you would have to do it for the Kurds, you would have to do it for the Shia, and before long the whole concept of a unified Iraq would be impossible to uphold. So, although negotiations were held, Iraq was not willing to accept the political leadership of Mar Shimun, or to grant the Assyrian tribesmen a degree of political autonomy. One group of the Assyrians, including Mar Shimun, escaped from Iraq and went over the border into Syria. Others remained in Mosul.

Just as the end of the mandate approached, fighting broke out around a village that lay between Mosul and the Kurdish hills, a place called Filfil. I don't know that I knew at the time what the immediate cause of the fighting was, but it was occasioned by this Assyrian movement—taking refuge in Syria and seeking autonomy—and its clash with local authority. There was a massacre, which led to wholesale military action on the part of the Iraqi government against the Assyrians, and there were some very difficult and bloody times indeed.

Faisal was out of the country. He had left the government in the hands of his only son, Ghazi, a very inept young man. The Assyrians did not take the Iraqi police action lying down. They fought back very bravely. It was the first challenge in many ways to the authority and stability of the new Iraqi government. Then Faisal died quite unexpectedly in Switzerland, reportedly of a broken heart because of what was happening in Iraq. This may be too simplistic an explanation, but in any case the country exploded. It was just a reaction of pure rage venting itself, and a very warlike spirit was everywhere.

I was in Mosul at the time and was acting as secretary for the mission. Our American Minister in Baghdad was concerned for our safety, so he sent me a curious telegram, which read—I think I can quote it exactly after all these years—"In view of impending thunderstorms, strongly urge you to hop Liz and skip." I looked at this thing and I couldn't make head or tail out of it, and knowing the poor English of the Iraqi telegraph operator, I was sure something had gone wrong. I went back to the operator and tried again, but I still got the same thing, "hop Liz and skip," so there was nothing to do but to go and find out.

I took a car and went down to Baiji, which was the railhead, got on the train and went down to Baghdad. I went in to see the Minister, who skinned me alive. He said, "I thought every American knew what 'hop Liz and skip' meant. It means get in the Ford and get out. Any American knows what a Lizzie is, doesn't he?" Perhaps I had been out of America long enough to have forgotten.

What he wanted us to do was to get out of Mosul. I went back with this message to my colleagues, and we did, in fact, leave and come down to Baghdad, where we stayed until the troubles were over. Although it was not involved in any of the fighting, Baghdad was the scene of tumultuous patriotic marching to and fro. I remember one great parade of mixed soldiers and civilians going down the street; they expressed their bloody feelings—it was summer and watermelons were in season—by putting round watermelons on the end of sticks and carving them like human faces, supposedly the bloody heads of the Assyrians who revolted against them. It was a tense time.

Then came the funeral of Faisal, and it was said at the time a hundred thousand tribesmen came from the desert around Baghdad, and a great emotional funeral was held to bury the man. The Assyrian rebels were in the middle. It was a kind of explosion point.

There was an Assyrian community in Baghdad of perhaps 500 families living together. They were not touched and continued to live there, during the years that I was there. Eventually, the whole question of Assyrian autonomy died down, and the Assyrians were integrated into Syria and other lands. Mar Shimun came to this country, where there were a lot of Assyrians who had emigrated, and the Assyrian question never again rose to trouble the country.

* * *

My colleague, Roger Cumberland, a graduate of the McCormick Theological Seminary, had been in the field about seven years before we arrived. He learned the Kurdish dialect called Kermanji. I learned a little bit of it with him at one time. He went out and lived among the Kurdish tribal people, journeyed among the mountains, and then in the year we went out, he married and brought out his wife, a missionary's daughter from the Philippines, who remained a very close friend of ours until her recent death. They settled down briefly in Mosul.

Roger, who had some money of his own, went into a village that lay on the slope of the Kurdish mountain facing Mosul, called Dohuk, where he bought a small acreage on which he could grow oranges. He came from Southern California and was interested in citrus. He built his own house and set up his residence there, and did his work among the Kurds. On one or two of his trips I accompanied him on muleback, a very interesting experience indeed.

He was a very shrewd political observer. The Iraqi government was not happy to have a foreigner in that area during these troubles and, as I recall, at the time of the Filfil massacres Roger and his wife came down into Mosul. But he never really enjoyed too much confidence on the part of the local officials, because he knew too well what was going on.

We left Iraq in 1935, and Roger stayed on. Then, in either 1938 or '39, Roger, living up there with two children and his wife in his house, was murdered by what appeared to be a Muslim fanatic. He had a room in which he met visitors, a *majlis* as it is called. As I recall it, two Kurds came to see him, not local Kurds—he had done quite a lot for the village. He had piped water in and generally tried to make himself useful. Anyhow, two Kurds came and said they wanted to talk to him, and they ended up by drawing a revolver and shooting him, and then fled. After lingering for the best part of a day, Roger died.

The Cumberlands had a great many friends among the British officers in the British air base outside Mosul; they flew a plane up there, and brought the body back. Subsequent investigation never fully cleared up that incident, but I believe there was evidence at the time, and I think the general view of our State Department was, that this was done with the connivance of the Iraqi government.

Roger was a member of the Royal Asiatic Society and had been in London in the months previous to this. He had, as I recall, written an article in the *Journal of the Royal Asiatic Society* about the massacre at Filfil. He was frank and he knew what he was talking about, and I think this disturbed the Iraqis. It was proof of the fact that he knew what was going on and was not afraid to say so, and our best judgment was that it was this fact that led them to play upon the innate feelings of fanaticism of some of these Kurdish groups, and if not to instigate the assassination, at least to encourage it and allow it to go unpunished.

* * *

I haven't been in Iraq for quite a number of years. My last visit to Iraq must have been about 1965 or 1966, after I was at Columbia. I stayed a couple of nights in Baghdad and had a chance to talk with our Ambassador there, Robert Strong, a very good observer, and *a propos* of nothing, it led to a very interesting experience.

I was a guest at the Embassy residence. The next morning I was walking down the hallway to the Ambassador's office, when an old Iraqi with grizzled hair, wearing a blue Embassy uniform, came down the passage, turned around and looked at me, and without saying a word, folded me to his bosom and began to kiss my cheeks.

I found that this was our houseboy, Ahmed. A harum-scarum rapscallion desert boy, he was about eighteen when he was our houseboy in Baghdad in 1934-35. He now had a family of 12 children and ran the mimeograph machine for the Embassy, for USIS. He fell on my neck and wept in true Biblical style.

That was the last time I was in Baghdad, and I did not have much of a basis on which to evaluate the situation intimately. However, it seemed to me quite clear that the Kurdish people are never going to amalgamate into the body politic of Iraq as long as it retains completely the stamp of Baghdad-dominated, Arab control. I do not see the possibilities of their forming a separate country, but I think they are going to continue to be a thorn in the flesh, and each time there has been a standoff between the Kurds and the Iraqis, including the last one, when there was an Army regime in Baghdad with a good deal of power behind it, the Baghdad authorities have not been able to bring the Kurds to heel.

This is entirely understandable. It is partly the mountain against the plain, and the mountain peoples often are ruggedly independent. It is partly deep, historical, racial difficulties. The Kurds are not Arab; they don't speak Arabic. They are an Aryan, Indo-European people whose language is akin to Farsi, and to them the Arabs are alien. The authority of the Arab has never been thoroughly established over Kurdistan. There was Turkish control of Kurdistan—how thorough I do not know—but there wasn't Arab control. Therefore, the Kurds never have been in the position historically to say they were part of a national Arab government. I would surmise that the chances of lasting accommodation are very slight until the Iraqis are prepared to give a large degree of autonomy, culturally as well as politically.

CHAPTER 3

DECISION IN BAGHDAD

Baghdad was quite a different scene. I had finished my study, although I continued to work on Arabic, in which I was interested. As Secretary of the Mission, I had a certain amount of administrative work to do. My assignment was as an evangelistic missionary, which meant essentially not education but the general conduct of religious services. There was a boys' school attached to the mission in Baghdad, run by two men and their wives, but I was not responsible for the school.

The first thing I did in Baghdad was to build my own house, making it large enough so it could be used for the purposes of our work. As an engineer by training and being young and brash by nature (although I had never built anything I decided I could), I designed and built a house in the area of Baghdad called *Sinak*, down by the old South Gate. It encompassed a residence, a meeting hall that would hold perhaps 75 people, a small library, and a *majlis* or sitting room, in which I could meet people.

I had an Arab *colporteur* who worked with me, a man who himself reflected the multiplicity of cultures in Iraq. A *mardinli* Christian, he spoke Persian, Armenian, Syriac, Arabic and English. He spoke the Eastern languages so well that if he were speaking in Syriac and an Arabic word appeared he would unconsciously shift and finish the rest of the sentence in Arabic and not know he did it.

He was a fine man, wise and patient. I learned a great deal from him. And he had groups, principally of young men who came and talked to him, with whom he conducted Bible studies. He assisted at a Protestant Arabic church in Baghdad, and we had Arabic church services in the little chapel I had built for these and for other people.

I did quite a bit of traveling around Najaf, Kerbala, Shamiyal, all over on the Euphrates. I am not sure that I did any good, but I learned a lot and came to know a lot of interesting terms. Curiously, the one thing I did which seemed to me to be of most benefit and gave entrée to the community was to design camp toilets. While I was there, the Boy Scout movement had reached Iraq and had opened a summer camp in the Kurdish foothills, and I had grown to know one of the cabinet ministers interested in this. His name was Daud al-Haydari, from the well-known Haydari family of Baghdad.

I was talking to him one day, and he said they were having trouble getting this camp together. "Well," I said, "I've been to camp. I will design you some toilets." So I made a simple drawing of a communal outhouse and how it should be taken care of and made sanitary. I had, after all, been a sanitary engineer in my training. And the Iraqi government very gratefully put it into effect. I learned to know many people in that connection.

I studied a good deal. I was interested in traveling around the country, and I got increasingly involved in the problems of young men who were trying to move out of their traditional background—not merely their traditional Muslim background, but their traditional cultural background—into the modern world. As I look back now, I think it was that involvement that stimulated the interest that finally took me to the American University in Cairo, where in the classroom you dealt with these problems much more directly.

I remember an incident that put it very directly. I used to go sometimes to the coffee houses and sit. I wanted to pick up conversation and learn some Arabic, and I would often take along the Gospels in Arabic, which were easy to read and in which I was interested, and then I would have a conversation with somebody.

A young student saw me, a foreigner, struggling with this, and he came over and said, "What are you trying to do?" And I explained. "Oh," he said, "I will help you." So we were reading along, and it happened that the reading was in the Gospel of Matthew, the temptation story, and we came to the verse, "Man shall not live by bread alone." These were Jesus' words. *"La yahya al-insan bi-khubs wahdahu."* He said, "What does that mean?" and I tried to tell him. He said, "I do not understand that." He said, "Here you are. You foreigners come out here. You tell us this. You live by bread. You live by motor cars. You live by nice houses and things. This is what we want. We want the bread that you've got. We have got the other things. We want the modern bread."

That made me think. In a sense, this was the nub of the problem—how you passed from one economy into another. While I was there, for instance, the first factories were being built in Baghdad. I think one of the very earliest was a cigarette factory, to make cigarettes by machines instead of by hand. This led to the emergence of a laboring class. I became very interested in these issues, and tried to follow them.

* * *

Early in my Baghdad years, on the occasion of some state holiday, I and other members of the foreign community, which was almost entirely British, were received by the King.

In his Arab robes, Faisal was a very impressive figure. Like some of the Saudi princes, he had the thin hawk face of the true desert Arab, and great dignity of bearing. But unfortunately, at about this time when he held his public meetings he eschewed his Arab robes and put on what the Arabs described as a *redincote*—from the French version of the original English "ridingcoat"—a cutaway, as we would call it. So when I met him he was dressed in striped trousers and a cutaway, wearing the national hat of Iraq, which was the *sudara*. The *sudara* looked like nothing as much as the little hat they wore in British prisons, a very undignified headgear. And the visual majesty of the Arab monarch in his flowing robes quite disappeared before this slight man in Western clothing.

Nevertheless, he was warm and wise, and he traversed a very difficult path in Iraq. It was hard for the Iraqis to forget that he really had been placed on the throne of the country not by local vote but by British fiat. I remember seeing one carefully guarded picture in Baghdad that showed the stand on which Faisal had taken his oath of office when he was crowned as King. It was a stand covered with bunting and so forth. This photograph was taken from the back. And what was the stand built of? Of beer boxes from the local British camp, which were stacked there and covered with bunting and so forth, and some bitter Arabs said, "That shows what he's standing on, you know. He's standing on British beer boxes. This is what put him in power."

To a large degree he succeeded in surmounting this view, partly because, in my opinion, he was very wise and partly because he had unusual ability, the same ability that his great-nephew Hussein of Jordan has, to deal with the tribal element that was so important to the country.

I think it was the lack of this ability in those who succeeded him, especially in Ghazi, his son, that led to a great many difficulties. These desert shaykhs, especially the people from lower Iraq, would come in to see the King, and he did not put on any of the trappings of royalty and was not *"Ya Jalalatikum al-Malik"*— Oh, Your Majesty, the King. They would say, "Ya, Faisal." And he would respond, "Ya, Abdallah," in the same way.

I remember one delegation had come to complain about taxes. When he had heard all their complaints, instead of citing the law and saying, you know, we have got to send out tax collectors, he said, "Please, for my sake, that I not lose honor in front of my people, that my face be white. Please, do not make a fuss about this and I will try and straighten it out." That kind of personal diplomacy with the tribal people really carried him through, and I have the feeling that had Faisal lived, the subsequent history of Iraq would have been quite different, because I think he was really the only man who could have bridged many of these gaps.

His funeral was a tumultuous affair. Everybody was there; a hundred thousand tribesmen came in. He was buried out in the northern suburb of Baghdad, Al-Muadhdham, about five miles from the center. There was a parade five miles long. All the different communities were there and the different guilds in the bazaar: the Butchers Guild and the Bakers Guild and the Leathermakers Guild and what have you. And bands. And just unrestrained hysteria.

Yet, in the midst of it, there were bright spots. I walked with the foreign British-American community, and right before us came the butchers, and the butchers had hired a band to play for them. And what did it play? It played to a very quick marching beat, "Oh my Darling Clementine." So we marched out to Muadhdham to bury King Faisal to the tune of "Clementine," and that cheered us up a little bit.

* * *

I had been in Iraq for almost seven years and been through a variety of experiences. I ended up doing some administrative work as mission secretary and quite a bit of building for the mission, and it was in the connection as secretary that, in the spring of 1934, I had to go to Jerusalem to attend the conference of the Near East Christian Council, which was the interchurch, intermission body of the Middle East.

I went over by taking a seat in a mail truck that was running from Baghdad across the desert into Jerusalem twice a week, ostensibly to carry mail. Actually, its chief freight was a load of Tigris salmon, a large fish caught in the Tigris and greatly prized. I joined that and took a two-day journey from Baghdad over to Jerusalem, going by way of Rutba Wells, which is in the middle of the desert, and then turning south into fairly uncharted country and getting so lost that for the best part of the night we had to just drive around in circles to pick up a track, and finally getting into first Amman and then Jerusalem on Palm Sunday. At that conference, Dr. Charles Watson, who was then President of the American

University in Cairo (AUC),* was also present and we met for the first time. On this trip I also made some contacts in Jordan which I sustained through most of my life in the area. We stayed in Amman for a brief period on our way over, worn out with the desert journey, and I met a man who then was a young teacher, but I believe had just become the Assistant Director of Education under the British-controlled government of Jordan. He was Samir al-Rifai, and the al-Rifai family proved to be very important. Samir moved up in the government ladder under the British, and after the Kingdom of Jordan was formed continued to be closely associated with the King. He was Prime Minister a number of times, and indeed was usually called in by the King when he wanted a strong hand to keep the restless Palestinians in order. Off and on through the years I knew him, and several of his nephews were my students in Cairo later.

That first time I went into Amman, Samir took me out to meet the then Amir Abdullah. I was only a pilgrim and a stranger, and the Amir was kind enough to receive me in his tent. I, of course, had known something about tribal life, because I had traveled among the tribes on the western side of the Euphrates in Iraq, where the Bani Tai and Bani Musa and Bani Amrar all wandered up and down. Abdullah was the kind of figure I knew.

At that time he was still keeping court in his black hair tent, spread on one of the hills of Jordan, in his Arab robes, open to people to see him as the traditional shaykh he was, and when I met him he was playing chess. I was introduced to him. I had very little chance to do anything more than be impressed with meeting a man of this character. As I mentioned, I had known his brother Faisal in Iraq slightly.

Jerusalem was not too different in those days from Baghdad. Physically, Baghdad too was an old city, with some modern suburbs, but Jerusalem seemed more sophisticated. There were many more goods on sale in the bazaar. The spoken Arabic was

---

*The American University *in* Cairo was originally the American University *at* Cairo. We have used the current name.

slightly different, which both interested and sometimes puzzled me. The British influence was infinitely more pervasive than in Iraq, where the mandate had terminated in 1932.

Anyhow, after I returned to Baghdad I had a letter from Dr. Watson, suggesting that I consider joining the staff of the American University in Cairo as a teacher in the field of philosophy and religion. It was that invitation which led to my leaving my first appointment in Baghdad and going to join the AUC.

I had a year to finish my assignment in Iraq. I was not due for furlough until the spring of 1935, and as a matter of fact, it took me the better part of that time to make up my mind what I was going to do. In the first instance, I was not particularly drawn to teaching, but the more I considered it, the more it seemed to me to be wise. In Baghdad I had become very interested in the problem of the younger generation, passing from the traditional milieu into the modern world—the student generation. Students used to come in and see me and talk about their problems, and I thought that probably I would be more effective and make a greater contribution in the setting of an educational institution. Finally, with some reluctance, I decided that was the thing to do, and in the spring of 1935 we finally left Iraq and came home for a year of study in this country.

Dr. Watson had asked me to come to AUC in the field of religion and philosophy. I had a theological education, but I had never studied philosophy as such. However, I had read a great deal and I think some of my own interests led in that direction, even without the formal training. So I spent the year in this country between Columbia University and Union Theological Seminary, doing something of a cram session in philosophy and also working on my Master's degree in the field of Arab thought. With the completion of that year, I went to Cairo in 1936.

The year of study was pure delight in a great many ways. I had been out of the intellectual swim for six or seven years and enjoyed the study simply as an intellectual exercise, but beyond that I had just enough immersion in the Arab world to have abiding experience upon which intellectual discovery could play. I have come to feel that in many ways experience ought to precede knowledge, because you have something then to chew on.

Philosophy I did at Columbia. This was in the heyday of John Randall, their well-known teacher of philosophy. I suppose his *Making of the Modern Mind* is one of the great classical books of the generation. I took a good course in the history of philosophy with him, together with assorted seminars clustering around it, and while it did not in any sense make me a Ph.D. in philosophy, it did prepare me for the beginning of the work I had to do in Cairo.

Then I went to Union Seminary to get some work in philosophy of religion, as an aid in rounding out philosophic knowledge. Also, since the graduate thesis that I was working on had to do with a treatise by the philosopher, al-Ghazali, which technically could be considered as a philosophy of religion, it seemed appropriate that I do that under the umbrella of Union Seminary, which had a good philosophy of religion department. I worked on Arabic with E. E. Calverley of Hartford Theological Seminary, who had been a missionary in the Persian Gulf area and had come back a fine scholar. He helped me, partly with my going to Hartford, partly by correspondence, in completing my annotation and translation of the work that I had undertaken—one of a series of small essays attributed to al-Ghazali. I don't suppose one could be sure that they were all actually his. They were published in a volume still in current circulation in the Arab world, which shows that they had a lasting value.

The one I worked on was called *Al-Adab fi al-Din*—Fitting Behavior in Religion. It purported to give instructions as to how a pious Muslim should act under all circumstances. On the one hand, if you will, a book of etiquette—on the other, a book concerned with what is the moral and right thing for a religious person to do. And it ranged all the way from very directly religious topics, as the fitting behavior of the believer when he prays during the month of Ramadan, to proper behavior when taking a Turkish bath. What you had in effect was kind of a panorama of the 12th century life of which al-Ghazali wrote, and I found its interest not so much in what it added to a technical knowledge of Muslim formal thought but as a picture of how Muslims lived and what they did.

A great many years later—in fact, only about five years ago—

when we were putting together a memorial volume for Dr. Aziz Atiya, I went back to this translation and worked it up into an article which I called "They Lived Once Thus in Baghdad." For instance, there is a section discussing the fitting behavior of a teacher. Al-Ghazali was fairly shrewd; he said teachers should not be influenced in their decisions by gifts that are brought by their students. A teacher should not be ashamed to stand in front of his class and say, "I don't know." And when the teacher is asked a question, his concern should be to rid himself of the question, not the questioner. On the other hand, the student is bidden to pay attention to the teacher when he is talking, and when the lecture is over, not to follow him down the street, touching his robe and asking questions of him.

It was an interesting picture of how people lived, and in some ways I was more interested in seeing people as people than I was in the formal philosophic material that might be found in the work.

One of the difficulties in translating this work was its extreme brevity. It is divided up into sections, such as the proper behavior for a teacher, the proper behavior for a student, the proper behavior for a husband, the proper behavior for a wife. Instead of finding a fully explanatory paragraph, you simply have a series of little phrases that come in between the sections. It is rather staccato and therefore a little difficult to translate. Calverley suggested that it was really not intended for widespread circulation. It was rather designed as lecture notes, headings upon which al-Ghazali then expanded.

Being a teacher myself, I at once saw the validity of this kind of explanation. It made sensible the particular form, and read in this way it becomes more germinal. One sees what lies there. One can imagine al-Ghazali walking up and down, lecturing on the notes at greater length.

Of course, the ultimate education is the one that you give yourself. One starts with that, and all the formal training does is to place certain weapons and tools in your hand.

What the Columbia education did was to introduce me rapidly to a wide circle of material and its sources. Randall's class was a large one. He was a magnificent lecturer, and as a result of the purview given by this lecturer, I read voraciously during the year in the various philosophies, so by the time I finished I felt that I had gained about as much in one year as one could. To be sure, it would have been better to go on into a more intimate learning experience in a very small seminar with a man like this, but I did not have the time.

I have always believed in the validity of good lecturing, and Randall was very good. It seems to me that there are two kinds of lecturers. One is the professor who really does nothing more than recapitulate what is in the book, and I think that one of the most deadly things is for a professor to use as a textbook a text he has written himself, because all he does is to repeat what he has already written down. This kind of lecturing is not contributory to growth and knowledge. But if a lecturer really assumes that you are reading the material and then goes off into interpretation and related questions and setting a framework within which you do your own thinking, then there is no substitute for the experience.

In Randall's case, I remember quite clearly his whole discussion of the Socratic role in Plato, as to whether, in fact, something like Plato's *Republic* was ever meant to be a serious view of a possible political state, or whether it was really Plato taking an ideal to the ultimate with the precise aim of stimulating you to see how impossible it is. To raise that kind of a question with students is to enliven their own reading, and I was fortunate in having this kind of teaching.

Union Seminary was different. It was very small. A great deal of my work was on my thesis. It had some good people—a good man in comparative religion, another in philosophy and religion. What I got there was the personal contact with the teacher, rather than, I would say, the stimulation of a mind broadly running over a body of material.

CHAPTER 4

CAIRO BEFORE THE WAR

We went to Cairo in September of 1936, in time for the opening of the academic year. I had earlier visited Cairo only for a couple of days to meet Dr. Watson and people in the university and to gain a physical acquaintance with the institution, and then had gone back to Baghdad. For all essential purposes, I came quite new and fresh to the experience.

There were very obvious differences. Iraq was not only a new country, but a country in which tribal origins were very close to the surface, where the desert stretched between Baghdad and the Syrian coast, and formed a certain barrier. Therefore it was very Arab, and medieval in a great many ways.

In contrast, Cairo was a large city, a very modern city in certain parts, and much more sophisticated politically. A person living in Cairo is much more insulated from the countryside, from the movements of the countryside, than a person living in Baghdad, where the smaller size of the city makes it easy to walk immediately into the country, and where the country comes into the city all the time. The countryside came into Cairo as well, but it was a different thing, and the Egyptian peasant was very different from the peasants I had known before.

Cairo was a much more cosmopolitan city, where the man in the street was much more aware of the outside world, where the politics of government were much more apparent and much more dealt with, and where the variety of business enterprises, and certainly intellectual enterprises, was far greater. In Baghdad there was the beginning of what became a university, but it was then a very modest teachers' college. When I arrived in Cairo, it had a university, and in addition to that it had large foreign communities: the French, Greeks, and the British, all of whom had their own schools, their own institutions. All of these cosmopolitan aspects separated it very much from the Iraq experience.

In 1936 the American University in Cairo was just beginning to pick up after the first impact of the American Depression. The original concept of an American university there had been broached before World War I. Dr. Watson had been born of missionary parents and had grown up in Cairo, and then had gone to the United States, entered the church and had become a pastor in that country. But during his stay there, he retained a desire to do something in Egypt, and he believed that a university was where the greatest contribution could be made. So, before World War I, there was some consideration and discussion of how a university could be started.

One ought to say at this point that at that time there was no national university in Egypt. There was an institution known as the Egyptian University, which was a purely private affair. The chairman of its board was Prince Fuad, later King Fuad, which led to some very interesting contacts between myself and his son Faruq. But it was a small, free, fairly insignificant institution, and there was no university, aside from al-Azhar, which really was a medieval theological institution. So the founding of an American university at that time appeared to be a necessary step.

World War I intervened, and not until 1918 was it possible to begin, at which time Dr. Watson got some backing from various people in the United States. The University was never a church-related institution, although it very definitely represented a general church-going interest. In 1918 the start was made. Curiously enough, and not by plan, the institution began in, and still retains to this day, the central building in which the old Egyptian university had begun to flourish. The building is Victorian Arabesque of the 19th century. It was originally the residence of a pasha, then taken over by a Greek manufacturer of Egyptian cigarettes, Gianiclis, a very well-known figure. He owned and kept up in rather handsome style this ornate building in the very heart of Cairo, next door to Parliament, on one of the principal squares of the city.

When Dr. Watson and those who were with him began to look around, they thought that this might be a good university building, but they were unable to purchase it. Then in 1919, if I remember correctly, when in the course of the Peace Conference there was a great deal of controversy in Egypt and a number of street demonstrations for the Wafd and for Egyptian independence, the plaza on which the building stood, *Midan Ismailiyya* (Ismailia Square), was the favorite meeting place for the demonstrators and Gianiclis was frightened. He was a foreigner, and here was a wave of intense nationalism, and he was ready to sell out. So he did sell to Dr. Watson and his associates, at a very reasonable price, and that building is still used as a central building in what became the American University.

When Dr. Watson first planned all this, he thought of a fully rounded university with medicine and agriculture and engineering, and plans were drawn up for all these, but the institution had scarcely gotten underway when the Depression struck in the United States. This caused dismissal of staff and reduction in the budget, and at the same time the Egyptian University had begun to emerge as a national institution. By the time I reached there in 1936, the university had passed through a very low ebb indeed and had just begun to fight its way upward. It consisted of a secondary school, which was necessary as an English-language feeder to the college, and on the same site the College of Arts and Sciences, a School of Oriental Studies, and a Division of Extension. In addition, there was a School of Education.

All this was very deliberate. Dr. Watson was a remarkable man, with a wide-ranging mind. When the Rockefeller Foundation was first brought into being, John D. Rockefeller, Jr., asked Dr.

Watson to become its first head, and he refused. He did not want to leave his work. That was a tribute to the kind of broad thinking that he represented, and he went on one hand into education and on the other into extension because he felt that these were places where Egyptian life needed to be served. This was only a small portion of what had originally been envisioned, but it was all that could be developed at the time, and as a matter of fact became the basis of university life. The enrollment was only a few hundred at that time, and although it built up gradually, it became apparent that the university would be an adjunct rather than a competitor to national universities and would not occupy a place of preeminence like the American University of Beirut.

Ewart Memorial Hall has a very interesting history. A hall that seats 500-600 people, it played a leading role in the contribution that AUC made to Egypt, because it was the chief site for the activities of the Division of Extension. The Division of Extension is not an accurate translation. I use the term because we have, or at that time had, nothing quite like it in American life. In Arabic, it was called the Division of Public Service, and the idea was adult education, not in the academic sense, in giving courses and degrees, although that later developed, but in the sense of raising issues and providing a platform where the public could come into touch with the questions of the day. Consequently, the platform of Ewart Memorial Hall became the leading site for the discussion of a series of problems that have to this day been of great interest, such as the population problem, which was repeatedly discussed and lectured on.

The emergence of Israel, for instance, occasioned a whole series of meetings, and the policy of the University was to insist that this represented a neutral platform. This was one reason why it was used so much, because this kind of discussion could not take place in a government institution, and on the other hand, the University was sufficiently apart from the American official presence that it was not an American platform.

The funds for this hall came in one of these accidental ways that always leads the Egyptian to say, *"Rabbuna byidabbir,"* (The Lord has a way of doing it). Sometime in the early 1930's, a young woman came to Egypt with her traveling companion. She was a Miss Ewart, perhaps in her mid-20's. Her grandfather had been very ill and had come to Egypt, as people did before World War I, for its sunshine and its warmth, and to recover his health. This had stimulated her interest in Egypt, and she decided to make a visit.

Dr. Watson never allowed a promising tourist to get out of his hands. Miss Ewart had inherited her grandfather's fortune, by whose will it passed not to her parents but directly from the grandfather to her. She suddenly found herself a very rich young lady; she turned up in Cairo; Dr. Watson knew about this and he called on Dr. Wendell Cleland, who was then directing the Division of Extension program, to act as her host. Wendell squired her around Cairo, and she saw the things that she wanted to see.

She was in the city perhaps a week. In any case, the time came for her to depart, and Wendell was to drive her to the railway station. Before they left, her companion said to him, "Dr. Cleland, Miss Ewart is very grateful for what Egypt did for her grandfather, and she likes the work of the University, and she would like to leave some kind of memorial to her grandfather, just to remember this."

Wendell said, "Well, what does she have in mind?" He didn't know whether she wanted to leave an encyclopedia or a bronze tablet or what. And the companion said, "I really don't know. You'll have to talk to her."

So on the way to the railway station, which was about half a mile away, Wendell finally said, "Miss Ewart, I understand that you would like to leave some kind of a memorial to your grandfather." And she said, "Yes, I would, and I think the University would be a nice place to leave it."

"Well," Wendell said, "what did you have in mind?"

She thought for a moment and said, "Well, I really don't know. What do you really need?"

Wendell, who had dreamed about this for a long time but had no concrete plans, said: "Well, I'll tell you what we really need. What we really need is a fine public hall."

Miss Ewart replied, "How much would it cost?"

Wendell did not have any hard architectural fees. He more or less grabbed a probability out of the air—let us say, $300,000, which used to be a great deal of money. She thought for a moment and she said, "All right. I'll give it to you." And before she had left, she signed a little statement to this effect. Presently the money was forthcoming, and Ewart Memorial Hall, which was built in the Arab style, was constructed, and so far as I know Miss Ewart had no contact with the University at any time after that. She never visited it, she never returned to Cairo. She disappeared into the night, but she left behind her Ewart Memorial Hall.

One of the interesting things about the American University then (I cannot speak for it now), in contrast to some of the other foreign institutions, was the fact that although it was American in origin and American in educational philosophy, in contrast to the French and English institutions, in no sense was it there to advance American cultural interests. It was there to contribute what a group of American educators could contribute within the Egyptian milieu. Consequently, not only was a good part of the staff Egyptian, but Egyptians were from the very beginning drawn into its life and work. The Division of Extension was a particularly good example of that. The program had been set by a committee composed entirely of Egyptians with the exception of Dr. Cleland, the Director of the Department, and Dr. Watson, *ex officio*.

The Egyptians on the committee, through the years, were some of the most eminent people in the country. I think that as long as I was with the University Dr. Taha Husayn was a member of the committee. Lutfi al-Sayyid was a member, in his lifetime. The Minister of Education was almost always a member. Ahmad Husayn, Egyptian Ambassador to the United States at the time of the Suez Canal incident, had been a member of this committee for some years. Leading members of the Wafd were on it. It was an eminent professional group of Egyptians who were in the process of dealing with national problems, and it was they who set the program and very largely staffed it. Everything was in Arabic; there was nothing in English. Throughout the winter we would have a series of weekly lectures for which the hall would be filled, and at which one or more Egyptian leaders would take up questions of the day.

The University certainly did have a higher percentage of non-Muslim, non-Egyptians than their proportion in the population. This was to be expected. My recollection is that at the time I went to

Egypt in 1936, about half of the education was in private schools, which were either Egyptian or foreign, or a mixture of both, and there was a tendency for all of these schools to have a particular clientele. Certainly, the Armenian, the Coptic and the Greek communities would have taken over AUC had they been allowed to do so. There is no doubt about that. They were ambitious, they recognized the value of learning in English, and there was still a certain charm about the American imprint that attracted them, and this easily could have happened.

It did not happen. There was a general conviction that we should insist that every student in the institution had to study Arabic, had to read and write it, because we felt that whatever their origin, their future was there and that was what they should study. If they did not pass their Arabic, they could not be moved from class to class. This certainly repelled a considerable number of non-Arabic speaking people who, however much they might chatter in street Arabic, had no intention of wasting educational time on such a mundane subject.

Roughly, through these years before World War II, about half the undergraduate body was Egyptian. Add to that the fact that there were always quite a number who came from Transjordan and who would be largely Muslim, with almost no Christians among them. Palestinian Arabs came as well.

One reason for this was that Cairo was the great Arabic Muslim capital, toward which everyone flowed. Also, living conditions among those attending the new Egyptian University were not always very good. There were no dormitories, and foreign students, such as Jordanians, would tend to rent a house together and hire some local girls, ostensibly as housekeepers, and their parents were not very happy about this.

We had a dormitory and made some attempt to direct and develop this side of life. These facilities attracted a continuing group from Transjordan, and from Palestine. Now, with the troubles of recent years, I find that old students of mine have been on both sides of the lines.

As for the Egyptian group, I would say that we tended to enroll perhaps three different kinds of people. On the one hand, there was the ambitious parent and student who saw in the English language and in the introduction to Western ways and Western knowledge a chance for professional advancement. In this group one would find a large number of the Copts.

Then there was a smaller, but more select, group of Muslims who sent their children partly because of English; they wanted them to study abroad later. Another reason was that at this time the Egyptian educational institutions were deeply embroiled in politics and students were always going out on strike. Politics on the campus—we never had that problem. The greater discipline and the insulation from politics were reasons why Egyptian families sent their boys. This would be particularly true of the leading families, among whom the fact that our degree was not recognized was not a barrier at all. They were going to go on and study elsewhere.

In the third place, there were always students who had not done well in the rigid, somewhat French-dominated methods of the Egyptian school. They were often brought to us, as a sick patient is brought from an inefficient doctor, in the hope that the new doctor is going to do better. I am glad to say I think we did do better. In a number of cases we were able to get away from the rigidity and learning-by-rote characteristics of the local schools, and really produce conditions under which students could improve.

There were a number of innovations. Dr. Watson, with his vision, put it very succinctly: "We never can match the Egyptian University in spending. They have always got more money. But while they spend a hundred piasters to a pound, we ought to be able to get a hundred and ten piasters out of every pound, and two new ideas." We were constantly working and experimenting in this field, and a number of educational developments were introduced in our institution which were gradually picked up in Egyptian institutions. We never claimed credit for this.

One important factor was that the AUC was right next door to Parliament, where parliamentarians going back and forth saw what was going on, and on more than one occasion what they had seen got onto the floor of Parliament. For instance, we had intramural sports, based on the idea that the school was responsible for health as well as for education. We had gymnastic classes, running classes and tennis out on the property. Sometime in the 1930's an Egyptian, on his way to the senate, had seen this and asked, "Why is it that the American University can do this? Why can't we do it?" Our program was also accompanied by medical records, which were new. We had the first coeducation in higher education in Egypt, and now the Egyptian institutions are all coeducational.

This desire for some kind of pioneering was carried over into the academic process itself. We tried—and we certainly had a degree of success, although it became rather expensive—to look at our bachelor's degree, not only in terms of the normal amount of credits and standards that one has to have for graduation, but to ask, what are the skills that a university graduate ought to have? In the end, it seemed to us that we were trying to transmit skills rather than semester hours.

For a number of years we had a system in which in each year there was a requirement over and above the ordinary routine courses and routine semester count. This system called in the freshman year for a series of extra classes in language and writing skills, partly of necessity, but partly intended to fuse the whole process of education. One had to satisfy and complete these courses, as well as the course work.

In the sophomore year, this led on to a series of courses in which we tried to correlate knowledge, and at the end of the year there was an examination in which a student was asked to handle material from the standpoint of two different disciplines. For instance, in my field of religion and science, the two factors often clash with each other. We got together as a group and looked at these problems and tried to bring science into one side, religion into the other side, and then, at the end of the year, we had a comprehensive examination which cross-referenced these fields of knowledge. A student had to show that he had some comprehension of that before he moved on into the junior year.

There were some interesting examples: Mustafa Amin and his twin brother Ali. They became journalists, running the *Akhbar al-Yawm* newspaper. I suppose in this country they would have run the *Daily News* in its heyday. They were that sort of vigorous people.

Mustafa used to laugh. He said he found the American University a puzzling place. He, as well as his brother, had been put out of an Egyptian school, I suppose partly for being obstreperous, but partly because he could not pass the examination. When he asked his instructor why he had not passed, the instructor said, "Well, when you answer the questions, you put in a lot of ideas of your own that weren't in the textbook, and that's wrong. The examination is on the textbook."

Mustafa said: "The first term examination I took at the American University, I failed, and when I went to the teacher, I said, why did I fail? Well, he said, all you did was put in what was in the textbook. You didn't put in any ideas of your own. What's a poor fellow going to do?" It was precisely to get that emphasis that we had designed these courses.

In the junior year we had what was called the library project. Students were working all year in the library with faculty assistance —and at the end of the junior year each student was given a topic which he had never studied, so that he had no classroom knowledge of it, and was given one day in the library to take the topic and find out what was in the library on the subject. Not to read the material, but simply to go to the card files, find out what was there and to make such judgments as could be made from the card file references. We felt that at least a man going to the university ought to be able to research a simple problem. This, too, was a requirement for passing into the senior year.

And then, in the senior year, we had a research project, partly oral and partly written, which again took a question that was meant to cover two different fields of knowledge, and on which a student worked all year. At the end of the year he came up before a committee and took an oral examination on it.

Some of these projects were quite remarkable. For instance, there was the Lebanese playwright, Najib al-Rihani, and Rihani was in his heyday. He wrote a great many popular comedies and plays, and there was a Najib al-Rihani Theater in Cairo. One girl spent the year trying to study the social, as well as the literary, content of Najib al-Rihani's plays. It happened that something like two days after she had made her report, he died, and as a matter of fact, her written notes, which I believe finally went to the Library of Congress, contained some material nobody else had. Not everything was as good as this, of course, but this series of extracurricular activities were all designed to supplement and go beyond rote education. In things like that, which were not necessarily copied directly, we stimulated the interest and concern of Egyptian educators and Egyptian people and made a contribution in this way.

So far as I know, the first courses in journalism as an academic discipline offered in Egypt were given by us. The Journalism School kept on until the early 1960's. By that time journalism had been introduced into all the Egyptian universities, and the American University folded up its work. The Egyptian universities still teach it today, but not a few of the journalists in Cairo went to AUC.

As a matter of fact, when I went back to Egypt as Ambassador in 1961, one of my problems was that I was hounded by journalists who felt that they all should get an inside scoop from me because they had been AUC students. I didn't always oblige them.

We had got into journalism in what I would call a typical Watsonian manner. When I went to Cairo, the University was just getting over the effects of political party fighting in the country. In the early 1930's, King Fuad had suspended the Constitution and had ruled directly through Prime Minister Sidqi Pasha; in consequence, all the political parties were up in arms against the government, and they were looking for issues to embarrass the government.

We had a student from the well-known Husayni family of Jerusalem who didn't do very well, and when it came to the second semester of his senior year, he simply didn't make the grade. It was a very ticklish business, and it was finally decided that he would repeat the semester and pass, and in order to save face, he was allowed to appear on the platform with the other students who were going to graduate.

In the middle of the graduation ceremony, this lad stood up after he had been passed over in the degree-giving and said the reason he did not get his degree was because he had exposed the American University as an enemy of Islam. What he had done was to go through the library and find all the books in which statements appeared about Islam that some orthodox Muslims might not accept. This was not difficult, since we had a School of Oriental Studies with all kinds of books. He went to the newspapers with these stories, which were all printed, and the opposition party picked this up and used it as a political issue with the government, to beat them over the head and say, look how the government is favoring this enemy of Islam.

The affair reached its climax when one of the newspapers published an article about the American University, saying that the only way it could get students to come there was to provide the free services of prostitutes. Dr. Watson, a good moral Scots Presbyterian clergyman, was absolutely outraged, and his outrage was compounded when during the week, at his open-house, the editor of the newspaper, whose son was an AUC student, came to his tea party. Dr. Watson, who was a very patient man, finally said, "I do not understand how you can come and drink my tea and eat my cake. I should think you would choke on it, after what you wrote in the newspaper." To which the editor replied, "Doctor Watson, you were born and brought up in Egypt. You know there is nothing personal about this. This is simply journalism."

Dr. Watson said afterward to us, "If this is journalism, I am going to do something about it." He brought out Dr. Lyle Spenser, Dean of the School of Journalism at Syracuse University, to survey the situation, make suggestions, and start us on the road to teaching journalism.

* * *

I ought to point out that a good deal of my analysis really represents later thought and study, playing back upon the experiences of the time. I did not go to Egypt as a student, nor was my chief concern to analyze its life. I went to become a member of its society, hopeful of being of some service to it. It became my home, and in the first instance my interest dealt with my work and the people that I met.

I think that this points to something that is important in

Middle East studies, and that is a certain dichotomy between the analytical scholar and the person who is practically involved in the life of the area. The analytical scholar, by reason of his interests and the nature of analysis, must, I submit, retain a certain degree of separation from events, so that he can look at and judge them, see them in the round as it were, from the outside, and not simply from the inside. Only so is it possible to make the kind of political and historical judgments that are illuminating.

On the other hand, this very stepping aside, from without the scene, is apt to deny to him the understanding that comes when one lives from the inside and sees a situation, not so much in terms of analysis, as in terms of experience. And I found in later teaching that there was a constant need to correct the rather rigid intellectual view of a situation that came only by analysis. Very simply, it was very easy for students to look at the Middle East as if it were a problem in political science. It is not a problem in political science. It is people. People who are alive. People living. And how to combine that with analysis is a problem.

One of the great examples was my good friend and colleague and late great scholar, Dr. Joseph Schacht, probably the most eminent authority on *sharia* law. Yet, and I hope I do him no injustice, he really had no feeling whatever for Islam as a system of human values, of *sharia* law as a code of conduct and help to people, and when you asked him questions in that realm, he was disinterested and indeed would get rather irritated with them, feeling that this was not scholarly investigation. I would maintain that it is, and I think it has to be remembered that in this, as in all that an oral history tape records, I was living on the inside, and I saw things in terms of incidents, in terms of friendships, of people, not so much in terms of analysis.

The year 1936 was indeed a significant one in which to come to Egypt. It was the year King Fuad, the first modern King of Egypt, died. He had been placed on the throne by unilateral declaration of the British at the end of World War I, and by the same largely unilateral action Egypt had been given a Constitution in 1923. The Constitution, while based on European practice, and establishing a Parliament and a parliamentary system, in fact placed a great deal of authority in the hands of the Throne, and it was really the Throne, backed by British power, that formed the effective center of political power in Egypt. It would be wrong to say that the democratic process, as practiced in a parliamentary system, was at work. I think Egypt is a prime example of the failure of the parliamentary system in the Middle East, one which has not been adequately studied.

Because of this characteristic of the Constitution and the British backing of the Throne, at least in the beginning, in the early 1930's it was possible for the King to dispense with Parliament, to suspend the Constitution, which he had every right to do, and to rule without the Constitution through appointed lieutenants, politicians who identified themselves with the Throne. This had caused a first-class political crisis in Egypt. It led to a great deal of resentment in the rising political life of the country, especially in the major political party, the Wafd, which stood in relation to Egypt the way the Democratic Party always used to do in the South of this country. If you were not a Wafdist, you were not really a true country Egyptian.

When King Fuad died in 1936, it meant not only the end of the first ruler of Egypt but also of the first phase of Egyptian royal authority. Putting the young Faruq on the throne seemed to promise the opening of a new chapter in the development of political institutions in Egypt. Faruq came in on a wave of very great popularity. He was a slender, attractive young man, 17 by the Western calendar, 18 by the Muslim Arab calendar. He married into the very well-known Zulfiqar family. The father was a judge and the daughter, Farida, was a beautiful and cultured woman, and they came from the old Turkish-Egyptian aristocracy. A very attractive royal couple was on the throne. With the accession of a new and untried monarch, even though he had received no education whatever to fit him for the throne—it was said he was brought up by the barbers and the donkey boys of the palace—there was a general feeling of euphoria and a chance to begin again and develop democratic parliamentary institutions.

I did not find a great many of my colleagues at this period keenly responsive to what was going on. Cairo is a big city, and it is amazing how in a large capital city you can have political currents swirling around, you can have riots, and not be terribly aware of them. When they are headlined in the *New York Times*, they demand one's attention. Sometimes when you live in the midst of such events you are far less aware of them than the person abroad reading about them.

One's awareness of the political situation was largely generated by the Egyptian circles in which one moved and by their understanding of the situation. This varied very much among my colleagues. The group which lived out in the Cairo suburb of Maadi, originally the suburb for British administrators and very foreign in its atmosphere, was less in touch with Egyptian life than those of us who lived in the city, where we met Egyptians. I lived in the university itself, right down in the heart of "Times Square," *Midan Ismailiyya*.

I would say that the general outlook of my colleagues was certainly liberal. One was caught up in these years in the typical American reaction against British control. During the war, Dean Landis of the Harvard Law School came to Cairo as American Director of Economic Operations in the Middle East and he lectured the British on this American attitude. He summed up what the American often feels about situations like this when he said that there is a very old and respectable tradition in America, that every country has a right to go to hell in its own way. While everybody had British friends, respected the British and recognized that they were good administrators, I would not say that the American community was strongly in support of the British.

One example of the American reaction against British rule goes back to the Harding administration. Our first Minister to Egypt, named Howell, was appointed by President Harding. He was a veterinary surgeon from Ohio who, it is said, had been one of Harding's poker-playing cronies. He arrived in Egypt, in which we had no particular interest at the time, quite innocent of any diplomatic experience or indeed of any worldly experience.

In his train he left a wealth of stories, but the one that I enjoyed the most, which I think is not apocryphal at all, had to do with the fact that the British High Commissioner, at that time Lord Lloyd, was really the last of the great British imperialists. Steely blue eyes, courteous, a no-nonsense administrator, Lloyd was the *doyen* of the diplomatic corps by virtue of the fact that he was the British High Commissioner. But Howell did not see why the American Minister should take a back seat to any British administrator.

When the opera season opened every fall in the Opera House down on the Square, for whose inaugural Verdi had written "Aida," the diplomatic corps always attended the first night. It was understood that the space directly in front of the door was reserved for Lord Lloyd's carriage, from which he would alight and walk in. Howell thought he had no right to this favored spot, probably reasoning, "I am just as good as he is—I am the American Minister—the American Minister's just as good as the British High Commissioner."

So that night he went down and had his coachman lurk just in the shadows away from this spot. When he saw Lord Lloyd driving up, about to go in, he had his coachman touch up the horses and slide into that slot just in front of Lord Lloyd, so that Lord Lloyd's coachman had to rein in, and Lloyd got out on the street, walked around the carriage and went inside, Howell having preceded him.

The next day the whole diplomatic corps turned on Howell and told him he could not do this. After all, Lloyd was the *doyen* of the corps, as well as the British High Commissioner. Howell would have to make some kind of apology.

Howell felt that he had made his point, so he went over to the British High Commissioner's office, not far from the University and not far from Howell's legation, presented his compliments, and asked to be received. Lord Lloyd greeted him and asked to what he owed the pleasure of his colleague's visit. After hemming and hawing, Howell said, "Well, Lord Lloyd, I really came to apologize for the incident at the opera last night."

Lloyd said, "At the opera? Incident? Last night? What do you mean by that, Howell?"

"Well," he said, "you know, when you drove up there, my coachman got out of hand, and without meaning it he slipped in front of you and caused some embarrassment."

To which Lloyd replied, "At the opera last night? My dear Howell, were you there? I didn't see you at all."

* * *

During the period from 1936 to 1940, there was a great deal of political discontent, and in particular the students got out of hand. They were constantly rioting up and down the streets. This did not endear the national movement to young educators, and there was a tendency to react against these excesses, and therefore to stand, perhaps, somewhat in the middle.

I would say that the political leaders of the pasha class were not so well-known to me because I did not very often come in touch with them. Directly beneath them was the parliamentary group, and these one knew much better—deputies, who might be Wafdists or Saadists or even supporters of the Throne, but who were the up-and-coming modern people, speaking foreign languages and looking toward things American.

They did have redeeming virtues. I think the study of parliamentary legislation at that time would show that there was a good deal of progress. It is very easy to sit back under the impact of postwar conditions and of revolutionary developments and say, why didn't they do this or why didn't they do that? Well, we can go back to the pre-Roosevelt era in the United States and say the same thing.

This was the period in which there was the development—the foundation, at least—of a national educational system. A considerable amount of social legislation was passed. And while they could have done a great deal better, I think that any fair estimate would say that given all the circumstances that confined them, they did not do badly at all. I knew many of the deputy class, and they were really very much concerned with the development of a modern Egypt.

I think, however, in judging Parliament, one has to go back and look at the political forces that were contending for power in the prewar years, perhaps the postwar years as well, and it was the decay of those powers that I think created the revolution. I emphasized above the importance of the Throne in the Constitution of Egypt, and certainly this was the major power, but behind the Throne were the British—the British occupation and the British administration through advisers to the government.

The third political power in Egypt was the Wafd Party, growing out of the movement to independence during World War I. It was the largest political party, and under it I would rank all the other political parties, the Saadists, the Istiqlalists and the Destouris. The Wafd was the one power you really had to come to terms with.

Finally, there was the influence of al-Azhar, the religious university. Not merely al-Azhar as an institution, but al-Azhar as representing the religious establishment of Egypt headed by the Rector, who in these prewar years, with Faruq on the throne, was Muhammad Mustafa al-Maraghi.

There were, therefore, four centers of power, and at any one time you could have the King and the British against the Wafd and al-Azhar. Or, the King and al-Azhar against the Wafd and the British. There were all kinds of combinations. An agreed balance of power between these forces was never achieved, and consequently all during this period there was a good deal of confusion. I think Professor Nadav Safran chose a very good phrase for this period when he spoke of "Egypt in search of political community." They did not have it, and they thought with the coming of Faruq they might achieve it, but they did not.

There is another factor to be remembered: All during Egyptian independence, and certainly during the period I am discussing, the overwhelming political reality and concern of the country was the British occupation. The question for these forces—the Throne, al-Azhar, and the Wafd—was, what will we do about the British? This question dominated all the politics of Egyptian life. This meant that it colored and became a focus of political life on almost every level. One might be, for instance, Minister of *Awqaf*,* but in the end, if he did not have a proper stance regarding the position of the British, he was not apt to play a political role, although the

---

*Muslim religious trusts.

position of the British had nothing to do with the *Awqaf* at all. One might be Collector of Customs for the Port of Alexandria, but the major political passport to respectability was how one felt about the British.

This was the question that dominated Egyptian politics, that lay beyond the ability of the Egyptians to solve, and was therefore a constantly recurring disturbance and crisis within Egyptian life. It was one of the major reasons why the Egyptians never really did develop the kind of democratic institutions that they wanted.

The British themselves were in a great dilemma at this period. On one hand, they had provided the Constitution. They were, under the Labour Party particularly, socially and politically liberal. In principle, they believed in the democratization of these emerging areas and announced this as their interest in Egypt. On the other hand, the nature of their imperial interest was such that they could not thoroughly trust Egypt to use the democratic process, and therefore had to reserve some areas which could not be altered by Egyptians. The status of the Suez Canal, for instance, lay beyond Egyptian authority, as did certain matters in the conduct of foreign policy and the very difficult matter of Egyptian relations with the Sudan.

On the one hand, the British were pushing Egypt toward parliamentary democracy, and on the other, they had continuously to interfere to prevent parliamentary democracy from working, because had it worked, it would have ejected them from the country. This was the turbulent sea into which Faruq came, and through which the political forces of Egypt tried to find some reasonably safe and quiet course until the outbreak of World War II.

Popularly, I would say that the sense of euphoria which came with Faruq's accession to the throne lasted pretty well into perhaps 1938 or 1939. One did not hear much popular criticism of the King. By 1939, the King was beginning to gamble rather heavily and not always staying home with Queen Farida, and while these are the prerogatives of royalty in any country, and certainly in Egypt, it began to be noticed and people began to respond to it.

Long before that, however, there was a loss of euphoria in the political scene. I am not sure that the masters of strategy in the Wafd ever felt as euphoric as they appeared to feel. As soon as the King was crowned, it was quite apparent that the Wafd, sometimes aided and abetted by al-Azhar, was very anxious to prevent this new King from ever attaining the power and the ability to exercise it that his father had.

This was shown in a variety of ways. One was the attempt of the government to dominate appointments to the royal cabinet. Not very long after Faruq was crowned, there was a bitter political struggle between the Wafd and the King over who would control the appointment of the King's political advisers and directors.

A second tactic that was tried was to encourage the King in the kind of irresponsible playboy development that would on the one hand keep him busy and on the other hand would worsen his image with the common people. This was not too difficult. The King did not have a gift for picking good people around him. The Lebanese, Karim Thabet, is generally said to have been his evil genius. He was known all over Cairo and popularly seen in this light. What happens, of course, is at first one says: "Well, a man in authority really, he is not responsible, it is the people around him," and people like Karim Thabet came in for criticism long before the King did.

It was then that the King began to display in public some of the attitudes that lost him popular favor. His thinking went something like this: "You're the King. You run Egypt. You go into a jewelry shop, you see a nice watch you want, you don't have to pay for it, you're the King. You take it and go home. You see a girl you want. Take her. You're the King, aren't you?"

One incident that caused a great deal of talk was at the Royal Yacht Club in Alexandria. There was a little brass cannon that was fired to start the yacht season. It was quite old apparently, and a highly prized piece. The King saw it, liked it, tucked it under his arm and took it home. He was encouraged in all this. He may have had a natural bent in this direction, but he was certainly encouraged by the people the Wafd put around him. Thus, in the late 1930's, he began to develop a playboy image which certainly took away a lot of the original good feeling.

Mustafa Nahhas was leader of the Wafd party. He was not visually very inspiring. There is a great deal of trachoma in Egypt, and Nahhas Pasha had been afflicted. One eye was very badly out of alignment, so that he looked at you with only one eye; his other eye looked yonder. I met him a number of times when he was Prime Minister, partly on behalf of the University. Nahhas was a popular politician who appeared on the balconies and exhorted the crowd, an orator who stirred up national feeling.

In 1936, when the Ethiopian crisis had almost broken up the League of Nations, Egypt concluded its first treaty with Great Britain—another reason why 1936 was a significant year. It was a treaty which somewhat diminished the prerogatives of the British presence and altered at least the façade behind which the British operated. The High Commissioner became an Ambassador. Egypt became an ally of Great Britain, instead of an occupied country. Nahhas Pasha negotiated this, despite the fact that the policy of the Wafd had always been for complete evacuation. He read the signs and recognized the situation. Egypt felt threatened by the Italian presence in Ethiopia, so he went to England and rather successfully negotiated this treaty; I think he was a shrewd politician.

When Nahhas came back from England in 1936, he came back in a wave of popular enthusiasm. There was now a Treaty, Egypt could call itself independent, and he was hailed throughout the country with great acclaim. Indeed, he saw to it that he was hailed with great acclaim, for he had claques of young street boys who would clap and cheer and call for him wherever he came out in public in Cairo.

The Egyptian is an absolute master at ticking off political events in stories. This was one: Nahhas was asleep one night with his wife in their bedchamber, and Madame Nahhas awakened in the early hours of the morning, felt ill, and pulled the bell rope beside her bed to call the servant. He did not come, so she sat up in bed and did what every Egyptian did to call servants, she clapped her hands loudly. In his sleep, Nahhas sat up, put his hand on his nightshirt bosom, and gravely bowed right and left to the adoring "crowds."

At a later period, toward the end of the war, when Nahhas was back in power, brought back by the British, another story shows popular reaction toward him. We had many shortages and everything was rationed during the war, and when the Nahhas cabinet came in, in 1942, Egypt was in the grip of these war restrictions.

The story was told about a poor man in Cairo who went down to the bank of the Nile and caught a fish; he brought it home gleefully, threw it in front of his wife and said, "Hurry up now. Cook it." She said, "I can't cook it." He said, "Why not?" "Well, I don't have any *nabatin*." (*Nabatin* is like Crisco, a fat.)

She said, "You know, the *nabatin* ration has been reduced and we finished ours up a week ago."

"Well," he said, "don't stand there yammering. Go cook it in butter."

She said, "Are you crazy. Do you know what butter costs at the bazaar? It costs a pound a kilo. I can't possibly afford that."

"Well," he said, "don't talk about it. Go cook it in olive oil."

She said, "In olive oil? The only olive oil we get comes from Syria, and since this present Cabinet is in power, they won't allow us to use any foreign exchange to buy it."

Very sadly, he took the fish to the banks of the Nile and threw it back in the river and stood watching it regretfully. It lay wan and white on the surface and gradually floated out of sight. Then it suddenly came to life again, stuck its head out of the water, waved one fin to the fisherman, and called out, "Long live Nahhas Pasha."

One of the devices that the Wafd turned to, shortly after Faruq became King, was to create a youth branch, like the Fascist Youth or the Hitler Youth; they called it the Blue Shirts. They intended to mount political action through this kind of movement. Then there were the Green Shirts, whom I believe to have been the Azhar-Throne counterweight to the Blue Shirts. They copied storm trooper tactics, rioting up and down the streets, getting into brawls with each other. The King still had sufficient authority finally to force the Wafd to give up the Blue Shirts and to neutralize them with the Boy Scouts, one of the King's special interests. There was another group called the Young Men of Muhammad, a rather militant "young men's Muslim association." All of these were devoted to the use of nondemocratic, violent means—of riot—we would call it today protest—with some desire to inject a strong Islamic note into the government.

The Muslim Brotherhood did not emerge on the popular scene until the closing days of the war; we know now they had been present and were operating. Had one been in government, one would have known it, but they were not particularly talked about. One did not have friends who were Muslim Brothers.

It has to be remembered that of all the political forces in Egypt the Wafd was the most secular. It was the least Muslim; it stood for secular government. It had very important leadership in the Christian community, and when in power there was a general feeling in Egypt that it was less discriminatory toward minorities than other governments might be. Over against this various other movements claimed to seek the reinstitution of Islamic elements within government life.

Some of my Egyptian friends believed that Maraghi, the Shaykh al-Azhar, had persuaded the King that royal power could be maintained, in the face of Wafd pressure, precisely by resuscitating a more Muslim state. I have no evidence that that is true, but I think there is some evidence that either the Palace directly, or people who represented the Palace, such as Ali Mahir,* put some money and some organization into this kind of religious group.

I never felt during this period that there was a great deal of attraction to totalitarianism *per se*. I think where you touched circles that were deeply concerned over the Palestine question—and this would be very much closer to the beginning of World War II, say in 1939—then those people tended to welcome German Fascism, because it held in check the forces they saw as bringing a Jewish state into Palestine. But as to general acceptance of Fascism or Nazism as a philosophy of government—I am not conscious that that was ever looked on with much favor. One has to remember that the Middle East has its own tradition of centralized power. I think it is a great mistake to think, for instance, that Nasser is explained by Tito, or by European Fascism of some sort. After all, the tradition of power in Egypt during a long memorable period

---

*Ali Mahir was several times Prime Minister.

was what we would call today "Fascist" authority. The strong man was a native ruler, and was not surrounded by a particular philosophic devotion to a political system.

There was a larger tendency in Egypt to judge in terms of nationality. The Italians were not popular and I remember in the opening days of World War II going down to my garage one morning and seeing standing up against the wall a row of beer bottles, filled with something. At the time, I had a driver—I did not usually have one—and I asked him what those were? "Oh," he said, "these are Molotov cocktails, and when the Italians march into Alexandria, we are going to go down there and throw these at them." That kind of attitude was not pro-Fascist by any means.

The Italian colony in Egypt was accused of welcoming and indeed of working for Fascism, and to that extent, it tended to repel people rather than attract them. I do think, though, that movements like the Blue Shirts and the Green Shirts and the *Shabab Muhammad* were copied, to a degree, from Fascist practice. But as in Nasser's later adoption of certain practices found in Communist states, I would be very careful not to assume that these devices signified a political philosophy.

* * *

When I went to Cairo in 1936, Arthur Jeffery was there, heading the small School of Oriental Studies, which was also the setting for his own research work on the Quran, to which he was then devoting himself.

Jeffery had come to Cairo, I think, between 1920 and 1930, before I had. He was an Australian, a Methodist minister, and had gone, I believe under the Methodists, as an educational missionary to India. While in India he had become interested in Indian languages and began his long career in philology. While he was a fine Islamacist, it seems to me that essentially he approached matters philologically.

When I became President of the University, I looked through Dr. Watson's correspondence; I found his original correspondence suggesting that Jeffery come from India and join the staff in Cairo, and Jeffery's response, which was genuinely modest. He said that he really did not think he was fitted to do this work because, while he knew Arabic, he was only then working in something like 28 different languages and did not think this was enough for a thorough scholar. It was partly witness to the fact that his standards of scholarship were very high indeed, standards which appeared again when he came to Columbia.

Of course, all kinds of stories gather around such people. Jeffery was married in Cairo. He married Dr. Watson's secretary, and they went out to spend their honeymoon at the Mena House, at the foot of the pyramids, and knowing the penchant of this scholar for study, the young American teachers at the University got hold of his suitcase, took all the clothing out, and filled it with texts in Arabic. And the story was that when he unpacked that night, he had nothing to spend the night in but Arabic manuscripts.

That may be true. It certainly was true that Mr. and Mrs. Jeffery would go out for the evening and after dinner Jeffery would excuse himself and go home so that he could study. This was understood. Mrs. Jeffery would remain. Despite this rather austere devotion to scholarship, he was also a very gracious host. Among the delightful experiences were the Shakespeare evenings that he had in his apartment in Cairo, where friends would be asked in, largely the University staff. It was always a black tie affair, and we spent the evening reading Shakespeare's plays, playing the different parts. And he was a man of infinite humor. He had the greatest string of stories that I remember anyone having—a very good raconteur indeed. He was altogether a delightful person and a very fine scholar.

He left Cairo about 1939. It was very interesting why he left. After all, Cairo was the natural spot for a scholar doing his research. He had come across a very early commentary on the Quran. I think it had been in one of the mosque libraries in Damascus. In any case, he had got hold of it and brought it to Cairo and was working in it; its value was that it contained variant readings of the Quran text that are not otherwise in existence.

So Jeff got one of the shaykhs of al-Azhar to come down and do work with him, and they were working through this commentary, annotating and translating it. He never would use a typewriter, and wrote his notes out in longhand in a series of notebooks. One of the things that Jeff would not have was a telephone in his office. He abominated it, and the telephone was at the end of the hall.

After some months of work, he and the shaykh had had a session; the notebooks were piled on one side of the table. The telephone rang, Jeff's secretary came in to tell him he was wanted, so he left the room and went to the telephone. When he came back, the shaykh who had been helping him was gone, and all the pages were ripped out of the notebooks and torn up. The shaykh could not stand the heresy of being confronted with these variant readings of the Quran. Apparently it had been bothering him for some time.

In effect, Jeff said, "You know, I simply cannot do this kind of work in Cairo." At that time, Columbia had lost its Arabic scholar and approached him, and he left the American University and came to Columbia, where he remained until he died.

We all knew Creswell* in Cairo. Creswell, you know, was one of those absolutely unique people. He had been a captain in the British Army during the war, brought out to the Middle East. He was not a university man. I think I am right in saying that he did not complete his university degree, and he did not have any specialized training. But he did get very interested during his military service in the Middle East, Palestine and Egypt, in the architecture of mosques.

When he got back to England, he did not know quite what to do, because he did not have any training. Somebody said to him, there is something anybody can do. You can start a bibliography. He went to the British Museum and, for any publication that had more than a certain number of articles in a given period dealing with Muslim architecture, he would go back to the original publication, and enter on little cards a bibliographic file of all the articles that had appeared in that journal since it had first been published.

This, of course, was a very painstaking piece of work, but it laid a foundation of knowledge that was unique and had the great advantage that anybody could pick it up and add to it.

Through this door he got into the study of monuments and of

---

*Sir K.A.C. Creswell, author of a number of works on Muslim architecture.

architecture, and by the time I arrived in Egypt he was teaching Arab architecture at the Egyptian University, and the first or second of his great tomes on Arab architecture had come out.

Despite the fact that Creswell was, I suppose, the leading authority in English on Muslim architecture—and when he finished a building, it had been measured and described to the point where nothing really could be added to it—he was not an Arabic scholar at all. He depended for his Arabic upon students. While he knew some Arabic, it was very little.

Furthermore, he was a thorough English colonialist and to an extent one must almost say a snob—he looked down on the Egyptian. He always carried a little bamboo cane, and when he was walking around the walls of Cairo and encountered street boys, he would just lay about him, and use extremely intemperate language to them. He always wore a very high starched collar that stretched his neck up. Very dapperly dressed, impeccable, he was the Piccadilly Englishman, out in the sticks, bringing knowledge and enlightenment to the natives. Strangely enough, the Egyptians understood this and accepted it. Of course, they tended to laugh at the incidents and say, who is the *magnun* (the crazy one)? But they accepted his scholarship and even during World War II, when the British did not fare so well, and later at the time of the revolution, Creswell was very kindly dealt with by the government.

In the latter part of the pre-World War II years, if I remember correctly, he lived in a little room up beyond the Muski bazaar in the very old part of Cairo. There are some very old houses there and he liked living in the old section of the city. Beneath him lived an Egyptian family; the woman had a radio which she played during the day, and the radio disturbed Creswell. He had his little library up in his apartment and as he worked the radio would go on and on, wailing Arabic songs. He finally lost his temper, as he did ten times a day, and went downstairs and pounded on the door, and when she opened it up, he cut loose in his broken Arabic and demanded she turn it off.

When her husband came home that night—this was a very conservative part of the city—he was outraged, and he took Creswell to task. Creswell finally said, "Well, you are right. I should not have done that." So he put on his best clothes and went down and knocked on the door and made a very abject apology to the woman.

I had an experience something like this at the University. In the early days of the War, I was in Cairo alone, and had an office in the School of Oriental Studies, in the center of which there was a quasi-courtyard so you could look over the railing and down at the front door. I was up in my study one morning, and I heard the most unholy yelling and shouting downstairs, what we call in Egypt a *dawsha* (disturbance). I looked over the railing and here was Creswell with a little bamboo cane, on the end of which he had skewered the *bawwab* (porter); he was absolutely incoherent.

I went down to see what had happened. We used to ask Creswell in to lecture, and he was going to lecture that night on the Dome of the Rock, with slides. He had come early in the morning to be sure that everything was set up. The door was closed, as it was a warm day, and we had a relief doorman—every doorman had one day a week off—who did not know Creswell.

Creswell had knocked at the door, the *bawwab* had opened it to this Englishman, and had said to him, "*Min inta?*" (Who are you?) And Creswell shouted back at him, "Not *inta* (you), but *min Hadratukum*! (Who is your presence, Your Honor?) You should say who is Your Honor!"

These Sudanese *bawwabs* are pretty tough themselves, so he proceeded to repeat, "*Min inta?*" And Creswell was shouting, "*Mush* (not) *inta! min Hadratukum!*" And when I went down there, he turned to me, absolutely livid, and said, "He called me *inta*! You must discharge him immediately! I have been insulted."

So I discharged the *bawwab* immediately to the next room, and took Creswell upstairs to my office. I was just about to have morning coffee and by great good fortune—the Egyptian would have said Allah ordered it that way—I had a plate of chocolate cookies from Groppi's,* which were called *diables noirs*. I did not know it, but Creswell was passionately fond of them, and underneath the influence of hot coffee and black devils, he calmed right down, especially since I had fired the doorman.

So he went off and that was over. And then I brought the

---
*A famous patisserie and restaurant in Cairo.

bawwab up and winked him up a little bit and raised his salary half a pound a month for having been insulted, reinstated him, and everything was all right. That was Creswell.

Much later, when I went out to Cairo as Ambassador in 1961, I was again reminded of him. I had been immediately preceded by Frederick Reinhardt, a holdover from the Eisenhower administration, who stayed in Egypt for a short time and went on to become Ambassador to Italy. In talking over Embassy matters and what had gone on in recent months, Reinhardt asked me if I knew Creswell, at which I smiled and allowed that I did know him a little. He said he knew him too, and he had never known anyone like him.

What had happened was that he had had a dinner for the various American archaeological expeditions that were operating in Egypt, of which there were quite a number, and he had a table of perhaps 16 or 18 guests, including Creswell. He was the only one who was concerned with Arab history, while most of the others were in Egyptian archaeology, the Pharaonic period.

Reinhardt said the talk flowed fast and furious around the table, but it all dealt with the ancient period, and the longer they talked the more uncomfortable Creswell apparently became. He coud not get a word in edgewise. His subject matter was not under consideration. Finally, in the middle of the dinner, he raised his hands and brought them down on the table with a resounding whack that made the silver and glasses all jump, and bellowed out in a loud voice, "A.D.!, A.D.!, A.D.!" With that, the conversation came to an end.

* * *

A hobby of mine for all the years I was out there was the mosques of Cairo, not primarily because of Creswell, although I learned a great deal from him, but somewhat because of the nature of Cairo itself.

Baghdad was an older city than Fatimid Cairo by some 200-250 years. It gave the impression of being very old, in that it was dilapidated, but it had very little of continuing interest in it. There were very few spots at which it seemed that the past lived on into the present, through buildings or through organizations. This was partly due to the fact that it had been sacked by the Mongols under Hulagu in the middle of the 13th century and really never recovered. From the 13th century—really down to the founding of modern Iraq—Baghdad was little more than a mud village of superior size on the banks of the Tigris.

By contrast, Cairo, founded 250 years later, had never been sacked by anybody, and consequently there was not the amount of destruction of buildings that had gone on in Baghdad, where there was so little left. Cairo was full of architecture that reached back to its very beginning. Not only public architecture, but buildings set in a social situation in which they continued to have life. You could almost think of Cairo as a core, adding layer after layer, growing outward, each layer reflecting the age during which it came into existence, and to a certain extent continuing some of the characteristics of that age. You were very much aware of living on the edge of, or with entrée to, a more traditional urban society than you were in Baghdad, and certainly, in this, a large number of mosques played a real role.

My interest in the great mosques was generated partly by the fact that as an engineer who had done building myself, I was interested in building practices, how the stresses and strains were carried, how the designs were laid. But I was really interested in much more than that. After all, a building is in a certain sense the materialization at a particular time of a whole series of influences, and if you look at a building not only as a problem in stresses and strains but as the confluence of historical forces, a building begins to lead you back into the age from which it came. As I have said several times, I was much more interested in life and in people than I was in formal culture.

Let me give an example. There is a mosque that stands within the Citadel that was built by al-Nasir Muhammad, the son of Qalaun. He had built a mosque down in the center of Cairo and then built this mosque, now somewhat restored, that sits up back of the Citadel. The interesting thing about the mosque is that the minaret has what looks to be Persian tile around the outside, and there is almost never any tile on minarets in Cairo. There is tile in the interior of mosques in plaques, but this is a departure from the ordinary, and a departure that was not followed up.

How did that tile get on that minaret? As far as I could determine, it was built during the time when life in the Middle East was being dislocated by the Mongol invasions. Al-Nasir Muhammad married a Volga Tartar princess said to have become his favorite wife, (Umm Anuk) and faience tile begins to appear in Cairo monuments in her era. One can almost picture the scene in which he decided to put up the mosque, and she says, "You know, please, I'm homesick, we always have tiles on our minarets. Why couldn't I have some tiles on my minaret?" So he put some tiles on the minaret.

I can't prove that historically, although the facts of her origin are well known, and every time I see that mosque I am led back from it into the whole dislocation of the Middle East by the Mongol invasion and into family pressures of women. Who knows what historical decisions may have been made on just such a basis? As you go over the various mosques in Cairo, you see not only their architecture as a purely engineering problem, but if you take each one, it becomes a living embodiment of the age in which it was set.

Then you go beyond this: a mosque was not only an architectural achievement and a point in history, it also had a use, and the use very largely determined the functional architecture of the mosque. As you look at the architecture, you get some understanding of the religious community and of the purpose it served, and this can carry you back to the society.

For instance, all of the early mosques, of which Ibn Tulun, which dates back into the ninth century, is certainly the most complete, are very simple. The Ibn Tulun Mosque is very simple indeed. You almost feel as though you were in a Gothic abbey in Europe when you stand within it. And when you go from that to, let us say, the little Mosque of Qait Bey, out in the Old Cemetery, which is small, highly ornate, very highly decorated, you see not only the natural evolution of style and decoration, but you see the reflection of something that was going on in Islam itself. In the eighth century, Islam was still relatively simple. It had a straightforward creed. Its theology was becoming elaborate, but still it had many of the marks of straightforward simplicity.

By the time you get to Qait Bey (1468-96), Islam, like Christianity 15 centuries after its birth, had become highly elaborate, filled with scholasticism, filled with all kinds of theological speculations, and the mosque becomes somewhat confusing at this point because, I think, it reflects the image of the community that was about it.

One can say either that the Qait Bey Mosque came at the pinnacle of development, or just when things began to turn sour. I base that on a good many things, but I think one of the interesting marks of it is the fact that in all of the medieval mosques, beginning with Ibn Tulun and becoming more and more elaborate as you come down through the centuries, the use of great Arabic inscriptions in bands around the walls was very common. This was not only decoration. It was a kind of holy crossword puzzle. Very hard to read. It becomes an intellectual challenge. You sit and look at it and puzzle it, and suddenly you see it, and when you see it, you are rewarded by having a verse of God's revelation, the Holy Quran.

In mosques after Ibn Tulun—within a few years—one looks at an inscription to puzzle it out, but one cannot. Why? Because it goes around the corner. You have been tricked. It has become clever, and if you turn to the Muslim theology of that period, you would be just as baffled as you were by the inscription on the mosque.

These were the kinds of things that interested me in the mosques. As far as I had time, I used to go and visit them. Indeed, I used to take my students to see them, because I have found that the ordinary Muslim student really knew nothing about his architectural heritage and very little about the connection between the mosque and his faith. I found that they appreciated this. It gave me a chance to meet them in a non-classroom experience, and I think that every man should understand his cultural heritage as well as he can.

During the war, when I went back to Cairo for the best part of a winter under government auspices, on Sundays I took groups of American Army officers on tours of the mosques. My purpose there was somewhat different. These fellows were far from home. While Cairo was not in any sense a hostile city, it was dirty by American standards—it had a lot of flies. The irritations of war tended to show themselves, and the officers talked about all these damned gypsies and everything they did. If you take a reasonable man out and show him the fan arching in the Qait Bey doorway and point out what geometry is involved in doing that, they say, "Gee, these guys knew something didn't they?" And I hoped I was making some contribution, not only to general knowledge, but to an appreciation that Egypt as a country and Islamic culture as a civilization were worthy of respect. While I never had the time to go into it as deeply as I would like, still I had enough to give myself a great deal of satisfaction.

I like the great middle period—the Muayyad (1416-20) Mosque at the Bab al-Zuwayla gate, and the great mosque of Qalaun, a magnificent piece of work, and Muhammad al-Nasir, who was the son of Qalaun, and of course Sultan Hasan (1356-64), who built the big mosque in the period—all the ripening of mosque architecture into its great period.

Ibn Tulun (876-79) is impressive because the Muslim community in Cairo at the time—Cairo really had not been founded when Ibn Tulun was built, but what became Cairo—was still small enough so that everybody who counted could go to the mosque at one time. If I remember correctly, Ibn Tulun covers about six acres of ground. You can get 10,000 people in it, and there you had the worshipping Muslim community together at one mosque.

Ibn Tulun I keep coming back to, and some years ago, when I could, I painted a number of pictures of Ibn Tulun, because it just had a charm. One of the reasons I think is the fact that it reminds me of many aspects of Gothic architecture—being one of the earliest buildings in the world to use the pointed arch.

On the other hand, mosques like the *madrasa* or school of Sultan Hasan give a different impression. It is not big enough to take large groups of people, and at this point what becomes fascinating about the mosque is the skill with which the architect uses decoration.

Indeed, I think one has to say that most of the mosques of

Egypt and the Levant—that is, excluding Iran and Turkey—rarely reached great architectural proportions. There are a few. There is Sultan Hasan; there is the tomb mosque of Barquq, outside the city, with minarets and domes and balance; but that was rare.

What the architects loved to do was to decorate, and this is where they were superb, because the decoration was related to and grew out of the natural lines of stress, and that is almost an infallible guide as to whether a mosque of this later period is a good mosque or not. If you look at its decoration, its inscriptions, its stalactites, and feel that you can take a putty knife and scape them off the wall, that is a bad mosque. If somehow they grow out of it, so you could not scrape them off without seeing the wall crumble down, there you have a good architect. At its height one had this integration of decoration and of stress line that did make them very impressive indeed.

There were two or three things that the architect in Cairo never really solved. He never really solved the problem of achieving great height within the mosque. The Turk did, partly because he inherited the Byzantine tradition. It was also, in my opinion, partly because he lived in a rainy climate and had to cover his courtyard. You do not have to cover your courtyard in the Middle East. I think one thing that the architects were quite conscious of, though I have no documentary proof, is that the blue sky of the uncovered courtyard becomes an integral part of the color scheme of the mosque, and as you look at it, you get this blue ceiling, provided by God in his grace, that melts right into the mosque. You tend to have large courtyards, which are very hard to roof over, and therefore the mosque never attained that soaring sense that you feel in the good, large Ottoman mosques with the domes, and certainly nothing that corresponds to the soaring feeling of Gothic architecture. They were flatter.

Perhaps this itself is a reflection of the fact that in many ways Islam is a very earthy religion. God does not require what is difficult, but what is easy, says the Quran, and while one should not assume that being a good Muslim was an easy task at all, in many ways I think it was a very humanistic view of life. Perhaps the mosque sat close to the earth and served a great many purposes other than worship, and not very often, at least in this local tradition, greatly reaching upward toward the unknown. Perhaps that is just a reflection of the character of Islam.

The so-called Muhammad Ali Mosque (1824) bears the same relation, in my opinion, to the best of Turkish architecture as Victorian Gothic does to real Gothic. There are some Victorian buildings which are impressive and I believe they are now more in favor. Certainly, if you look at the Muhammad Ali Mosque from the city, in its balance of dome and minaret on the spur of the Citadel, it is a very impressive feature of the landscape. On closer inspection, one finds there is a lot of *ersatz* about it. For instance, alabaster or brick is painted to look like marble. This kind of deceit is never good in architecture, and most particularly in the house of Allah.

The mosque itself was built of alabaster and is called "the alabaster mosque." Alabaster is an abominable building material. It has a very high coefficient of expansion. It swells in the summer, it shrinks in the winter, and there are cracks all over. It was very difficult to make it endure, and in fact the mosque has had to be under restoration ever since it was built.

I think it is perhaps peculiarly fitting that the whole Muhammad Ali period itself had this characteristic, of the ancient and modern, the façade of modernity, which reached its height perhaps with Ismail, in his attempts to, as he said, make Egypt a part of Europe. So I do not decry it, if you know what it is, but I do not think it is a really great achievement in the field of architecture.

There have been some attempts to introduce a modernistic note into mosque building, as there have been into churches. Here I confess a personal prejudice. I rarely see a very modernistic church that moves me particularly, and I rarely see a very modernistic mosque that moves me particularly. There is a relatively modern structure, in traditional pre-Turkish style called the Rifai mosque, which is the burial site of the Royal Family. It is not considered to be great art, but I like it better than the modernistic style.

Then there were a number of mosques, from the Turkish conquest of 1517 on, built in the Ottoman style. It was an imported style, whereas the Cairene style was native. I do not mean by that

that it was composed entirely of Egyptian elements, it had elements from all over the world, but they coalesced in Cairo and I think represented something of the Cairo atmosphere and of Egyptian weather. Nevertheless, there are some good Turkish mosques, and the turning back to the pre-Turkish style really dates from the latter part of the 19th century with the revival, not really of the Arabism of Egypt, but of Islam in an Arab setting.

CHAPTER 5

EGYPTIAN FRIENDS AND ASSOCIATES

During this period I gradually began to know groups of Egyptians. Many were Egyptians who then or later had significant roles in government. I was living and working in Egypt, not standing on the side-lines as an observer, although I followed with interest what was going on in political terms. I made many friends, and they were practically all Muslims. I did not meet the Christian community very much. Perhaps that was a prejudice on my part. I did have good Christian friends, of course, but it seemed to me that if one was going to deal with Egypt, one had to deal with it in terms of its dominant culture, which certainly was Islamic.

Mansur Fahmy, when I knew him, was an older man. He had been either an early Minister of Education or a Secretary General of Education—I am not sure which term was used. He was very much the French-educated, Turkish Egyptian. He dated from that period and, like many of his contemporaries, he was deeply moved by French culture. He was educated in France, and he had been affected by what I would call the ornate artificiality of a certain amount of Turkish culture and literature.

When I knew him, he was not in education. I think he was retired, although he was well-known as a writer and lecturer, and he would come to the American University and lecture, especially in the Extension courses which I have alluded to above. He was a fine Arabic scholar, but he showed, I think, his Turkish background. As he lectured, he would grow more and more ornate in his language, like a Belgian lace-maker, starting with a single thread and then going round and round and round until it was so tangled up that you could not see the pattern at all. This reminds me of someone who overheard him and said, "What beautiful Arabic! I do not understand what it means." His friends used to smile at him somewhat for this penchant; it was a reflection of the cultural period out of which he came. When I went back to the Embassy in 1961, he was no longer alive.

But he was not without his perceptions. I thought he was a very good example of what I would call the 19th century, French-trained, liberal-minded Muslim. As a leader in education he was responsible for sending the first delegation of girls to Europe for modern studies, a real mark of liberalism. On this occasion he made a remark that has always seemed to me to be the essence of the attitude that he and many of his contemporaries took. In speaking to these girls, he said, "Remember, you come from a country with a past, and while you may change that past, you can never deny or despise it."

In that combination of seeking change and development in the modern world, yet having the thread of connection with the past, I think he correctly represented a certain type of Arab. I enjoyed him very much, and would go over and have tea with him and practice the gentle art of conversation, which had been practically unknown in the America that I grew up in.

This immediately brings to mind Taha Husayn, principally for the same reason. Taha Husayn was also French-educated, very French-educated, but unlike Mansur Fahmy he spoke the most beautiful, crystal-clear Arabic. Even I, with my halting knowledge, could follow him. I think that this was due partly to the fact that he was blind, and had no script to read from. He had to form each sentence in his mind before he spoke it. I think he had been deeply impregnated with the preciseness of the French language and with the French passion for clarity itself, so that in a certain sense he spoke French Arabic. That is, he spoke Arabic imbued with this desire for clarity. It was a delight to hear him lecture for an hour and a half, very deliberately, because of his blindness, in which *kilma-kilma, jumla-jumla* (word by word, sentence by sentence) his ideas would unfold. Whereas one got lost in the clouds of Mansur Fahmy, admiring the colors of the sunset as they glinted on the mists, not really going any place, with Taha Husayn you got clear presentation of a thought, an idea, in very moving language indeed.

Taha Husayn was *baladi*, that is, he came from the village, and Mansur Fahmy came from the group of Turkified Egyptians. I am sure Fahmy's family had Turkish blood—almost all of those older families had had Turkish women in them some place or other—but I think it was also a difference in their ages and in the men themselves.

When Taha Husayn became Minister of Education, after World War II, and I was President of AUC, I went to him one day to have a long conversation about the University. I was always concerned that we should never continue what we were doing unless the Egyptian government saw some value in it. We were not there to force anything down the Egyptian throat, and on more than one occasion, Dr. Watson, my predecessor, and I had tried to emphasize this. I had a long talk with Taha Husayn about what we were doing.

He said, "Well, I have one great criticism of what you are doing at the American University." I asked, "What is that?" He said, "You are not sufficiently American."

This rather surprised me, because after the war, with the restlessness against the British, Egypt was beginning to move very rapidly into cultural nationalism and insist that all books be kept in Arabic and all street signs be in Arabic. Taha Husayn was a great figure in cultural Arabic affairs, and here he was saying we were not American enough.

"What do you mean?" I asked.

"Well," he said, "if we want to know something about Egypt, we can do that, we can teach that, we can teach Egyptian culture. If we come to you, we want you to give us the best that you have, and I look at your curriculum and you do not have a single course in American history." This was quite true. "You do not have a single course in American literature." This was quite true. He said, "Why don't you put in a strong course in American cultural affairs? That is the thing that we would most appreciate."

We did not do that. I did not quite accept this point of view myself, but I thought it was a very interesting revelation of the attitude of a man who was deeply Islamic, certainly deeply Egyptian, toward another culture, perhaps in part because of his own sense of indebtedness to French culture.

Incidentally, this is something I have found in more than one country in the Middle East. Once, when we were discussing the relative merits of French colonialism and English colonialism, the Lebanese Ambassador to Egypt, Nadim Dimashqiya, a very able man, said: "There is one great difference between the French and the English. They are both imperialists and they are both bad and we want to be free from both of them. But the trouble with the British was, they never tried to impose their cultural system on us, and so when they departed they left us a good civil service, but we had not gained much culturally."

He continued, "The French are cultural imperialists and we want our own culture. But under them, we had entrée to another culture and its values, which has been of enormous importance to us." I suppose, in effect, that is what Taha Husayn was attempting to say to us.

Almost all of Egypt's intellectual—indeed political—leadership was strongly marked by a knowledge of or interest in European culture. Because of its location on the southern side of the Mediterranean and its openness toward the West, Egypt, it seems to me, has always been more in contact with the Western world than has Iraq, buttressed behind 500 miles of desert.

Almost all of the political leadership, and I would say the cultural leaders, of Egypt—outside of the religious circles, the

Azharites—were products of some type of Western civilization. The generation that stemmed from the 19th century was largely French-trained. It was really not until well on into the 20th century that you began to get people who were English-trained. So most of the younger people were marked by their English training, whereas more of the older ones were marked by their French training—not an invariable rule, but generally valid.

In this connection, it is worth pointing out that Nasser was really the first major political leader in modern times who was purely Egyptian-trained. He never studied outside of the country. He did study in the military school in Egypt, and I often felt that some of his judgments and appreciation of world affairs showed that fact, in contrast to his somewhat more sophisticated predecessors, who had, if not formal training, at least traveled enough in Europe to know something about it.

Another good example of the French-trained mind was Ibrahim Bayyumi Madhkur, one of the finest Egyptians I have ever known. When I first knew Dr. Madhkur, he was a member of Parliament and headed, I believe, the Parliamentary Committee on Education. This was in the 1936-37 period, because after the treaty was signed between Egypt and Great Britain, which gave at least a façade of independence, Egypt began to take a greater interest in developing its own institutions, and almost immediately there was an interest in putting into practice that article of the 1923 Constitution which called for universal education. It was very hotly debated in Parliament at the time, and I first had my attention called to Dr. Madhkur because he made a speech in Parliament in which he ended up by saying: Before we make education universal, let us be sure that the education we have is worth universalizing.

This was really the nub of the matter. Was education going to be urban-centered, and largely French-dominated, or would something genuinely Egyptian emerge?

He was a member of the Arab Academy, members of which I knew. The British scholar Sir Hamilton Gibb was one of them, for instance. I got to know Madhkur in that capacity, and through the years we continued to be very good friends. He was a good scholar and is presently President of the Academy. He had specialized, I believe, in Ibn Sina. He was a lawyer by trade, not a politician, and not a political leader. And he too was French-trained and had something of that same clarity of thought and approach and speech that you found in Taha Husayn.

A contrast to this kind of French-trained person was Shafiq Ghorbal, the historian, particularly of the Muhammad Ali period. Shafiq must have been nearly Dr. Madhkur's contemporary, but he had been trained in England and had a degree from an English university. I believe he had taught in England. He may have known French, but he had none of the French culture, and the difference between these two men was very apparent.

Ghorbal did do some writing in English, although not a great deal, and in talking with him I felt more at home, because he shared this cultural background. He was a very fine scholar, and one of the things that he did, and did very successfully as he decreased his teaching responsibilities as an older man, was to carry his history on to the Cairo radio. Radio had become quite a powerful instrument, even before World War II, and he put on continued programs every week with historical studies and historical background.

Another man of very much the same type was Mohammad Khalfallah, Dean of the Faculty of Arts and Sciences in the University of Alexandria. I grew to know him because, after I became Dean of the Faculty of Arts and Sciences of AUC, I was invited from time to time to sit on the examining committee that was questioning graduate students of the Egyptian University on their theses. And once I was invited by Dr. Khalfallah, whom I then did not know, to go to Alexandria and to sit with a committee to hear a young man defend his thesis on the influence of Islamic elements in Spain upon early French culture.

Khalfallah proved to be a delightful person. Like Shafiq Ghorbal, he had been English-trained. Indeed, he had an English wife, as did Shafiq Ghorbal. He brought to his work what I would call the typical intellectual disciplines of the English university. I was interested in him not only because he was a stimulating friend and I was interested in what was going on in the world of university education, but also because he had a very special interest in looking at modern literature as the mirror for contemporary social problems. Like Shafiq Ghorbal, he too took to the air, and after World War II there was an hour a week, in English, in which he would take some good contemporary Arabic novel of Egyptian life and view it from the standpoint of what it told about the society and its tensions and strains. Very good indeed.

Later, when I came to Columbia University, I tried very hard to get Khalfallah over as a visiting scholar for a year, because I myself felt that in modern literature we have an entrée into modern Arab life that has far too long been neglected. Unfortunately, by that time, he had become head, I think, of the translation section of the Arab League, and I was no longer able to get him.

There was a whole group of people of this kind that one could mention. Dr. Ismail Qabbani I first knew when he was a young man about my age just before the war, and he was principal of what was called the Demonstration High School in Cairo, a secondary school pursuing a curriculum different from that prescribed by the government, an experimental curriculum. This says something about Qabbani, because not many Egyptian educators were willing to cut themselves loose from the safety of the textbook and the curriculum and go out on the uncharted seas of personal thought.

I used to visit him and we would talk about problems together; after the war he became the first Minister of Education under the Revolution. Ultimately he went, because the Revolution got rid of most of the people from the early years. But he was a good choice, because he was very much in sympathy with trying to evolve a distinctly Egyptian pattern that would fit the needs of Egypt, and not simply be a reflection of either the French or the British system that somebody had studied.

I sometimes think that many of the developing countries have the same problem that you find theologically among Christian missions. Somebody has said that the trouble with the conservative church doing work in Africa or Egypt or some such place is that it tends to create a native church so much more conservative than *it* is, that it loses relevance to the situation. I think that this second-hand importation of European and Western ideas often did not work to the benefit of the country. We all do that. We are undergraduates, we take a stimulating course, we go out and get a job and the first thing we do is teach a course like the course we took. It is a very natural thing. I think that Egypt suffered rather largely from this creation of a university system that was far too rooted in the Western world to reflect many of the Egyptian needs and practices.

Let me be more specific. The French intellectual influence was by far the earliest, much earlier than the British, and it is still largely the most pervasive. University organization was on the French model, with the interest in examinations, the emphasis upon rigid factual/memorial approach to learning. This did not produce the kind of intellectual stimulation and development that all could benefit from. There were some brilliant students who came through the Egyptian University, just as there were some brilliant teachers. The Egyptian is a highly competent scholar, but the university, in those days, did not give him quite the setting where scholarship would flower into good education.

In making a judgement on any university, certainly an Egyptian one, you have to break it down into its faculties. One of the problems was that the entrance requirements to the different faculties were on a graduated scale. If you wanted to get into the Faculty of Science you had to be in the upper 10 percent of the high school graduates, so the Faculty of Science tended to get the best men. Then Medicine might be below that, and Arts and Sciences below that. Then you got down to Law, another step down, Commerce . . . and Agriculture was at the bottom.

The result was that while there was good agricultural experimentation in Egypt and good Egyptian agriculturists, many of the students who were enrolled in agriculture did not intend to be agriculturists at all. That was where they could get in, and once they got that magic degree, that baccalaureate, they could then be employed by the government at 15 pounds a month, doing anything the government wanted them to do. Yet some very able students turned up, and most of them went on to take their graduate work abroad. How far that contributed to their success I could not say.

As for the Azharites, the fact is that whereas a generation earlier they had often been civil servants, as inheritors of the culture, this was not true in monarchical Egypt after World War I. They tended to be found in certain specialized areas. For instance, almost all the teachers of Arabic, at least up to the secondary schools, were people with al-Azhar training, whether or not they completed it. This was a basic fault. Almost all the teachers of religion in the secondary schools were from al-Azhar, and after 1936 or thereabouts, Islam as a subject was required by the Egyptian government.

The primary school system out in the villages still had a large number of the *kuttabs*, which were schools taught by the local *mullah*, who was usually an Azharite. When you went into the Ministry of *Awqaf*, you found it staffed by people with religious training, and of course there was the whole system of religious courts, the *sharia* courts. This is where you found the al-Azhar people, and while there were a few people like Taha Husayn, who had come out of al-Azhar and gone on, I do not recall many. There was Ahmad Amin, whom I knew only slightly; his era was a little earlier. Muhammad Abduh had had a group of disciples, and I think many of these had combinations of European and al-Azhar training. By the time I got there, one did not find them very often.

We did have, for instance, as Head of our Arabic Department at the University, an Azharite, a very fine man indeed, a great friend. It says something for both the content of our education and the attitude toward it that when he finally left us to go to a government institution, he reported that the first thing the principal of the school said was that he did not want him to infect his institution with any of the educational methods of the Americans, who did not make the students stand up every time the teacher came in the room.

In our School of Oriental Studies we had six or seven Azharite shaykhs who taught Arabic. They were rather specialized, because many of them had been there for quite a number of years. But in moving through Egyptian intellectual life, you did not run into identifiable Azhar people except in the circles that I mentioned.

* * *

I was due for furlough. I had come out to Egypt in 1936 and I was due to go home with my family when World War II broke out, and it was uncertain as to what should be done.

In the spring of 1940, when things began to heat up, it was decided that I had better take my family and go home. I was then Dean of the Faculty of Arts and Sciences. And so we made arrangements to travel, just as Italy was beginning to act restless. Clearly we were approaching something of a crisis, so I gave up my apartment over in Zamalak and came and lived in the University, poised for flight, as it were.

When Italy suddenly entered the war on the side of Germany, the American Export Line informed us that its ship, then leaving Beirut, would be the last of the Export ships in the Mediterranean and would pick us up in Alexandria on a given day. We had to pack up and go off right away. Indeed, I really only had the definitive word on the morning of the day we were to sail.

The day before, Dr. Watson took me out to the Mena House. We had a long conversation together about what the war might bring and what University policy should be through it, and what I should present to the trustees when I got home. He was generally priming me to carry this message.

And Dr. Watson, in true Watsonian style, which was very philosophical—and the Mena House is right at the foot of the pyramids—said to me, "You know, Badeau, I really do not get very disturbed about these things. When I do, I come out and have tea at the Mena House. Then I look up at the pyramids, and I say to myself, Watson, these pyramids have been here a long, long time. Lots of wars, a lot of troubles in the world. They always go on and Egypt does too. So I am really not worried."

My son was a baby, and the *tarmargi* (nurse or nanny) had done the washing and hung the baby's clothes on the roof. Early in the morning we got the message that the ship would be sailing at noon. So we rushed down to Alexandria in such a hurry that we left all the baby's laundry fluttering in the wind up there. The ship did not sail until about three o'clock in the afternoon. It was the last American ship out of the Mediterranean.

Back in the United States, my plan was to take a year of study. I did so in New York, partly at Union Seminary and partly at Columbia University. I was beginning to get ready to work for a doctorate. But I took enough time out to do what one rarely has a chance to do: I took some courses at the Seminary and some at Columbia that had no degree requirements whatever. I was thirsty to pursue certain things, and from that standpoint it was one of the most enjoyable years I ever had because I waded in, did what I liked and was enormously benefitted by it.

As the year went on, it became clear that I was not going to get back; we very shortly got into Pearl Harbor. I was at the time raising money for the University, and was up in Providence, Rhode Island, on Sunday, preaching in a church there, when word of Pearl Harbor reached me.

We had settled in Princeton and the Foreign Policy Association wanted me to write something for them, so I sat down and wrote one of their little Headline Series books,* which was the first serious concerted political analysis I had turned my hand to. I very much enjoyed doing it and was stimulated by it.

Just as the book came out, I was called to go to Washington and subsequently went into war work with the US government. The Office of War Information was just being formed. It was the great American propaganda agency, and I was called to Washington and asked whether I would be interested and available to be what they called a regional consultant to the Middle East section. I got a leave of absence from the University, the family stayed in Princeton, and I went to Washington. The Office of War Information was thrown together out of newspapermen and advertisers, and it probably had more nuts per square inch than any other agency in Washington.

I was also approached to join the staff of the strategic studies group which later grew into the CIA. This I did not do; I did not want to do anything that I could not tell my Egyptian friends I was doing. I felt that this would imperil my hope of returning to Egypt

---

*Entitled *East and West of Suez.*

and being honest with them. White propaganda, yes. Black propaganda, no.

I will give an idea of how bizarre the OWI could be. I was hastily called to Washington to replace a man who had just been fired. He had been a war correspondent for some newspaper or other in the Balkans, and when OWI was formed, it was thought, since he had been in the Balkans, he knew something about the situation. So he was brought in, and he lasted not very long, two or three months, and what finished him was a propaganda proposal that he put forward to OWI.

One of the effects on Turkey of the war was to reduce imports; certain basic commodities, like candles, soap and sugar, were very hard to get. So our friend, the former reporter, suggested that America could create good will in Turkey by supplying such items. And the way he first suggested supplying them was to buy several million cakes of soap, of the size that is used in hotels, each one to be attached to a little parachute made out of a Kleenex, with a propaganda message printed on it. Then an American Air Force plane would fly over the Turkish countryside and drop this soap on the countryside, and the grateful peasants would pick it up and bless Allah for America. That was too much even for the OWI. He went the way of all flesh, and I was called down.

I don't know exactly why the OWI asked me to join. I had no particular contacts with Washington. I had not written much, although I had done a good deal of lecturing; one of the techniques of raising money for the University was to try to create a healthy interest in Egypt as such, and not merely to go out and speak about the University. I suppose somebody, as a sort of last resort, thought of my name and I was pulled down there.

I did not know Elmer Davis; I did not know any of the people at OWI at all. I did find later that a distant cousin of mine was employed by them, but this was a surprise to both of us, and I never found out who it was that suggested me.

I spent about a year in this work, three days of the week in Washington, two days of the week in New York. I do not know how valuable it was to them. It was valuable to me because it immediately put me in the flow of a great deal of information, and for the first time I began to think more connectedly politically, and I began to collect material. I do not have all my card files now, but I used to clip out newspaper items, and quotations, and maintain a file of them.

A good deal of one's work at the beginning, as I said about my predecessor, was simply to prevent a man from making a fool out of himself—and America from making a fool out of itself. I found that there were all kinds of materials that had been prepared for propaganda purposes. One of the favorite techniques of the American advertisers was the giveaway, and as soon as they started to deal with propaganda, they introduced this advertising technique. And we had all kinds of giveaways—chocolate bars, cigarettes, etc.

I discovered that one of the giveaways was a pin cushion. The argument was that everybody uses a pin cushion,—regardless of the fact that in the Middle East, at least, every tailor keeps his pins stuck in his *galabiyya* (robe). But it was said almost everybody uses a pin cushion, so a pin cushion would be a good giveaway.

How do you get a propaganda message into a pin cushion? Well, the way you do it is to make a figure in cardboard, a silhouette figure, about five inches high, an eighth of an inch thick, which when you look at it this way is Mussolini and when you look at it that way it is Hitler, wearing brown velvet britches stuffed with sawdust, a sort of a pin cushion. And of course the psychological effect of sticking pins in the derrieres of two dictators was absolutely wizard, as the British would say. Here I found we actually had a couple of hundred thousand of these things.

I managed to stave it off, saying "Let us take another look at this." I took some and sent them off to Cairo to friends of mine there, especially to Dr. Wendell Cleland, who ran the University Division of Extension that I have mentioned, and asked him to do a little sleuthing on it. He presently wrote back, citing an incident that I was able to take to Elmer Davis, and it really quashed the idea. Cleland had taken this figure, not on the streets of modern Cairo, but up into the Muski, into the old city, and he had stopped somebody on the street and said, "See this? Who is it?" The fellow looked at it for a while and said, "That is Mussolini." He recognized Mussolini from the papers. He turned over to the Hitler side and then he looked at Cleland, and said, "Well, that is either Churchill or Roosevelt. I am not sure which." When I told that to Elmer Davis, he said, "Let's cut this out."

A good deal of the beginning work was at this level, and then later it was to provide guidance on material that went out to the Arab world, to make constructive suggestions and, much more, prevent mistakes being made.

It was a liberal education for me. For instance, we had a motion picture division. And in Iran, at that time, the head of the New Jersey State Police, whose name was Norman Schwartzkopf, was aiding the government. He was out on a mission to Iran to help them upgrade their gendarmerie, and he wanted an agricultural film. We had a very fine film about growing corn, fertilizing and so forth, and it had a lot of good stuff in it. But the trouble was, the film had been turned out in Iowa, and it began with pictures of chute after chute of hogs going to market, because this, of course, was the great export of the state. What do hogs eat? Hogs eat corn. So if you grow better corn, you get better hogs, you make more money, and then you take off into corn.

I said, "You cannot send this out to the Muslim world. Just take that film apart and cut the hogs out."

"Well," they said, "we cannot do that. What is usable in American must be usable any place, and we cannot cut this."

So I had to veto it. Again and again I ran into that strange kind of cultural blindness that went on the theory that you cannot tailor these kinds of materials to local cultural needs. But I needed to get back to Cairo. I made arrangements with Wendell Cleland, and we more or less spelled each other off. I went out to Cairo in November 1942, and Wendell came back to OWI in Washington to take my place.

This was only a relatively short time after the battle of Al-Alamein, and I came across North Africa by plane, very much aware of the fact that we were traveling through the immediate aftermath of battle. Indeed, when we spent the night in Libya we stayed in the German Officers' Club, which only a month before had been occupied by German officers, and it was in the only part of the city that had not been plastered flat by bombs. The reason, I was told, was because the British and the German flyers had a gentlemen's agreement that they would not bomb each other's clubs. So it survived and we were able to stay there.

CHAPTER 6

EGYPT AFTER THE WAR

The Cairo to which I returned—I had left in 1940, so I had only been gone two years—was obviously quite different. For one thing, there were American troops everywhere. We had just come fully into the war and were beginning to make Cairo the main bastion of our supply route, a supply line which undergirded the successful British effort in North Africa.

The US forces were not only physically apparent, but their presence led to a certain degree of tension between the British and the Americans. The British soldiers resented the fact that their pay was low; things were expensive in Egypt; the Americans could afford them and the British could not, and one was conscious of this fact.

Furthermore, the defeat of Italy and the rollback of the German tide had created something of a vacuum. There had been those in Egypt who had lent a certain measure of support to the Axis powers—not, in my opinion, so much because they were pro-Axis, but because they were basically anti-British. For instance, there was the well-known Aziz Ali al-Misri, the Chief of Staff, who had a long record of anti-British activity, and indeed was accused of being in treasonable correspondence with the Germans at this time.

So there was a good deal of realignment of objectives and questions about the British presence, and those Egyptians who had pinned their hopes upon a successful German-Italian drive now had to readjust to the fact that this wave had gone as far up the beach as it would ever go. In general my American colleagues and myself had a much more sympathetic attitude toward the Egyptians than the British did. There were many fine and able Britishers who understood, and felt a sense of service toward, the Egyptian, but it was always within the context of the British contribution, the British leadership. The Americans had never quite taken to that approach. On the other hand, Egypt had escaped from the Italian-German drive by the skin of its teeth, and the desire of the British for stability was entirely understandable.

The incident of the ultimatum from the British Ambassador to Faruq took place in February 1942.* By this time the King's reputation had suffered a good deal, both because of the political squabbles in which he was involved and because of his playboy habits, and there was less popular sympathy for him, but there was an American feeling that Britain had perhaps somewhat injudiciously reinforced its presence in the country.

Looking back in retrospect, I think it is quite true that that incident was in many ways a turning point in British-Egyptian relations that almost inevitably led to the final troubles and to the Egyptian revolution. There was a very real sense of outrage. You have to place this against the background of what the situation had been. There was mention earlier of 1936, the year I came to Egypt, and of the 1936 Treaty, and the fact that it marked a certain advance in Egyptian-British relations. A treaty was signed, at least on paper. The two countries were equals; they exchanged ambassadors; there was no longer a High Commissioner. This had all been accomplished within the context of the Italian presence in Ethiopia, when Egypt really felt threatened in many ways by the adventurism of the Italians.

*To protect what Britain perceived to be its wartime interest, the Ambassador told Faruq to ask Nahhas Pasha to form a Wafd government. When the King at first refused, British tanks surrounded Abdin Palace.

One has to remember that Egypt has a very special, and curious, relationship to Ethiopia. The Ethiopian Church, a Coptic Church, and therefore doctrinally and historically related to the Coptic Church of Egypt, until recent years had always had its Patriarch chosen by the Coptic Patriarch of Egypt. This was a national right, and even a Muslim government was very anxious that that right should not be interfered with. When the Italians officially Catholicized Ethiopia, and the link between the Ethiopian Church and the Coptic Church was cut, the Egyptian government reacted strongly, because one of its historic Egyptian privileges had been done away with.

The British and the Egyptians seemed to be adjusting to each other, and the general outlook that one felt in Egypt, outside of the extreme nationalist political parties, was that they were on the way to adjustment. One thing that the Palace incident did was set back the clock of that adjustment; it returned to the pre-1936 days. Indeed, it seemed almost to roll all the way back to the original Urabi Pasha incident in the 1880's, and this was the first thing that Egyptians noted, that the hope of finding a *modus vivendi* between British interests and Egyptian desires was pretty well gone.

If the first effect of the Palace incident was in general to impugn the motives of the British and to dash hopes of adjustment, the second was that it marked the beginning of the end of the Wafd Party. It is curious that Nahhas and the Wafd were willing to come to power under these conditions, because the Wafd's great strength had always been an anti-British position. Again and again it had gone into opposition and remained in opposition on that point.

I suppose I would have to say that the Wafd had been out of power so long and had so little patronage that it simply could not resist the temptation to come to power. Furthermore, I believe that because of the skirmishing between the Wafd and Faruq, and the general attempt of the Throne party to curtail the Wafd, the Wafd saw this as a chance to get back at the King. So the accession of the Wafd and Nahhas to power, under these circumstances, did raise a great many questions indeed. I do not think the Wafd ever regained its reputation, and indeed immediately after the war, it became beset with financial irregularities and with very questionable personal dealings on the part of Serag el-Din and others. Its disintegration went on.

I think a third effect of this was, temporarily at least, to create in Egypt great sympathy for the King. His image, from that of a playboy, fooling around with other people's wives, spending money lavishly, was suddenly changed to the brave hero, representing the independent wishes of Egypt, who had been done in by the British. And while this picture did not last long—certainly, by the time the war ended, it had begun to fade—at the time, it was noticeable.

Sir Miles Lampson (later, Lord Killearn) was the British Ambassador who submitted the ultimatum to the King. Lampson was not very popular in the American group. We did not have close contacts with him. I had been there to dinner, but in general he represented the kind of domineering figure that fitted into the American preconception of what a British imperialist was like. He was physically a very large man. And while not the same kind of steely blue-eyed imperialist that Lord Lloyd was, nevertheless he took no nonsense, and when he had to read the riot act to Faruq, he read it in a very straightforward way.

As I recall it, my Egyptian friends were not as much affected by Lampson as the American group, because this is what they expected. This was the way British people acted. In a way, they were somewhat in sympathy with a man who did what he had to do—it was the expected pattern. It brought the Americans, however, face to face with their unresolved feelings about the realities of international imperial life.

* * *

In the spring of 1945, Dr. Watson, the founder and first president of the University, resigned, and the trustees asked me to take his place as president. It was something to which I'd given very little thought. I had looked around in the United States for other things to occupy me, but I finally decided, with my wife, that we should go back to Cairo, so we prepared to pick up and go, and to get there at the earliest possible moment so that Dr. Watson, who was not very well, could be relieved to come home.

We sailed on V-E Day—not knowing, of course, that it was V-E Day until we were at sea. While the war was theoretically over, there was enough concern about lone wolf submarines in the Atlantic that we sailed in convoy without lights all the way across the Atlantic, until we got through Gibraltar. We went on a troop ship called the *Athos II*. It had, I think, been a rather large liner, converted to a troop ship, now being used to carry all and sundry, including some troops, back to the Mediterranean. It had a French crew, who almost mutinied because the captain would not allow them to come to the dances with the young lady passengers.

We arrived in Cairo in time for commencement at the University. Dr. Watson left and I took up my duties.

Egypt was then beginning to blow up a squall. The incident in 1942 had brought about immediate stability. It had shown that the British were not prepared to stand any nonsense, and while it certainly injured the reputation of the Wafd, nevertheless the Wafd was, and remained, the majority party. The hopes of Italian-German pressure on the British were gone, and Egypt settled down to its wartime regime.

By the time I got back there in the summer of 1945, this period of relative stability was beginning to come to an end. The King had by this time dismissed Nahhas. Faruq was obviously not prepared to allow Nahhas to be forced on him any longer than necessary, and with the dismissal of Nahhas and the Wafd, the whole kettle of Egyptian politics was thrown back onto the hot stove again to see where it would boil over.

During most of the war Egypt had been neutral, technically. One reason was that by remaining technically neutral, with Cairo an open city, there was much less chance that either the Italians or the Germans would bomb this great city of the Arab-Islamic world. With al-Azhar and all the monuments, it was felt that this was a degree of protection. While there was some bombing when I was in Cairo during the war, it was always off in the outskirts; the city was never really hit.

Incidentally, one of these bombing attacks out past Heliopolis showed the enterprising nature of the Egyptian street urchin. Barely half an hour after we heard these little bombs fall 10 or 15 miles away, in front of the University there was an urchin selling what he claimed were hot bomb fragments, just picked up from the ground.

The political climate of Egypt was very rapidly beginning to change. The United Nations was coming into existence, and Egypt did not want to see a world body formed from which it had been excluded. It had been a member of the League of Nations. In the proposed Charter of the United Nations, it saw an opportunity to counter the 1936 Treaty and to press the British for withdrawal. So a Royal Cabinet, headed by Ahmad Mahir, always a King's man, was brought in, and one of its first acts was to declare war on the Axis powers, thereby giving Egypt the right to become a member of the United Nations. The actual declaration of war was in February 1945, and the result was the assassination of Ahmad Mahir by an Egyptian nationalist fanatic.

By this time there had begun to be a great deal of restlessness, especially among students in Egypt, in regard to the remaining British troops. One thing I became immediately aware of on returning to Egypt this time was the great weariness of everybody. Understandably so, with the war, with high prices. Everybody had a different gripe. The servants had their tea and sugar rationed. The servants *had* to have tea and sugar—they had nothing else. Food shortages were not bad, but everything was under rationing and control.

One day when I was driving in my own car just outside the University, the end of the car was swiped by a British Army lorry, simply because the military driver refused to obey the signal of the Egyptian traffic policemen to stop. I got as angry as the Egyptians did. This kind of thing had created an atmosphere of great weariness. Together with the dismissal of Nahhas and the flareup of feeling connected with the assassination of the Prime Minister, everything very rapidly began to lead to fairly open and widespread opposition to the general course of events and to the position of the British.

It was at this time that there began to appear the slogan that was constantly repeated over the next few years, "Evacuation," and then later, "Evacuation with blood." It was quite apparent that the British would have to negotiate some new position in Egypt. The

Egyptians felt that they had really been loyal during the war; they had not acted treasonably. There had been some people around the King who had perhaps so acted, but in general Egyptians felt they had helped the British, as indeed they had, and that the time had now come to reexamine their relationship and try to wipe out the aftermath of Britain's forcing of the Wafd on the King. The British did not show much appreciation of this feeling.

It seemed to me that this was a prime example of what has often been British policy in these cases. Never move until you are pushed, and then move as short a distance as possible. The Egyptians began to push, and particularly apparent were the student groups.

We were still able to keep the AUC students almost entirely out of this—much to my surprise, as I look back on it. I think one reason was that while all Egyptian students were naturally volatile, with cultural dislocation and economic problems feeding that tendency, those in the state universities were also the target of organized political activity by the major political parties. The Wafd had a student group; the Istiqlal had a student group; the Saadists had a student group. You could buy enough students at ten piasters a head to have a riot any time you wanted. I think, undoubtedly, behind these student riots there lay pressure and a degree of planning by the political parties, who used student unrest as a tool against the British.

Many of the current political leaders had been student dissidents themselves when young. It was a tradition in Egypt; there had been student riots ever since World War I. The students represented a politically conscious, somewhat upperclass, group and while one would have much more difficulty stirring up the countryside or moving among the shopkeepers of the city, the students were ripe for this sort of thing. Added to this, it was much more difficult, in my opinion, for a government to act sternly toward students than toward almost any other class of people.

A good example of this occurred a little later, when a group of students at the Egyptian University protested against an action of the government and started out for a demonstration. The University lies on one side of the Nile while Central Cairo is on the other, and the students started across the bridge which runs over Rodah Island. They were met by the riot police with their shields and their sticks; they were beaten up, and I believe one of them may have been killed.

In any case, the government took strong action to contain the students, and the result was that the Cabinet fell within two days' time, because you could not go out and beat up students without arousing a great deal of sympathy for them. Thus the use of students was both a tradition in Egypt and a good political tactic.

One has to remember about these riots that, serious as they are, they are always more serious in the *New York Times* than they are if you live in Cairo. I do not mean to say that the *Times* ever misreported them, but in Cairo they are set in the general flow of city life. Cairo was even then a very large city, and you could hear about riots and never see them. That is what we did. We would get inquiries from home or clippings from newspapers abut riots in Cairo that we had never seen and had only heard of as, say, a murmur on the horizon.

It used to be said that nobody rioted before ten o'clock in the morning, because everybody had to go to the bazaar and buy provisions for the day. And nobody rioted after two o'clock in the afternoon usually, because that was the time one took a siesta. There was some degree of truth in this.

I had a job to do at the University, and there were various problems to deal with. With Dr. Watson's departure from Cairo, in a certain sense the first phase of the University was over. It had been his vision. It had been a vision that was not fulfilled. I do not say that in criticism; it was simply that the times had changed. As I came to the University I had the feeling that it was necessary for us to rethink our functions radically. That does not mean necessarily to change it, but the time had come for a master reappraisal of what we were doing.

Furthermore, the war itself had had a certain effect on the University, because it had stopped the sending of Egyptian students abroad. They no longer went to study in England or France, or Germany, and we began to get a somewhat different type of student, students whose families would have sent them to the United States or to England, and now, not being able to do so, sent them to the AUC because of its English teaching, its foreign character, and I think a general recognition that, modest as it was, it represented a real contribution in the field of education. So we came out of the war in some sense more deeply imbedded in the local Muslim element of Egypt than we had been when we went in, although I do not think we were ever as far separated as some people have thought.

Furthermore, it was quite clear that as Egypt became increasingly self-determining in its policies, however that might work out, the Egyptian government would more and more extend its authority over the field of education, and this was quite a new factor. The concept of a fully responsible Egyptian government, less dominated by the British, began to emerge after the 1936 Treaty, and after the war it extended to the right to direct and control education. This would of course involve the AUC in a new relationship with the government, creating factors that had to be examined.

Finally, there was the sheer matter of finances, which besets everybody. Dr. Watson was a very competent money raiser. I had not raised money particularly. For my sins I now had to do so. How we were going to run a university and make both ends meet was a problem.

Watson had known government people well and was very highly respected, but he did not have to negotiate with them. Indeed, it is worth saying at this point that when the University was originally opened in Egypt in 1919, it was not with American help but with British help—a very interesting fact. Dr. Watson and his colleagues had gone to the US authorities—we had only consular representation in Egypt at that time—and found no interest at all. Egypt was of no interest to us at that time and there was no reason why the United States should have helped. Then he went to the British and discussed the venture with them, and they in effect gave it their blessing. And that was really the basis upon which the University was launched.

Another factor that had to be looked at—and it became quite important—was, as I have indicated, that World War II brought lots of Americans into Cairo. It involved the United States in a diplomatic presence, which was soon to become a very important factor. What would this do to the American University? We had always been an independent, private organization. Since so many of the other foreign institutions, like the British schools and the French schools, were related to or arms of their governments, was the American University an arm of the American government?

In the prewar days that was not a very vital question, because there were no very important American interests in Egypt. But America came out in a big way, and in a certain sense began to exercise a function somewhat along the lines of the British presence. That was a question that had to be considered, and indeed it played a not inconsiderable part in many of our decisions.

There was still the tradition of separation between the US government and this kind of institution. Different ministers and ambassadors took different attitudes toward it. They certainly did not actively move to control the University but rather, I would say, tried to maintain friendly relations with it.

The one point at which there was a more direct approach was when the Point Four* program was launched, in 1950, and there was a desire to get something done quickly. The Embassy called me up, some time in early March perhaps, and wanted to know if I could spend $300,000 by the first of June. I said no, I could not spend that much money by the first of June—not and do anything with it—and they felt really quite urgently that we ought to do so. This, of course, was an attempt to set up a program with which they could go to Congress. We had that kind of relationship with the Embassy, and at a somewhat later period—that is, in 1952-53, when Jefferson Caffrey was Ambassador—he was concerned that the University be an asset to the American presence.

I think I can explain best what that means by an incident which involved the Ambassador, and which indeed was somewhat unusual, because on the whole the Embassy had never really touched our affairs. Earlier on, Abd al-Krim al-Rifi† had escaped

*The name originally given to the US foreign aid program, from the "fourth point" in President Truman's 1949 inaugural address, promising to provide technical assistance to developing nations.

†Abd al-Krim al-Rifi was the leader of the northern Moroccan revolt against Spanish, and eventually French rule in the early 1920's, and was exiled. During a transfer of place of exile, he escaped from a French ship in Egyptian waters in 1947.

from his detention by the French, become a refugee in Cairo, and settled down there, much to the annoyance of the French.

We had in the American University an International Relations Club, and they wanted Abd al-Krim al-Rifi to come and speak to them. I knew he was a controversial figure. On the other hand, I believe very strongly in freedom of investigation, and the University had a reputation of having a free and open platform, tested on more than one occasion, so I was not prepared to turn down this suggestion out of hand.

So I went and called on Abd al-Krim, who really was a lovely man—the old-fashioned scrupulous Muslim, dressed in beautiful white robes, an Arab gentleman. I talked to him at some length. And he said, "I am very glad to come. I will not cause any trouble." I did not really place any conditions on him, but he said, "What I would like to talk about is *al-taqarrub bayn al-shuub* (the drawing together between the peoples)." He said, "I spent my life fighting the French. The French have fought me. We cannot go on fighting each other all the time. The time has come, after this great war, for people to get along with each other."

I thought that was a pretty useful topic, so I told the International Relations Club, if they wanted to ask him, certainly they could ask him. And they did ask him and he came to the University to give a lecture.

When this was announced in the paper, I had a call from the American Embassy, from, I think, the First Secretary, a man who had long been a personal friend of mine; he said he was calling for the Ambassador to inquire whether Abd al-Krim was going to speak at the University. I explained to him what I had done and said yes, he is going to speak at the University.

"Well," said the voice, with a certain degree of asperity, "the Ambassador is inquiring because he is interested in this."

That evening I went to a cocktail party of some Embassy people, at which the First Secretary was present, and he got me in the corner and rather laid me out. He said, "You should have known from that call that the Ambassador did not want Abd al-Krim to speak there, because he has had a note from the French Embassy protesting against the appearance of an avowed enemy of France on an American platform."

I said, "Well, he did not tell me he did not want him to speak there." He said, "You should have known." He was really very huffy about it.

The interesting thing is that when I was back in Cairo as Ambassador, the French reopened relations. The French Ambassador found this incident in the files of the Embassy and told me he had noted that afterwards the French cut the whole American University off their invitation list, and no longer invited any of us to any official French function in Cairo, because we had become an avowed enemy of France.

Ambassador Caffrey was a very skilled diplomat, and the inquiry he had made to me was very much like him. He never would put himself in a position of being refused. On the other hand, I can well believe his feeling that the mere inquiry should have immediately resulted in action. This was the kind of relationship we had.

* * *

I mentioned the growing political restlessness among students. It was the February after Ahmad Mahir had been assassinated. Sidqi was Prime Minister. The students organized Evacuation Day, on which they were going to demonstrate against the British, demanding their evacuation from Egypt, and the slogan was, "Evacuation Before Negotiation." It was not to be subject to the negotiation process.

I have mentioned that the University was on the *Midan Ismailiyya* and, right across from the University, the Midan was fronted by a triangular piece of land, which had been enclosed by a broad fence, inside which lay a British military encampment. I believe it was largely concerned with the keeping of order in Cairo.

Early on the morning of February 21—I believe—1946, mobs began to gather right in front of the University, and my wife and I went up on the roof where we could have a bird's eye view of everything that went on. The Midan is a large square. I cannot say how many thousands of people were there, but it was a substantial group. Not all students, by any means, because as soon as this sort of thing gets going, all kinds of people from the city join in.

It was fairly orderly until a lorry came down Qasr el-Aini Street, a British Army lorry. This I saw myself. The road was blocked by masses of people, and instead of turning off into a side street and avoiding the crowd, as all the other traffic was doing, the lorry plowed right into the mass of people. Whether the driver lost his head or lost physical control of the car, or whether he was just angry—was not going to have these Egyptians act this way—one cannot say, but we saw the lorry plow in, knock down numbers of people—I do not know whether anybody was killed or not—and this really set the crowd off.

They attacked the boarding that protected the British encampment—tore it down, set fire to it. The British opened fire; some people were killed, some were wounded. The wounded were carried into the University, where we set up a little dressing station to take care of them, and there was absolutely a first-class riot, the memory of which even now is very, very disturbing. This became really the first of the post-war riots, and in two or three days there was rioting in other Egyptian cities as well.

Yet, caught in the middle, I saw something that I thought was very typical of Egypt and a reminder of the realities of life amidst the unrealities of politics. Qasr el-Aini is the main street that runs along the Nile, down which all of the carts bearing peasant produce come in from the countryside. When this riot started, there was a stream of these carts coming in as usual. Right in the middle of the riot, when things were really getting hot, one of the carts came down and pulled off on a side street, and an Egyptian peasant woman, a *fallaha*, got out and got down in the crowd, completely oblivious of what was going on. She was not out to shoot or hurt anybody. What she wanted to do and did was to pick up broken pieces of that fence as firewood, and when she got enough to wrap up in her *abaya* and put on her head, she trotted off, put a load of firewood in the cart, and off she went home again.

I thought this was very typical. There are two sides of Egypt; on the one hand, the continuing peasant need and oblivion to politics, and on the other hand this really frightening experience. The roar of an enraged crowd is really something one does not forget. Fortunately, we never had another riot as close to the University as this.

* * *

The Palestine question was embedded in many ways in Egyptian politics. It is interesting to note that in the earlier stages, at the end of World War I, after the Balfour Declaration, the various reactions of the Arab communities to Jewish settlement in Palestine included very little overt Egyptian opposition.

In Egypt, while you found some individual reactions in the 1930's and early 1940's, it was not the kind of burning question that it had been in Iraq when I lived there, which was far earlier. The emergence of the Palestine question in Egypt was very largely a post-World War II phenomenon. It was geared to two things. One was the rise of the Muslim Brotherhood and of their quickened nationalistic and Islamic feeling, of their attempts to recruit fighters to assist the largely Muslim, Arab inhabitants, of Palestine. These attempts centered around al-Azhar. The Muslim Brotherhood was becoming an important political party—one the King may have had something to do with, as I mentioned earlier—and the mere fact of their involvement in and feeling about Palestine, I think, moved the government in different directions.

The other factor was that, as the Egyptian campaign against Great Britain and its position in Egypt mounted and feelings became deeper and deeper about evacuation, the growing Jewish influence in Palestine was looked upon as another example of the British imperial presence. How could you fight the British occupation of Egypt and not also fight the British occupation of Palestine? Out of these two feelings, in part, the reaction was born. Of course, in that post-war period there was a general heightening of religious feeling, and while I think it is a great mistake to interpret the Arab-Israeli conflict as a religious conflict in any sense, the fact is that when there is a quickening of Islamic feeling, there is a quickening of nationalist feeling. In particular, when Israel was launched under the sponsorship of the West, it was seen as essentially a religious state—a state that had a basis in an ethnic religion. This, I think, tended to feed the revised hopes of those who wanted an Islamic religious state. They said, if Israel has one, why can't we have one? So these things were closely knit together.

All during the days before the launching of Israel, there was agitation in Cairo and a growing resistance and resentment. Groups like the Muslim Brotherhood made it a political issue to embarrass the government, and with the spread of the Brotherhood and the general quickening of religious, political, and nationalistic sensitivities, this kind of question began to become important indeed.

We felt it in AUC, because as the troubles erupted in Palestine, many of the Arabs got out of Palestine, coming down to Egypt and to the University. We always had members of the Husayni family there, for instance, as well as a number of others. Indeed, after 1948, and the actual setting up of Israel and the disclocations in Jaffa and Haifa and elsewhere in Palestine, we had quite a contingent of Palestinian students in AUC. Thus, for the first time, students began to bring political feelings and political activity into the University and to raise questions about its policy of noninvolvement in political events.

* * *

The Arab League came into existence. Of course, it too was damned by the fact it was originally a British plan put forward by British Foreign Secretary Anthony Eden, and as I try to separate my memory from later observation, I do not remember that it was talked about a great deal. To begin with, it was not until the Nasser period that the Egyptians began to talk much about their Arabism. While they were formally a part of the Arab world, spoke Arabic, and were Muslim, one recognized that at the same time they had a strongly marked sense of local identity. They were Egyptians, Nilotes, and one was therefore not keenly aware of the Arab League. When Israel was created, then the League took on more of a political role and, curiously enough, the chief thing I remember about the League is that my Egyptian friends criticized it because it did not do anything.

I knew Abd al-Rahman Azzam* very well indeed, and he was an Arab, in the sense an Egyptian is not. I remember, during this

*First Secretary General of the Arab League.

period, with a League meeting in process, an Egyptian newspaper came out with a cartoon—the Egyptians are good cartoonists—showing Azzam Pasha assuring the heads of the resistance movement in Palestine that the Arab League was with them and would fight to the last *word*.

I think this is somewhat typical of the popular reaction. Indeed, all during my time in Egypt, I never found the Arab League to be terribly effective in that country. I think the Egyptians were pretty realistic about what it could and could not do. Although after Nasser introduced Arabism into Egypt, perhaps that changed somewhat.

* * *

Blame for the defeat of the Egyptian Army in 1948 was put on the British for not fulfilling their obligations of the 1936 Treaty and building up the army to strength, on the one hand, and on the other hand, on the government, especially the King, for the kind of crookedness, defective arms and everything else that made the defeat possible. The army was not blamed. It is the general penchant of people not to accept blame, and certainly the army was not prepared to accept it in this case. I remember, when I was a young teacher at the University, being very much impressed by a notice that was pinned up on the bulletin board by some student, who said, "A fountain pen has departed by itself from the pocket of Muhammad Ahmad. Anybody finding it will please return it." This is not an untypical attitude. The army was beginning to emerge in Egyptian life and Egyptian politics, and I heard very little criticism of it as such, but one did hear criticisms of the King.

* * *

In November, 1945, four of our representatives in the Middle East, including S. Pinkney Tuck, Minister to Egypt, who was able and well-liked, met with President Truman.

I had dinner with Tuck and his wife the evening before they left for Washington; I knew them quite well and he told me he expected to see the President. He got to Washington, saw the President and came back, and I had dinner with him a day or two after he had returned, at which time he told me that it had been a very unsatisfactory experience.

The President had allowed this group to wait about four weeks before he agreed to see them. When the spokesman for the group referred, among other concerns which they held, to the influence exerted by the Zionists on American policy, the President replied: "I am sorry, gentlemen, but I have to answer to hundreds of thousands who are anxious for the success of Zionism; I do not have hundreds of thousands of Arabs among my constituents."

In May 1948, a group of us in Cairo protested to Mr. Truman about what we felt was the overly hasty action of the United States in extending diplomatic recognition to the new state of Israel within eleven minutes of its establishment. Two of my colleagues at the American University and I drafted a cable to Truman, expressing this view. Our opposition was not to the establishing of the State of Israel, which was based upon a United Nations resolution, but it was the fact that the—as we saw it—hasty and injudicious recognition of Israel within a few hours would not only shake the American position in the Middle East, but in the end would not be good for the Jewish communities throughout the world.

It was a fairly lengthy cable. I remember it cost something like $45 or $50, which was a great deal of money in those days. But we sent it. Then, after it had been sent and received in the United States, it was released to the press of Egypt. It was not sent for that sake; it was not a public gesture; we felt this way very strongly. I suppose one has to say that because of our work in and identity with Egyptian society, perhaps we were infected somewhat with the feelings of that society.

In any case, the sending of this cable and the resignation at about the same time of Ambassador Tuck created an enormous impact in Egypt. The Prime Minister (who I think was Nuqrashi at that time) came to my office in AUC to call on me, which was very unusual indeed, and to express the gratitude of the Egyptian government for the stand we had taken.

I thought a most illuminating thing in this regard was that

one of my Egyptian colleagues on the staff—who had been on the American University staff for some 20 years, so presumably knew something about Americans—also came into my office and said that he was impressed with the great courage it took to do this. And I said, "Abd al-Nur, why courage?"

"Well," he said, "you will never be able to return and live in America again, will you?"

"Why not?" I asked.

"Because," he said, "you publicly have disagreed with your President. Nobody can be allowed to do that. We know that perfectly well. We know you will not be permitted to go home again." That was an interesting insight into a mind that I thought had grown accustomed to the Americans that were around him.

The resignation and the cable undoubtedly cushioned somewhat the effect of the recognition in Egypt, at a time when it was having its own problems with the Muslim Brotherhood and with defeat in Palestine. I repeat that we did not design it for that purpose.

The succeeding Ambassador, Stanton Griffis, was not a career officer, although he later served in one or two other posts. He was an American businessman, quite an able one. We had in Cairo what we called the American Club, a group of American businessmen who gathered informally for lunch once a month just to meet and talk. One of the things that we did was to raise money, which we gave to the Embassy as a contingency fund to help out Americans in trouble, a useful adjunct.

The new Ambassador was asked to address the club, which he did. He said that American policy had been stated by the President, and of course no American in Cairo would publicly disagree with his policy because such disagreement would be disloyal to the country. He expected that none of the men present would in any way criticize what had been done by the US government. He had not been back in his office ten minutes before his phone began to ring. Socony Vacuum, Mobil, all kinds of American businessmen let him know most emphatically that they disagreed and were going to disagree very openly, and nothing more was ever said about it.

I though that was an illuminating illustration of attitude, and whether it was due to lack of diplomatic finesse or whether the Ambassador really believed what he had said, I have no way of knowing.

In any case, the result was that the University passed through these difficulties relatively unscathed. At one time, we did have a few windows broken by students who were marching by and threw stones at the University in connection with an anti-Israeli riot. My heart was cheered and I felt we had accomplished something when after this had happened—the damage was very slight—the Palestine students in the University, headed by one of the Husaynis, Fuad, came to me and asked about the damage and how much it cost. I told them, and they said they wanted to pay for it, because, while they were in entire sympathy with the feelings expressed by the marchers, smashing windows in a university was not the way to express their feelings, and so they would like to pay for them. I felt we really had gotten some place.

* * *

Faruq's relations with AUC came from the fact that his father, before World War I, when he had no thought of coming to the throne, was the Chairman, or President of the Board, of the old private Egyptian University, and it happened that his office was in the building, the Gianiclis cigarette factory, that we later purchased and which was the main building of AUC. My office was actually the room that Faruq's father had used as his office.

After the war, there was some thought of moving the site of the University, or of doing considerable construction, which would affect this building, perhaps even tear it down. Somehow the King heard of this, and he asked me to come out and see him. He said, "I am interested in that room. It was my father's office. I would not wish to see it destroyed, and if any rebuilding is done, I wish you would let me know, because I would like to see it preserved and I would like to put up some kind of a plaque to commemorate it."

I remembered that, and presently I went off to the United States, as I did every year, to the meeting of the Board of Trustees. We then were considering the possibility of building a new institution out near the pyramids and discussing what would be done with the city property. When I got back, I thought I ought to inform the King about the result of these discussions, in line with his request.

So I put in a request to the Royal Chamberlain for an audience with the King, which you did by writing to the Royal Chamberlain in Abdin Palace and stating what you wanted. Generally it took about two weeks to get an audience with the King, unless it was some very urgent political matter, which of course this was not. I wrote to him, if I recall correctly, on a Thursday. The answer came on Sunday evening during an American church service down in the heart of the city, in one of the American mission churches down in Azbakiyah. We all took turns preaching, and it was my turn to preach that night. There was a six o'clock service, which I conducted, and I was just getting into my theology and homiletics. I do not remember what I was preaching about, but in the middle of it, one of the American ushers walked up the aisle in front of me and put a piece of notepaper on the pulpit under my nose; it said, "We have just received a telephone call from the palace. You were supposed to see the King at six o'clock. What happened?"

I said one of the fastest benedictions known in the history of the Presbyterian Church, and I got out and drove my car to the Abdin Palace, which was where the King's protocol office was located. I got a thorough "wigging" over there, because you do not do this to kings. I had to say that I never had received the answer to my inquiry and I was very sorry for what had happened and that I would look into the matter to see what was wrong. I got thoroughly dressed down.

I then went home. I lived at the time over on the island in Zamalek, and when I got home I found that my children were somewhat upset—my wife had been with me in church—especially my six or seven-year-old, Peter, who was walking up and down and more or less wringing his hands, and said, "Father, what have you done? Are they going to shoot you?"

"What do you mean?" I asked.

"Well," he said, "a little while ago, the Egyptian Army came here." Egyptian military people had come on motorcycles to inquire what had happened.

The next morning I inquired and found that on that Saturday afternoon the King's messenger had delivered the answer to my request to the University, which was closed Saturday afternoon, and the *bawwab* had put it in his pocket and forgotten to give it to me. So, armed with this, I went back to the palace to explain. The Egyptian is a very kind person; having thoroughly dressed me down Sunday night, on Monday the officials poured the balm of Gilead on my wounds and said, "Well, you know, *bawwabs* are like that. It happens at the Palace. Please do not let it displease you. We understand."

"Well, I still want to see the King," I said. I told them why, and they replied, "Well, we do not know about that. He does not like to be stood up." But I put in another request, and this time I received an immediate reply to come out and see him on the next Wednesday. That was only two days later.

I went to the Qubba Palace, which is out beyond Heliopolis, about a ten-mile drive from downtown Cairo, with some degree of concern, because I think it is a truism that the smaller the court, the more rigorous the protocol, and the Egyptian court was really rigorous indeed. The King received me. By this time, he had grown enormous, a very large man. He always wore a pearl gray Prince Albert coat, which wrapped around and made him even larger. When I came in he looked at me and frowned and said, "Badeau, is it really true that you were in church preaching when my message reached you Sunday night?" And I said, "Yes, Your Majesty." He looked at me and said, "I'll bet you had a bad half hour," and he lay back and laughed uproariously.

Then he explained that when I had not come, he was afraid there had been an automobile accident, and he had sent his motorcycle escort all the way from the Palace to my house in Zamalek, over the principal route, to be sure nothing had happened. That is why the soldiers had turned up at the house.

To make matters worse, in that week something else had happened. The King liked to go around incognito, and he used to go to the Gezira Sporting Club very often, and when he was there nobody was supposed to see him. That was the understood protocol. This same son of mine who had been concerned about the soldiers was over at the Gezira Club playing on a Monday or a Tuesday when the King turned up. Peter did not look at what he was doing, and he ran smack into the King. So much so that he knocked himself onto the ground, at which the King picked him up; Peter gave one look and, recognizing who it was, scuttled away like a rabbit. Peter had told me about the incident, and I said, now Peter, never mention that. You did not see the King, he was not there.

So the next thing the King said to me was, "Wasn't it your son that ran into me at the Gezira Sporting Club?" And I replied, "Well, Your Majesty, I see this is my bad day. Yes, it was my son."

"Well," he said, "I want you to tell that boy of yours something for me." He spoke excellent English, very colloquial. He knew a lot of American slang. He said, "You tell that son that the next time he runs into a fat man, what he should do is butt him in the stomach, and then when he bends over knock him in the jaw." Again he lay back and laughed. He put me at ease. He was almost everything people said he was, but I found it hard not to remember that under these difficult circumstances he was really very kind to me.

I told him what we were going to do at the University. He asked me again to let him know when the plans were complete, to send him the architectural drawings, and he would consider what might be done to commemorate his father's position.

We had a relationship there that was good. When Dr. Watson retired from the University in 1945, the King decorated him with the Order of the Nile. He was the first American, I think, ever to receive that order in Egypt. It was entirely unnecessary; it was a genuine expression of good will.

When I retired in 1953, the King—still the titular sovereign of Egypt although by the time I left he had abdicated—awarded me a similar decoration. These were not personal at all, but they showed a feeling of appreciation on the part of the Palace about what the University was trying to do. The King did have this side to him; one had the feeling that under different circumstances and with some proper education in the responsibilities and conduct of politics, he might have turned out very differently.

The King's penchant for young ladies was not unknown in Cairo. Therefore when he took to the habit of dropping into the flat in Zamalek occupied by one of the Embassy military attachés, who had a very attractive wife, word spread through the city that the King was up to some hanky-panky. The fact is that was not true. What he liked to do was appear there unannounced and unexpected early in the morning, six o'clock, something like that, before anybody was up. He liked to sit down in the living room and look at American magazines, which he very much enjoyed, and he would sit there until the family got up and came to breakfast. When it came to breakfast, he wanted and had always waffles, of which he was very fond, and he would just have a nice conversation and eat waffles and go off, and as far as I know he never made a pass at the woman at all.

Another situation illustrating the King's human side goes back to World War II, when an American officers' club was opened almost across the street from the American University. It was in an Egyptian villa which had been taken over. There was a formal opening, an open house, and I went over to attend it.

The streets were narrow and there was not much space, so there was a big sign out in front, "No Parking in Front of the Club," and there were places to park up and down the street. I was inside at the time, and presently King Faruq drove up in his little red racer, which he liked to drive around in, officially incognito. The King stopped his car in the forbidden area, got out and started to go in, when the American MP who was there said to him in effect, "Hey, buddy, can't you read? Look at that sign. Go on, go drive around the block and park some place else." And Faruq meekly climbed into his car and drove around and parked some place else.

* * *

There were changes that not only involved the AUC as a single institution, but the old relation between the Egyptian government and the process of education in Egypt. When we went to Egypt in 1936, something like a third of all Egyptian students were in nongovernment schools—private schools, either community schools like the Greek School, the French School, or the British School, or schools that were run by Egyptians, presumably for a profit.

As noted earlier, with the 1936 Treaty, and at least a change of façade in Egyptian life, the Egyptian government took a larger role in many internal matters, including education, while the British role decreased. As one of the older British administrators in Egypt once put it, "In Egypt, we didn't believe in universal education. We didn't believe we should educate Egyptians any faster than there was need for them. We tried to relate the needs of the country and the job market to education."

That may have been an efficient vision, but it was not one that would satisfy the growing concerns of Egypt. After the war, when Egypt took what I would call the second step in its independence, insistence on British withdrawal and assertion of its independent rights, education immediately felt the impact. One thing that was done was to bring all schools through the secondary level under government control, and a law was passed to that effect fairly soon after the war. All schools, without differentiation, were brought under the control of the Ministry of Education. Whether that control meant that they had to follow a government curriculum was a matter of question, but the right of the government was asserted.

This law affected AUC. We had a secondary school, the Lincoln School, which we created because we needed a feeder for the college, especially in English, and this raised questions as to its future. Ultimately, that school was abandoned in the post-war period, not because we, in any sense, were opposed to or feared government interference in the conduct of the school, but because we felt that there had been such a development of Egyptian education, especially at the secondary level, that conducting a school of our own was no longer justified, and that the time had come to gear the four years of college work directly to the Egyptian educational systems.

The question remained as to whether the law included the government regulation of education above the secondary level, and this affected two institutions only, I think. One was the American Girls College, a two-year, post-high-school institution, conducted by the American Mission. The other was the American University in Cairo.

The question was never definitively settled by the government, although later, during the Nasser period, government control was extended to the university level. But there was a good deal of negotiation during this period over that unanswered question, which brought me in closer touch with the Ministry of Education than I had been before. Government control was not extended over the university section, the post-secondary section. But there was a warning or a promise that we ought to integrate our work as closely as possible into the totality of Egyptian development.

At the same time the Egyptians were looking forward to the expansion of their own university system. Prior to the war, there were only two universities in Egypt, al-Azhar and the University of Cairo (which had a branch in Alexandria). After the war, higher education began to expand, and I believe that now, or at least a few years ago, there were nine universities in Egypt.

The question therefore arose: what is the place of AUC? This I took up with successive Ministries of Education, and while I never got a clearcut answer (I did not expect one) I was convinced that there was sufficient receptivity by the Egyptian government, as long as we were doing something unique, something that was not being done by the government, that we would be welcome and could operate on reasonable terms. Our School of Journalism was such a unique program. Our Division of Public Service, that I have mentioned, was another.

We had a School of Education that was designed for teachers who were already teaching, with night classes to bring up their standards and introduce them to a good deal of the educational thinking that characterized the Western world. One means was through the publication of the *Journal of Modern Education* in Arabic, which had an extremely influential role. These developments were all discussed in one way or another with the Egyptian government, and they led to certain fresh emphases in the university life.

A particular problem that bothered the University and all foreign schools in Egypt was the fact that their certification, whether at the secondary level or at the four-year bachelor level, was never accepted by the Egyptian government. This word "accepted" has to be understood. It did not mean that the government maintained any set of educational standards that had to be reached. It simply meant that if you had a baccalaureate or a bachelor's degree from the Egyptian University, you could be employed by the Egyptian government at a certain rate. The rate that comes to my mind, in the early post-war period, was 16½ pounds a month, which seems rather small compensation for four years of intense learning.

This kind of recognition was not given to any foreign school, which meant that as our enrollment after the war included a larger percentage of Egyptian Muslims and Christians, our students had a real problem on graduation, because they were not automatically eligible for a government job. They wanted to be assured that, having spent their time in education, they would get recognition for it.

The reason for this ruling in Egypt was interesting. It is not as irrational or as nationalistic as one might suppose. It goes back, I was told, to the latter 19th and early 20th century, when most of the schools in Egypt were foreign community schools, or at least when there were a very large number of foreign community schools, and these schools received their certification from their consular offices. The Greek School was certified by the Greek consul, etc.. A consular office lies outside the control of the government of Egypt, and therefore the government had no control at all, and there was no assurance that a consular office might not conduct a low-grade school or fudge on the examinations.

So the Egyptian government at some time during that period adopted a policy that no certificate of a foreign school be considered valid unless the students of that school returned to the country of the school's origin and took their final examinations, the standard final examinations, in that country, outside the authority of the consul and the consular courts. This was actually practiced in the case of the French Law School in Egypt, which was quite influential at one time. The students went to France and took their examinations. With that, they could come back and qualify for the Egyptian bar. Given the political realities of Egypt, this was not an unreasonable act on the part of the government.

Obviously, we could not send all of our students to America, and I finally took counsel with the legal adviser to the American Embassy, who himself was a very interesting man. He was Judge Jasper Y. Brinton, the senior American judge on the Mixed Courts, who, on his retirement, stayed on in Egypt, and died there a few years ago.

He was an institution in Egypt. Half the judges in Egypt had been influenced by him somehow, and when I talked to him about the problem, he said, "You want to remember that in most governments, in government circles, certainly in Egypt, it is always the contingent decision which lasts." He said, "If you go to an official of the ministry and you ask him to make a blanket decision about AUC, you're asking him to reverse the policy of 20 years. He's not going to stick his neck out and do that. But if you go to him with a specific case—here's Ahmad Mahmud (John Doe), and these are his qualifications, and the Minister of Education wants to hire him as a teacher. Will you consider Ahmad Mahmud's education as meeting the requirements for a teacher's appointment? Now, you can get a decision on that, because it doesn't involve anybody but Ahmad Mahmud." This was very good judgment indeed.

Through the postwar years, increasingly we would take these individual cases to the government, and if the student was defensible, get him cleared. The result was that by the time I left, there was the general expectation that any proper student holding an AUC degree could be employed in at least certain sections of the government, education being the most common one. Not as a matter of right, but as a matter of custom. I believe that this has never been changed. I think there is still no recognition of what one would call government employment equivalence between AUC and the Egyptian University. But as a matter of fact many of the students certainly found places in government employment. Of course, one of the results was that many of the AUC students did not work for the government, and I think this was an extremely healthy development. Socony-Vacuum always took a number of our people, and they went into entrepreneurial positions.

As one looks back as an educator, it is sometimes humbling to think what it is that really serves a boy when he gets out in life. The principal Egyptian representative of Trans World Airlines in Egypt was one of my students. He is now in this country. He came here after the revolution, in a very good and responsible position. He was, I think, a sophomore in college when his father died, and he had to go to work to earn a living. I got in touch with Socony-Vacuum and I told them about this boy. He was not brilliant, but a fairly good student.

Among the things he had done was to be very active in the dramatic club, and this too was something that was unique to us. The Egyptian University did not have these sorts of extracurricular activities. In the dramatic club, he had directed the building of scenery, as head of that crew. He could direct a group of people, and on the basis of that, Socony-Vacuum hired him. He went on to display a gift for administration.

There was still a favorable American image. Almost a hundred years of work by American missionaries, whatever may have been the Muslim reaction to the religious purposes, had created schools and hospitals, had brought a group of foreigners who learned the language or identified with the country, had created hundreds of graduates from these institutions in and through the government—this was the image of the United States.

Moreover, the American University at this time had no connection with the US government, unlike the Lycée Français next door, or the British School, and somewhat to the distress of some Egyptian authorities, was not engaged in cultural Americanism; it was serving the local community. Insofar as a foreign school could be integrated into local life, it had done a pretty good job. On top of that, I have the feeling that the incidents that surrounded the reaction to the creation of Israel were beneficial indeed to the general image of AUC, although I would say again they were in no sense concocted for that purpose. They were quite genuine.

We did not have any really xenophobic incidents, quite the contrary. I was rather surprised one day to receive a message that a group of al-Azhar students were downstairs and wanted to see me. This was sometime after the war. There had been some kind of trouble with al-Azhar. The students were on strike. I do not remember the exact circumstances, but the Azhar students were in conflict with their own administration, and a group came down *en masse* and wanted to enroll in the American University.

This put me on the spot, because I was sure their request was not genuine in the sense that it represented a thirst for education; I think it was part of the ploy. Somehow I had to deal with it, and fortunately I was able to point out to them that while we would welcome them and certainly honor whatever work they had done in al-Azhar, all our instruction, except for courses in the Arabic language, was in English, necessarily so, and they would all have to pass examinations in English before we could take them into the university, or else they would not profit from the education.

The one thing al-Azhar does not teach is English. It teaches Arabic. The group went back home again; I thought that this showed that there was not too deep a feeling against us.

There were some incidents around the time of the creation of Israel that did show stress and strain. I spoke of the lectures that we had in Ewart Hall on various social and national topics, under the Division of Public Service. One of these lectures took place very shortly after the creation of Israel and its recognition by Truman, and the speaker of the afternoon, who was lecturing on some social topic, was the number two or three man in the Wafd party. He spoke, and when he reached the end of his speech, he launched into a very bitter attack on the United States, for its policy—not on the University, on the United States—for which he was wildly cheered. I was chairing the meeting.

After the meeting, he came to me and he said, "I really apologize to you for speaking the way I did, but I had to do it." He said, "This has always been a free platform, and I felt that I had the right, on an American platform, to attack the American government." And we remained good friends ever after.

Some Egyptians boycotted a few University functions. I have a letter from Mme. Huda Sharawi, who was the grand old woman of the feminist movement in Egypt, who was invited to a reception and who sent a courteous, but curt, reply, saying that she could not attend a reception at an institution whose origins were in a country that had acted in such a way in regard to Palestine. That kind of thing we had, but any deep and lasting effect, no.

* * *

We have a good deal of alumni support in terms of returning to the institution, and we had an alumni association which had a certain number of meetings, but lacked financial support. I think there were two or three reasons for this. One reason is that there was no tradition for this kind of support for any educational institution, not the Egyptian institutions, not the other foreign schools and not the American institution. This was a new and a strange idea.

One would have to look at the whole pattern of charity and how charitable responsibility is discharged. For example: one of our students, after the war, came from a well-known Sudanese family of Khartoum. He did four years with us and went on, at Syracuse or Cornell, taking a doctorate, I think, and he was a great success because he ended up practically owning the Coca-Cola concession in Khartoum, which is enough to make a success out of any man.

He was a social science major, and he had a lot of trouble with his family in the Sudan, who gave away a very considerable amount of money. There is a real tradition of charitable giving in the Islamic world, but it is a tradition of giving it out in little bits and pieces to individual people. What he wanted to do was to organize his family charity and pick out a number of good causes in the Sudan and budget for them, and this they absolutely opposed as being against all tradition.

Alumni giving falls a little bit into that pattern—that way of supporting things was not common. You could get a little money for scholarships to help a deserving student, or something like that. But the continuing demand on one's finances, that we graduates of American universities know so well in this country, was absent in Egypt.

CHAPTER 7

THE EGYPTIAN REVOLUTION

Clearly the roots of many of the social developments which have characterized the post-Faruq period were laid in the postwar period, before 1952. A number of leading people in Egypt were very much concerned about and aware of the general need for some kind of social reform. I note again those lectures in Ewart Hall, which as early as 1936 explored things like the distribution of land and at times called for radical measures.

Sometime before the war a Ministry of Social Services was created, and this in itself was a significant factor. The traditional function of government in most of the Middle East, certainly in Egypt, had been to gather taxes and to enlist men in military service. While that broke down somewhat after World War I, the idea that a government should undertake responsibility for social development was relatively new. The creation of the ministry was evidence that something was stirring.

After the war certain social reforms were instituted. For instance, the government insisted that all institutions, Egyptian and non-Egyptian, operating in Egypt, establish pension plans. That had not been the case before. We did not have a pension plan at AUC. We did not have it for the Americans, nor for the Egyptians, because we went back to the heady days of free enterprise, and we had a Scots President. But after the war, the right of institutions summarily to dismiss people without compensation became illegal, and a rather carefully graduated law of compensation was put in.

At about the same time, perhaps a little later, Egypt installed something like our social security system in America. It was called a social security system, although I do not think actually it was quite that. Nevertheless, it showed an advance.

At about the same time, the government undertook to regulate and scrutinize all the charitable organizations that operated in the country, foreign and private, to be sure that there was no overlapping, that their funds were properly used, and that they were indeed a social asset. At the heart of this move was a group of government officials who, although they belonged to the elite of society, certainly had a concern for what we would call the old liberal tradition.

A number of them formed a society—I have the feeling it was right after the war—called the Egyptian Society for Social Work. My colleague Dr. Wendell Cleland was the sole American member. The other four or five members of the committee were people who revolved through the Cabinet. For instance, Ahmad Husayn, who was Minister of Social Affairs after the war, and Egyptian Ambassador to Washington at the time of the High Dam fiasco, was a member of this committee, along with people of equally senior rank. They raised a budget of their own and got some money from the government, because the government did contribute to charitable organizations, to try experimental social work. The chief scene of this work was in a village that lay on the north edge of Cairo, called Maniel, and the *Reader's Digest* published an extensive article—a good article in the *Reader's Digest* style—on the village. This experiment was an attempt to discover what could be done to lift the standard of living, cleanliness, and health of the village by the employment of a proper social worker and by providing a social center. It was a significant piece of work indeed. In the course of such work, young Egyptians were drawn into this field, so that by the time the revolution occurred there was at least a nucleus, a cadre, of social workers in Egypt concerned with such problems.

Another area that saw considerable advances in the postwar

period was the program for the blind. Egypt is beset with blindness, due to eye disease, an old problem. If my memory serves me correctly, James Breasted, in his book on ancient Egypt, *Dawn of Conscience*, quotes a papyrus letter, written about 1600 B.C., from a father in Upper Egypt to a son who was in the government, which said, "Lo, I want my eyes, and they are missing." A lot of eyes were missing, and some very good work was done for the blind. Within the confines of the general system, I think a good deal was stirring along these lines, and in a way precipitated programs of the revolution, at least identifying to the revolution the sort of things that might be done, needed to be done, and that perhaps were already under way.

There was some very good work, for instance, being done for women, on a purely private basis. The mother of one of my women students was conducting baby and birth control clinics during this period, and this was eventually carried on by the revolution, with a good deal of volunteer help from women's groups.

In general, the Wafd Party had the reputation of being more interested in social legislation than any other party, and, incidentally, of being—I hesitate to say less religious, because I do not want to cast aspersions—but of being less sectarian than other parties. Makram Obeid, number two man in the Wafd, was a Copt. Whether or not the absence of sectarianism lay behind the social interest, I am not sure. The area has not been adequately studied, and I think there is a good opportunity here for a scholar really to delve into the social momentum that was inherited by the revolution in the Nasser period.

Another aspect was the program that was publicized by the Muslim Brotherhood. While on one hand they called for the revival of the Islamic state and the purifying of Egyptian life from non-Islamic elements, on the other hand, perhaps somewhat like Gandhi, they did call for social justice, and in their newspaper, the *Ikhwan*, programs of social change were debated and put forward. Again, it would be interesting to have someone take Nasser's programs of social change and compare them with the content of the *Ikhwan*'s in the years just before the revolution occurred. I think one would find a continuity of thought there.

Certainly during this period there was a growing sense of

social malaise. The war, of course, had dislocated the economy and society. When the Egyptian government came out of the war, it lacked leadership. The Wafd had been largely discredited, and if that were not enough, it had in a way committed suicide by its own indiscretions in the few months just before "Black Saturday" (January 26, 1952) occurred: the continuation of all kinds of government controls on foodstuffs and the aftermath of the Palestine War. As I have pointed out earlier, it was not so much that Egypt had been defeated in a struggle with Israel, or that the army was at fault, but that the completely moribund character of the Throne had been revealed. One could say that it was really a Watergate tenfold. Suddenly the mask is torn off and the very center of government is shown to be corrupt, with all those around it.

That was combined with a series of assassinations—of course one has to remember that violence and assassination are no strangers to Egyptian history. During the years I lived there, there were no political assassinations until Ahmad Mahir was killed in 1945; still, there was a tradition of violence in Egyptian life.

This element returned, and its return seemed to me marked, and was so interpreted by the Egyptians I know, as a failure of constitutional government—the breakdown of the system of government, its incapacity and its unrepresentative character. Although I was busy at the University doing my work and was not poking around in the political situation, it was quite clear that we were headed for something.

I had returned to the United States before "Black Saturday." I had made up my mind that, for family reasons, I was going to resign from the University, and I had been home in connection with this decision, and because I went home regularly to raise money and do other things. I took a plane back to Cairo on January 25, 1952, a Friday.

Normally we would have arrived the next day, the 26th, "Black Saturday." Instead, our plane was grounded in Athens, and we were given some information, not much, that something was wrong in Cairo, and were advised to stay overnight.

I tried to get in touch with the American Embassy in Greece

but I was not able to do so. The next morning, however, the airline office called us and we took off again. I found that my seat companion, who had apparently come on another flight into Athens and then joined us, was the new military attaché at the British Embassy.

I must say that for a British veteran, scarred in battles around the world, he was very apprehensive. He had never been in Egypt before, and when he discovered I had lived in Egypt, he did little on that trip to Cairo except try to pump me as to how he was going to be dealt with when he arrived, whether he would be shot, hanged or burned, and I tried to comfort him as best I could. The interesting thing is that when the plane landed in Cairo, and you could still see some smoke in the air, he was met by a military delegation with a representative of the Foreign Office and given absolutely pukka-red-carpet treatment. You never would have known there was anything wrong at all. He was whisked off to the British Embassy; when I saw him afterward he still had not recovered from his shock.

We arrived in Cairo sometime on Sunday, the 27th, and I went to the University and confirmed that all was in good order. AUC had not been damaged in any way.

There were many rumors concerning the origins of the riots. Of course, there are always rumors in Cairo, as it happens, and when I got back into the city on that Sunday afternoon my *suffragi** told me what was being said on the street. Several rumors, as I recall it, were bandied about. One was that the Muslim Brotherhood was deeply involved; probably that was true. It was maintained that the Brotherhood had prepared lists, for instance, of storage houses and depots which carried liquor, because as conservative Muslims they were very strongly against the liquor trade, and these were usually sought out and sacked.

Then there was the Polish Ambassador, who lived in Zamalek, not very far from me, and who left town very shortly afterward. It was commonly believed, by more responsible people than *suffragis*, that he had been the principal element in providing backing and perhaps organization for the riots, which pointed to

---
*Male house servant.

the use of leftist forces in Egypt. I hesitate to say Communist, because at this time I was not particularly aware of a strong organized Communist movement. There were leftists, popularly called Communists, and he was accused of backing them, and his sudden departure from town was said to be clear proof.

It is quite clear that the Palace used the occasion finally and completely to discredit the Wafd and to allow the King to move into a position of power himself. But I do not recall any serious discussion suggesting the Palace was the origin of the riots. Certainly the King could have stopped the widespread rioting, if he had ordered the army out immediately on Saturday morning. This he did not do. He allowed the Wafd, and in particular the Ministry of Interior, more or less to hang themselves by failing to take the necessary measures, and only when they had failed did the King move in.

The Interior Minister, Serag el-Din, was a fabulous character. Later, when I went back to Egypt and the Embassy, he lived right across the street from me, and I would see him wandering in and out. His sister, if I remember correctly, had married Nahhas Pasha as a second, young wife, and during those spring days, prior to the rioting in Egypt, he had made a great deal of money, with Mme. Nahhas and other people in the Wafd, by rigging the cotton market. The common story in Egypt was that Nahhas in his dotage was very fond of this young wife of his, who led him around by the nose while her brother pillaged the coffers of the cotton trade.

Be that as it may, Serag el-Din was held responsible by a great many people for what happened because he was Minister of Interior, and he was either very inept or did not choose to act. The popular reaction was shown by a cartoon in a newspaper two or three days afterward. It showed a police station down in the heart of the city, with a police officer coming in the door. He had been sent out by his superior to get a match to light a cigarette. And he comes in through the door, dragging this huge, fat, gross Serag el-Din by the collar along the floor, saluting smartly, saying, "Sir, I could not find a match, so I brought you a lighter." That was Serag el-Din, of course, being held responsible for the burning of Cairo.

I think, like Nahhas, he was a demagogic politician. Both

knew the ropes of popular politics in Egypt. There were people in the Wafd Party who in my opinion were really principled people devoted to a cause. I would not place Serag el-Din among them. But the fact that he, after all these years, could emerge in a reborn Wafd Party (in 1978) and still retain some measure of political leadership, simply shows he was a smart politician. He would have been a Mayor Daley of Chicago if he had lived in the United States.

* * *

I was also in the United States at the time of the July Revolution in 1952. I had come home because I had made up my mind that I was going to leave my post at the University, and I had returned to attend my daughter's graduation from Middlebury College. I started back to Egypt at the end of July, so I arrived sometime in the first week of August.

Egypt has not had a series of changing governing institutions; it has been a highly stable country. After all, the Crown had existed from the time of Muhammad Ali, which was well over a century. In the spring of 1952, cabinet followed cabinet, but Parliament continued, and the King gave at least the image of continuity in leadership. But it was the end of the monarchy, and I think that was thoroughly realized.

The surprising thing was that it was done in a sense so quietly. The Throne simply flowed away, and there were no great convulsions. The King, as I said earlier, had become very unpopular, and the history of royal interference in government had led to such confusion that there was nothing but a vast sigh of relief, as though people were saying, well, at last it has happened. While there was very little evidence earlier in the year that active revolution was being plotted, and we did not hear about it on the streets or in the circles I moved in, when it did happen no one was particularly surprised. Everyone breathed a sigh of relief and settled down.

Shortly after the revolution, when it became apparent that it was indeed a Revolution, in the sense that it was going to attack some of the social institutions, one began to see resistance to it among the wealthy Coptic community, and the wealthy landowning community. This had not quite occurred when I got back. It was simply that an incompetent and rather gross king had finally sailed into the sunset.

I do not believe the story that the US government, or Ambassador Caffery personally, gave any support to the movement. Caffery certainly acted very correctly in seeing the King on his way. I think that one has to realize that the timing of the *coup d'état*—it is really better to speak in terms of a *coup d'état*, because it seems to me the revolution came later as a result of the *coup d'état*—occurred because the officers' group was on the verge of being uncovered and attacked by the King and the government. They were fighting for their lives, and they had to move, or the King was going to move. I did not see evidence that anybody, especially the Embassy, was privy to this fact.

The King had felt that Muhammad Naguib's election as head of the Officers Club, and the resistance to the King's candidate, had led to the rumor in royal circles that there was a free officers' movement in the army and that they were against the King. The King was going to move against them. So the officers said, "Look, let's do something." It was far more pragmatic, more clearly explained by domestic affairs, than by anything else. I have never subsequently seen any evidence that the Embassy was involved.

Naguib was not a figurehead at that time. He had not caused the revolution, although it was his action in the Officers Club election, in a certain sense, that precipitated it. He was not one of the originators of the action. On the other hand, I do not think he was brought in simply out of respect. I think he was brought in because this young group of officers was driven to take drastic action without having an adequate plan. It was very much a spur-of-the-moment thing—not in its ultimate reality but in its timing—and they found a confusing situation.

They met practically no resistance. The government had fallen into their hands; they had a great deal of good will. What were they going to do with it? They had all been young professional army officers, without any experience in government. How do you make a law? How do you handle decrees? How do you oversee administration?

They did not trust the existing politicians. Nasser had a very deep suspicion of partisan political life. Here, however, was Maj. Gen. Muhammad Naguib, who was greatly respected and who had achieved prominence in the public eye because of his military career. In addition, he was a trained lawyer with a degree, who had done a considerable amount of army administration. I think he was brought in to buttress and to provide a certain amount of legal and administrative know-how in the development of the revolution. Everything one can learn of the first year of Naguib and his contacts with Nasser shows that he was not, in fact, used merely as a figurehead. He did involve himself, and I think ultimately that his departure from the scene was due to very deep differences between himself and the revolutionary party.

Shortly after I got back to Egypt in August of that year, we had a large meeting of notables in Ewart Hall. (This was the first time I met Nasser, then a young officer.) Gen. Naguib was to make a speech. He had earlier made his first public address some place down in the city, I presume in Opera Square. So this was not his first address, but it was a carefully calculated speech to tell people what the revolution was about. I chaired that meeting, and met him for the first time.

He was very much a warm, informal man. Every time I look at Walter Cronkite, I see "Uncle Naguib." He smoked a pipe, and not only a pipe, but one of those queer, upside-down pipes, like Charlie Curtis, Hoover's vice president, used to smoke.

Even this early, mid-August, just a few weeks after the revolution, the government had begun to erase some of the familiar features of Egyptian life. The *tarbush* almost immediately disappeared, and nobody used the word pasha. It was understood that if you used the word pasha, you paid a piaster fine, just to remind you. Maybe it was five piasters.

Muhammad Naguib was on the platform in military uniform, of course, and he took off his hat and put it down on the lectern in front of him. He started his speech by saying, *"Bashawat,"** and then he took some coins out of his pocket and dropped them into

---

*"Pashas"—as we might say "your excellencies."

his hat. Perhaps this was a calculated gesture. One cannot be sure. What interested me was that he started to speak to the group in good, classical Arabic. He had a good education, and he spoke very deliberately, perhaps a little haltingly, but still good Arabic.

He had not gone very far in this vein before he stopped and slapped his hand on the lectern, and he said, *"Nahki Arabi"* ("Let's talk Arabic"). Then he lapsed, if you call it a lapse, into the ordinary spoken Arabic of Egypt, a very much more vigorous and lively language. He really poured out what he thought the revolution was about. The impression was made of an older leader. He imprinted this kind of informality at the very beginning of the revolution.

I noted a good symbol of rapid change when I went to Alexandria to stay with my friend, the padre of the British community there, who lived next door to one of the princes of the Muhammad Ali family, a cousin of Faruq. The padre went over there one afternoon for tea (I did not go) and came home chuckling to himself. He said that he has gone into the residence and found the prince walking up and down, more or less muttering to himself, holding what looked like a piece of pasteboard in his hand and saying, "This is the last straw. They cannot do this." The piece of pasteboard was an invitation to the first official party that the government was giving, issued by Gen. Naguib and saying at the bottom, "Business Dress Will Be Worn."

This was the collapse of a highly articulated royal society. For the prince to go to a command dinner in the palace and wear business clothes was unacceptable. It was indeed a symbol of what was happening in Egypt. Not completely, of course. Even as late as 1961 ot 1962, when I was in Egypt at the Embassy, there were still a few older men who wore the *tarbush*. I am not sure it was illegal, but it just disappeared. It was a symbol of the Turkish days, and they got rid of it.

All titles disappeared, and the prerogatives of rank. For instance, the Minister of Education was Ismail Qabbani, who had been principal of the model school mentioned above. He began to drive his own small British car to the ministry, and he got there at eight o'clock in the morning. This may not seem much, but in Egypt it was a great deal. It meant the dropping of privileges.

Although these were only surface indications, the whole system was really extremely hollow, and it took very little to eliminate it.

Of course, there were those who deplored this. I am inclined to think in retrospect that the wealthy Copt probably deplored it more than the wealthy Muslim. At least, he talked about it more, and those older Coptic families really never did become reconciled to the regime. Since many of them later lost land to the regime, I suppose this is understandable. The revolution robbed them of their position. One must remember that although they were a minority group, there was not much discrimination in Egypt. The wealthy Copt had his place, the pasha had his place. The egalitarian system, the limitations on land ownership—one of the very first things the government did—and the general disappearance of their society really moved them. I remember one Coptic lady saying, "It is even worse than 1936. You know, in 1936, in the middle of the Depression, I could not buy any fur coats, because my peasants did not work hard enough. Now the government is going to take away my land and my position, and maybe I cannot ever have a fur coat."

The older Muslim group undoubtedly felt it also, but they were not so inclined to talk about it as the Copts. Perhaps they felt less dislocated than the Copts. For one thing, there were very few Copts in the army, almost none. There were mostly Muslims. Robbed of one position of power, the Copt did not quite know whether he was going to find another position of power in the new regime. Then, too, the Wafd Party had been the most secular of Egypt's parties; Makram Obeid was a Copt, and the Copts had—I would not say a predominant influence—a strong influence, and had been accepted very largely as equals.

* * *

The general mood that I recall, certainly in Cairo, was that it was about time. Things had gotten as bad as they could get, and it was time to get out of the mess. But there were several challenges to the regime in its early days that caused a wide stir in Cairo, and they are interesting because of the sources from which they came.

One was the challenge which came originally from the labor

movement, in the large Misr spinning mills down in the Delta—I think it was at Kafr al-Duwwar. There was labor unrest down there, alleged at the time to have had a certain Communist inclination, and it very well may have. Certainly there were left-wing groups, perhaps not manipulated by the Soviet Union at all, but left-wing, that wanted in on the action, just as the Muslim Brotherhood wanted in on it. Denied any role, the left-wing groups became a source of threat. It ended in rioting, large-scale arrests, in a trial, if I remember correctly, by a military tribunal, and I believe there were two executions. This was very rare; there was very little bloodletting in the revolution. The new government policy seemed to be—when you have taken away their power and drawn their teeth, let them go; they are no longer a threat. So the execution of two people was notable and a symbol of how serious that threat was.

Having been through six months of constantly changing and inept government, and a much longer period, ever since the end of the war, of distress in government, and the revolution having occurred, as I recall it the reaction was—we do not want to rock the boat. It does not make any difference whether it is the labor union that rocks the boat, or who rocks the boat. We simply cannot keep on changing cabinets and changing governments, and I do not remember any particular outrage being directed at these executions, although I did not move among Communist circles.

The other challenge came from a different source. One of the first things that the government did was to pass a land reform measure, which sharply limited the size of the individual holdings. When one looks at it, it really was not as radical as it appeared. If I remember correctly, I think that one was allowed to own 150 acres. But this was not 150 acres per family; this was 150 acres per individual. Papa and Mama and Ahmad and Laila could each own 150 acres. When one remembers that at the time the revolution took place, good agricultural land usually sold for $10,000 an acre, this was far from a really egalitarian move. I think that the government instituted it partly to have some immediate, quick symbol of social reform that could be held up and shown to the people.

The other reason was certainly political. The landowner was

the government; the landowner was the Parliament. If you take away his land, you take away his power. And I think the government was entirely conscious of that factor. It may even be that it took this action to give itself political stability.

This move was immediately challenged, not by any of the large Turko-Egyptian Muslim landowners, but by one of the Arab families of Upper Egypt. There were some families there who had a more purely Arab origin than the Nilote Egyptian, and who had either actual tribal connections or tribal structure.

One of these was the large Lamlum family, who owned lands around Minya, above Cairo. When the land reform laws were promulgated, the chief of the Lamlum tribe, if one can call it that, rode into Minya with an armed escort and tried to take over the police station. He declared that nobody was going to take away his land. The government turned on him with massive military force. He was not killed, but he was put down, and put down absolutely firmly, and as far as I know, during that first year that was the only case of attempting use of force in order to preserve land ownership.

Like the disappearance of customs, it seemed to me that the confiscation of land progressed very rapidly, partly because ownership of vast lands was hard to defend, partly because the monarchy had fallen. The structure of influence and privilege which could have protected the landowners had gone. It was very rapidly accomplished, and once the Lamlum challenge was over, one heard very little more about real resistance, although there was a great deal of bitterness.

I was interested that a number of my friends and my students at AUC who were the children of large landowners had a case of bad conscience and said, "We're going to suffer from this, but it's our just due, we were wrong." Some of these fit quite loyally into the society; others did not.

If you look over the course of 3,000 years of Egyptian history, it is quite clear that it is not dotted by a plethora of revolts. An Egyptian friend, who is a historian, said that there had only been two other revolts in Egyptian history; I never could get him to say precisely what they were. But Egypt is very stable in terms of Middle East countries.

There are some very obvious reasons for this. One is the centrality of irrigation in the country. I think it has often been stated that highly irrigated societies tend to be highly centralized because they have to be. One mark of that in Egypt was that no matter what the government was, even in the spring of 1952, when they were having six or seven governments within three months, the one program that was virtually never changed was that of irrigation. A new minister, when he got into office, would change all other programs to show that he was new and progressive, but never the irrigation program. That continued and still continues.

Coupled with that, the irrigation program gives a government very large economic control over the countryside. All you have to do is to direct the irrigation water or close it off, and you have the country at your mercy. If this goes on over centuries, it does produce a certain state of mind.

A third reason lies in the fact that the margin of living on which the peasant subsists is so small that the only way he can be assured of certainty is to stick to what he does. When I went with the Near East Foundation later, I found this conservatism in marked contrast with some of the peasants we dealt with in other countries. An Egyptian *fallah* knows how to plant his grain in succession, and if you offer an innovation, he is not sure that it will work, and if it does not work he will starve to death.

Centuries of that kind of close living tend to breed out adventure from the soul. What the Egyptian peasant has done at times is to fly off into rioting. There have been several instances when there have been murders and mass movements, but these have been outbursts, not really organized revolutions.

* * *

Nasser was a shy, rather quiet man, to whom I was introduced at Ewart Hall. While it was clear that he, Anwar Sadat, Zakaria Muhyi al-Din and others had managed the troops in the coup, Naguib was seen then as playing a much more important role. People I knew who entered the government really supported it on the basis of Naguib and what Naguib stood for.

As that winter went on, it became clear that there were tensions between the revolutionary officers' group and Naguib; we kept hearing rumors of one kind or another of differences. That, of course, was the winter in which the Regency Council was dissolved, the monarchy was abolished, and the Republic was declared. While Naguib was the first head of the Republic, rumors began to go around of all not being well.

I was interested in the observations of Jefferson Caffery, the American Ambassador, made in the spring of 1953, just before I left Egypt and came back to the United States. Caffery had been very much sought out at times by the young members of the Revolutionary Council. He had been correct in relations with Faruq. His going out to the yacht in Alexandria to say goodbye to him had earned their respect; he was a very capable diplomat, and he was in a position to hear a good deal.

He said once at a dinner party that Naguib's problem was the fact that he tended to believe the last man he talked to, and that consequently his policies did not have the clearcut devotion to an ultimate objective that later characterized Nasser and his revolutionary comrades. This began to show, I think, in some of the government policies.

Again, there was the observation of an Egyptian friend, a former Minister of Commerce, Western-educated, very competent indeed, and incidentally a Copt—this was also just as I was leaving Egypt—who said that the real difficulty was that Naguib was an elderly reformer who felt that, having changed regimes, gotten rid of the King, run the rats off the ship, hosed down the decks, you could very largely take the same old officers back on board and sail on the same course. The course of the government in that year under Naguib was one of reform.

In contrast, Nasser and the group around him were revolutionaries. Not that they had a cut-and-dried plan of revolution, but they were convinced that there had to be broad, deep, fundamental changes in the structure of government and of society. What part personal rivalries may have played in the Naguib-Nasser picture is hard to say. But as I look back, it seems to me that that is an accurate statement of the fundamental differences between the two men.

One found it in the inability of Naguib really to control the remnants of the old parties. The Wafd wanted to come back; the Muslim Brotherhood was very anxious to get in. My impression is that he did not deal with them decisively, because he really envisioned a reform government in which all factions had a place; Nasser and Company did not.

Nasser did not impress me at all on first meeting. He always had presence, but he was very quiet, and even when I knew him much later, he was quiet, until the time came to talk. Then he became quite a different man.

CHAPTER 8

NEW HORIZONS:
THE NEAR EAST FOUNDATION

I left Egypt in June 1953. The Near East Foundation in New York had approached me and suggested that I come with them as President, and after looking into their work and what it offered, I decided to do so. I wound up my work in Egypt, made an extensive trip through the Middle East (Lebanon, Syria, Greece and Iran) to see the Near East Foundation projects in the field, and got back to this country about mid-July.

As noted earlier, just before I left, the government, still the Naguib government, awarded me the Order of the Nile. This decoration so kindly given to me was, I understood, the last one sanctioned by the royal government and the first one bestowed by the revolutionary government. It came just at that interval.

The decoration was presented to me at a dinner held on the roof of the Semiramis Hotel overlooking the Nile. I was alone in Egypt; my family was home. When I got back to my room that night at the university—11-12 o'clock—my telephone rang, and an Egyptian voice speaking in English asked for me and then launched into a bitter tirade—at the decoration of an American. We were dirty imperialists, the whole lot. I always assumed the call came from one of the radical Communist groups. This was for me the only instance in Egypt of any such personal attack or attack on an American presence.

I have been a very poor job-hunter all my life. I never got a job I went after. I made the decision to leave Cairo before I had any clear plans, and I thought primarily at that time of going into teaching, although I had not taught for a long time. I was in contact with a number of institutions when the offer from the Near East Foundation came, quite out of the blue.

I accepted it, after looking it over, believing that it would serve my purposes very well and hoping I could serve theirs. There were two or three factors in accepting the offer. One was the fact that it involved voluntary work for the general assistance of the Middle East. I hate to say charitable work; that is not quite the right connotation. It was my business—and after all, I had spent all my adult life in doing something with the Middle East—to express my interest in and concern for the area, and here was a program which continued in that vein.

A second thing was that it brought me back to the United States. Yet the job also would take me back out to the area probably every year, and while that was in no sense part of an agreement, it did work out that way, so that during the eight years that I was with the Foundation, I was still in contact with the Middle East even though I was living in this country.

A third thing that attracted me was that it broadened my contacts in the Middle East, not only for reaching into the Arab world, but from the Arab world into adjacent countries. The Foundation had under way then a very important program in Iran. It was just finishing off its work in Greece. It was interested in and was negotiating for some possible work in Turkey. This scope gave me a broader feel, and while that was not a major factor, it certainly made me realize that I was not only staying with the Middle East, but staying with the Middle East in a wider circle of acquaintanceship, which served me very well indeed later, when I came to leave it and do other things.

The Near East Foundation had been in the Middle East long

before the government was, and it was interesting that when President Truman announced Point Four, he used the Near East Foundation as the illustration of what he intended. That was in his original statement.

I did not know this at the time, but actually, when I got into the Foundation and began to read its documents, I found out that the concept of what we call technical assistance really first surfaced in any substantial way in the formation of the Near East Foundation, and I have been unable to find any other clear records in that connection, apart from the Foundation's.

It had grown out of refugee work during and after World War I, beginning with the work for the Armenians, Greeks, Lebanese and others. The old Near East Relief was somewhat like the refugee organizations of today. By the end of the 1920's, that refugee problem, while not entirely solved, had settled down to more or less its permanent aspects, and the group that ran the Near East Relief began to think about what ought to be done next. A commission appointed to study the problem included a man from the American Board of Commissioners of the Congregational Church, a man from the Teachers College at Columbia—quite a group of prominent people.

They made a study and issued a printed report, at the end of which they laid down what I would call the "charter of technical assistance." The report said that it must be recognized that no foreign agency can cure the problems of another country. This can only be done by the country itself. Therefore, what is needed is not an organization that goes in and starts farms, hospitals, schools, and all such organizations. What is needed is an organization that will go in to assist a local government to develop skills in this regard. It must be done by and under government auspices and not by foreign institutions.

As a result—and this is a very inadequate summary of that report—the Near East Relief was dissolved and the Near East Foundation came into existence. It became a foundation not because it had a lot of money—it did not—but because they did not know what else to call it. It was a new program, started in the early 1930's to run what we now call technical assistance.

We had no permanent staff that would learn the language of

the country, for instance. Because the object of every program is to dissolve itself within a certain length of time, the particular program that you institute determines the kind of people you want. For example, when we were working in Iran with the Shah in the land distribution program, one of the problems that came up was a credit union for farmers, and one of the things the Foundation assisted in doing was to set up a series of credit cooperatives. As far as I know, this is the only country, at least for the Near East Foundation, in which that was done. For the particular project you needed an experienced credit cooperative man, and you could not have one on your staff permanently. We went out and recruited people, under contract for a period of years, and while some of them worked in country after country, we did not have what one could call a permanent staff.

The smaller the bureaucracy, the larger the success. We had several criteria. One of them was that any man that came into our employ should have at least 10 years of practical and successful field service in his line of work. That way he could go out right into the countryside. Agricultural extension is a very good example. We assisted the government of Greece to develop its agricultural extension services, and now Greece probably has the best agricultural extension service in the Middle East—if Greece is in the Middle East. At least its food is.

What one does under these circumstances is to go out to our Western states, find the kind of farm agents at the level required, and see what they can do. Many could get a two-year leave of absence. Even after World War I, a certain amount of international adventure was in the air. This answered that spirit. I was a little surprised at the number of practical, hardheaded people in this field who really had a concern for others. There was no doubt that, while they had to be paid an adequate salary and given professional perquisites, they were partly moved by the fact that the world needed them. And they went out and did what they could. We put together teams under a country director, depending on what the particular program was, and as the program finished, then these people returned to their own niche.

I am thinking of a man we had in Africa, in the field of

community development, who had an extremely good position in the State of Idaho. He was able to take a three-year leave of absence, and when he finished he could go back to his position and be more valuable exactly because he had had the diversity of experience elsewhere. But if you hire a young man without experience—quite apart from possible ineptitude—and he comes out with you for two or three years and then goes back, it is difficult for him to get into service. His profession has moved on.

I did not do very much recruiting myself. We had an administrative staff of three people plus myself. One was a recruiter, one a program man, and one was essentially what we would call today a money-raiser, a PR man. While I was involved, I did not recruit.

I spent much more time helping to find programs, in which I was very much interested as an educator, and also in negotiating contracts with the local governments and seeing it through the various difficulties one is apt to run into. These contracts for new services often involved a great many problems. Usually, one was introducing a service for which the governments had no competent officials and no civil service rules. Thus, once the contract was negotiated, one was usually faced with a double problem.

On the one hand, there were the attempts of the established bureaucrats, in education or in agriculture, to get their hands on the project. There was money there, there was prestige, and there were jobs. When they got their hands on it, the experimentation would disappear. On the other hand, there was also the pressure to apply the fairly rigid rules of government employment to a totally new profession. So that when you start training, let us say, agricultural extension agents, and there is a general rule in the country that anybody who has a teaching function should have a bachelor's degree from college, you cannot get agents with that qualification; you have to get along with high school boys. Therefore you have to persuade a government to take this area of organization and set the rules aside until it has grown up.

This was one reason why they used the Foundation, because often the government was unable, because of its own rules, to make these exceptions. They could hire the Foundation and its agents and the Foundation could make the exceptions. In this area I had to do a lot of negotiating.

* * *

The Greek work had begun very early on. In World War I, Near East Relief had been in Greece and helped with its problems, and in World War II, when there was a new refugee situation, we went back into the refugee business.

In the period between the two wars, we had set up in Greece very good extension and home economics systems, and after we dealt with immediate post-war needs, Greece had reached the point where it could take care of itself. It had begun to educate very competent Greeks, and many of them in the field of agriculture would go to Cornell, some of them very outstanding men indeed. We kept a distant eye on them when the government asked us to do so. In some cases, it was easier for the government to have us do things than to act on its own.

The last thing we did in Greece was to help the government set up a rehabilitation program for Greek farmers who had been injured by land mines left behind by the Germans—a terrible problem. A farmer would go out in the field, step on a land mine and blow his legs off. What do you do with him? We worked with the government to give these people some rehabilitation, and then to make them into tailors or watchmakers. That involved the setting up really of a new department of government.

In northern Greece, the German retreat was so hasty they never dug up the land mines. Maybe they would not have, anyhow, but it was a very serious problem. The government wanted to deal with it, but had no agency for that purpose.

That work was completed and it was around 1955 that we left Greece and no longer had any really active work there, although we were represented on some boards. For instance, we set up an institution for the blind.

* * *

Syria was quite different. We never had the success in Syria that we had in Greece, which is not surprising because we were not able to work in Syria until after World War II, when the French mandate terminated. Syria went through a series of *coups d'etat*, Shishakli and the others. The political situation was very shaky. There was a good deal of suspicion of America and Americans, generated to a large degree by the American connection with Israel. That was one of the most important factors. Problems were also generated by the fact that Syria was still a country of large landlords, and of politicians who were landlords, who tended to treat the Foundation in terms of the political advantage they could get out of it.

We ran a program of extension and other things there, but the time came, around 1955 or 1956, when it was quite clear that we could get no further, because there was no base within the Syrian government that would continue to develop and carry on what we were trying to do, so we got out.

* * *

We did a great deal in Iran. We were still operating in Iran as late as 1978, despite the large oil revenues that it had—rural development work, not just agricultural extension. We did other things, but that has been the Foundation's central concern. For most of these countries there is much more progress in the cities than in the countryside, and modernizing tends to be an urban phenomenon.

After the Shah nearly lost his throne in 1953, there was a concerted effort on the part of Westerners to try to assist, not the Shah as an individual, but in the development of the whole country, to bring both political stability and economic growth. The Near East Foundation came in with that general surge of interest. When I became President, we were already carrying on a program with the Shah in this field.

What we had done was to take an agricultural area south of Tehran, called the Varamin Valley, where there were perhaps a dozen villages, and in connection with the Ministry of Agriculture, the Ministry of Education, and maybe the Ministry of Health, start building a village improvement program. This was just as the Shah was getting under way in his land distribution scheme, and while we were not directly involved in that scheme, which he himself had designed, the services that we were developing were intended to be spread to the new small landowners that the Shah's program was going to create.

So the Shah was very much interested in our program. He supported it in a variety of ways, and on a number of occasions—perhaps once every two years—when I was in Iran I would have an audience with the Shah, who was always interested to know about what was going on. And indeed, one of the things that I did early on was to see to it that a report was sent to him every year, on how our work was progressing, even though technically speaking we were under the ministries rather than himself.

I came to the Shah with a rather interesting connection. The Shah had married King Faruq's sister, and I had come there with my background in Egypt, and I recall that the first time I met the Shah the matter was brought up. It was shortly after the revolution in Egypt, and the Shah reminded me of this fact and said that he had known Egypt, had known Faruq, and his questions were direct political questions. Why did I think Faruq had lost his throne? He said, "I have my own opinion of him, but why do *you* think he did?"

I told him I thought it was essentially because Faruq had tried to govern without having the capacity to govern well. It was not resistance on the part of people to a royal government; it was resistance to inept government. The Shah at that time was in the midst of some of his early difficulties with the people, and I remember quite clearly his saying, "That's very interesting. That's something to think about."

I hope he thought about it, because it seems to me that in a sense, it is also the problem of any monarch or person at the center of power. I was always sensitive to the fact that the Shah was really very well informed about Iran. How deep the information was I do not know, but he certainly kept abreast and knew what was going on in terms of economics. I never talked with him politically about Iran, because it would have been improper for me to introduce the subject, and he never did. Almost always, therefore, my time with him was spent in talking about the Foundation, what its success was and how things were going.

The last time I saw the Shah, if I remember correctly, was after I had resigned from the Embassy and had gone to Iran in the course of one of my trips for Columbia University in the late 1960's, and I had quite a long conversation with him. We went back to my diplomatic experience in Egypt, in connection with some of the problems he was having, which were quite different.

I suppose I share the difficulty of making an accurate appraisal of the Shah at this point. On one hand, there is no doubt that the royal government, in terms of what we call today civil liberties, was very repressive. There is no doubt about this at all. The secret police—*Savak*—were present and operative. There were many illustrations of this that I ran across from people I knew, friends of mine—quite genuine impressions.

On the other hand, the Mussadiq period had so furiously shaken the throne that I think it was very understandable, in the early part of the 1960's, that the central government should take a rather tough line and try to keep law and order. The royal government was threatened from two different sides. One was the liberalizing, left-wing, more radical group, and I do not mean that as jargon. The other was the extreme right wing, *mullahs* and religious organizations. And he used very repressive measures against both.

Is one right in doing this or not? Sometimes, it seems to me, you have to have order and that is that. Even St. Augustine recognized that the mark of government is, in the first instance, order, and without it there is no divine order in the world.

The Shah did not give the impression of just hanging on. I think he was quite determined. But on the other hand, he did not give the strong, clearcut, magnetic impression that you got from a Nasser. One was very impressed with Nasser; one was not so impressed with the Shah.

The Shah had suffered under two disabilities. One was the

fact that he was brought back and supported by the Americans, and he had to rely on them, and yet that very reliance created problems for him, since Iran had had such a long experience with foreign domination. Secondly, he suffered largely in comparison to his father. He was very conscious of this, in my opinion, and I think that much of what went on in Iran is to be explained by the necessity on one hand of carrying on the line of growth and development that his father did, and on the other hand of really surpassing his father in doing it, in order to establish himself.

The groups of people that I worked with in Iran, the Iranians from the Ministry of Education and so forth, were all reasonably pro-Shah. I do not mean they were strong partisans, but I think they were all moved by the belief that Iran had pretty well to choose between some kind of orderly process, or go into chaos, chaos aided and abetted by the Russian pressure on the northern border, and what they saw as the threat of Communist penetration into the country. Iran has dealt so long with outside powers; my Iranian friends would rather cockily say, "We will take care of ourselves. We know the Russians very well. We knew the British. Neither one ever conquered us, and we have to play one off against the other." Which they did, indeed.

* * *

The Iranians are story-tellers par excellence, and a couple of Iranian stories, which I think are illuminating, have come to me about the present situation.*

In the first place, an Iranian senior government official, an old friend of mine, who used to be associated with us in the Near East Foundation, was in this country to investigate matters concerning Iranian students, and he visited me one day during the crisis which became the revolution.

When I asked him about the situation, he said it's like the story about the man who went out to buy a house. He found a

*This section dates to a January 4, 1979 interview.

house, rather decrepit, but he decided to buy it. Before buying it, he made a bargain with the house, saying, I'm going to spend money on you and fix you up and put you in shape, but all I ask from you is that if you ever feel you're going to fall down, warn me in advance.

So he moved in and after a week a very large crack appeared in one of the walls, and he made some mud plaster and wiped it over so it didn't show. Another came and he did the same thing.

Shortly thereafter, just as he was leaving the house, it suddenly fell down and he barely escaped with his life. He turned in anger to the house and said, what's the matter? We had an agreement that you were going to tell me before you fell down. The house replied, but how could I have talked? Every time I opened my mouth, you plastered it up with mud.

This is a reminder of the fact that actually there had been many rumblings of discontent in Iran, not merely in the five or six years prior to the revolution, but indeed almost from the time that the Shah took the throne—certainly from the early 1950's, with the Mussadiq period.

One has to recognize that many of these went unheeded, and one is dealing with forces that, whatever may have caused their immediate flare-up, are really fairly old.

I remember a Persian friend of mine in Baghdad, who was a *lahafji*, a man who made bed comforters. He would come in and tell me stories, and one of them was that of the Shah who argued with his prime minister as to whether education or heredity was definitive in life. The Shah maintained that education was, that education could change anything, and he made a wager with his vizier and set a date for the proof.

The date came: the Shah assembled the court, the vizier was present, and the Shah said, I will now show you that education is much more important than heredity. And he clapped his hands, the door opened and in came twenty-four pussycats, standing on their hind legs, and each carrying a cup of tea, which was passed around the court.

Well, said the Shah, this is against the nature of the cat. I've proved my point. At which point the vizier took a mouse out of his pocket and threw it on the floor and the cats threw the cups up in the air and ran out of the room.

* * *

Iran and Egypt are quite different societies in a number of ways. Egypt is a highly unified society; it really has no important ethnic minorities. There is the Coptic-Muslim difference, but that is a religious difference, not ethnic. It seems to me that of all the people in the Middle East, the Egyptian is perhaps the most monolithic in his characteristics and in his sense of identity.

This is not true of Iran. Iran is very much regionalized. There is the central desert with a ring of states around it. Some are Arabic-speaking, the Ahwaz, down on the Persian Gulf; some are Persian-speaking; some are nomadic, up around the Caspian. There simply is not the unifying factor of culture. This is one very real difference.

In the second place, the fact that Egypt is pressed geographically into the valley of the Nile, where all have to live cheek by jowl, has led to a certain development of tolerance for each other, or at least getting along together. Iran is spread all over the lot, and I think there has been much more brigandage, violence, this kind of thing, because people have not had the local pressures to deal with it.

I found the Iranian peasant quite different from the Egyptian peasant. I don't think he was quite as conscious of the long centuries of living on the edge of disaster, although, goodness knows, he lived very poorly. He was much more dour. The Egyptian is much more open, more carefree. The Iranian is a sober and dour man, and I found more suspicion in the Iranian villages, more remoteness from the European scene, than in Egypt.

There is this difference as well. After all, the Shah claimed 2,500 years of existence for his throne. It was a long-lived national institution, and this was certainly one of the things, I think, that enabled the Shah to get by with many of his policies. They did not have anything like this in Egypt. The throne was of very recent origin. There was no great long historic tradition of government by that institution, and therefore there was no center of loyalty to it.

Once, going up the Nile, one of my friends tried to get a peasant to express himself about what was going on in Cairo and about the Prime Minister. Finally the peasant lost his temper: "We don't care who rules in Cairo. All we want to be given is our irrigation water and to be let alone."

* * *

From 1930 until after the war, the Foundation was a purely private organization, which meant that we furnished part of the funds and the host government furnished the rest. I may say that in Iran, once we got going, for every dollar we put in the Iranian government put in nine.

When Point Four came on the scene, it began to look around and to use a number of private agencies, and we were the private agency that was used there. They would write contracts with us for doing a certain specified piece of work. Here we had a program, say with the Ministry of Education, and Point Four would contract through the ministry to pay part of the cost as their contribution. Point Four did not inaugurate it. We had quite a number of programs of this kind in many of the countries where we were operating.

Almost at the same time we started in Jordan, where we had similar arrangements, and this meant that I spent quite a bit of time negotiating contracts in Washington. That always involved some difficulties. The pressure by Point Four, when it got going, and in a difficult political situation, was always for short-term results. "Get our people there, this government's got to be saved." Walt Rostow was always talking about the take-off point—how the heavy bird hops across the field until it gets going fast and then it soars into the air.

So there was a tendency on the part of Point Four to press for rapidity, for large-scale operations and results. In our own experience, this was not very sound. Any program you start is going to make mistakes—it's inevitable. It is necessary, because only if you make mistakes do you discover what needs to be done. The smaller the area the mistakes are made in, the less you have to undo afterward. If you have a very large agricultural extension program convering, say, a whole province of Iran, and it goes agley, then you have problems. So there was a certain amount of tension with Point Four over this matter of rapidity. Furthermore, there was a tendency, understandable enough, on the part of many government services, to want the best we in America had whenever we introduced anything. The best we had was sometimes far beyond their reach, however.

Let me give an example. At the time I knew Iran, the great majority of Iranian villages had no schools. So one thing the Ministry of Education was interested in was getting a village school system going. We worked out of Varamin then, and we started in with what was really a replica of the old-fashioned one-room schoolhouse, where one teacher had four classes, because there were not enough qualified teachers. This worked out very well.

Point Four very strongly opposed it. They said, we got rid of this 100 years ago in America. They were wrong. I went to a one-room schoolhouse when I visited my grandfather's farm in Middle-bush. They asked, why introduce this outworn system to Iran? The answer was, for Iran it was a step into the future, and once you get a school system set up and the necessary position for it in government as a turning point, it can gradually grow up into a more sophisticated system.

Let me give an extreme example. In one village in Iran we came into, the Point Four program had, previous to our coming, recognized the need for a bathhouse. That is always a problem in Iran, where water is scarce. So they had built a community bathhouse.

When we came into the village, which was incorporated into the area of our work, we found the bathhouse no longer operating. Why not? In the first place, when the Americans had built it, they brought in lovely, nickel-plated faucets and shower heads. Everyone in the village thought they were silver; people have silver faucets in America; the first thing they did was steal them all. They were poor people, they needed money. They found out they were not silver, but they could still get a good price for them. So there were no faucets or shower heads.

Secondly, the cost of heating oil to run that bathhouse was simply far beyond their means, no one could afford it; they could not buy oil. So the place was abandoned.

We got the Town Council to take it over and helped them raise funds, and they went into Tehran and bought a lot of locally made hardware. It did not work very well, but nobody was going to steal it. Then we got them to replace the oil heating with either cornstalks or wood, and it was arranged that every family wanting a bath would deposit a certain amount of wood or cornstalks, and that kept the thing going. This is an illustration of the two levels on which one could operate.

I do not wish to be misunderstood. Point Four did a great deal of good work, but these were the kinds of discussions that would go on, and this was the difference in emphases in the programs we were operating.

Our relations with the Ford Foundation were different to the extent, of course, that they were free from any governmental pressure. They tended to operate with longer-term goals in view. On the other hand, I have a theory that the Ford Foundation felt it was almost as good and certainly as big as the US government, and it was as little inclined as the government to take any nonsense from a private agency. We had considerable difficulty with the Ford Foundation at times, although we also had good relations with them.

Another example: The suggestion was made that we go into Iraq, and a colleague in the Near East Foundation, who was much more experienced than I, went to make a study of Iraq and what could be done; then he came back and wrote up a proposal for the Ford Foundation. This was the way one did things. Let us say that the figures for the first year represented 75,000 dollars, the second year 100,000 dollars, and the third year 150,000 dollars.

The Ford Foundation said, look, this is piffling. If we can't spend a million dollars on this, there is no use doing it. We said, you cannot spend a million dollars in Iraq in three years without making a mess of things. You cannot find out where you are going without trying it out, and if you do this for three years, then we will be ready to take off. The Ford Foundation said no. Either take the big program, or take no program.

This brought me back to one of the things that I learned and appreciated as an educator. At least, I think I learned it. It seemed to me very sound indeed, and that is that in this kind of development, in contrast to the formalized education, say, of our university system, you cannot plan in advance exactly what you are going to do or how you are going to do it, until you know what can be done.

I mention that we had an agricultural extension program in Greece. When this was started, what the Greek government wanted to do was to take the curriculum for agricultural extension agents from Cornell University and introduce it into the University of Athens. This assumed that a Greek agricultural agent would have to do exactly what an American agricultural agent would do, and we did not know whether he would or not.

So when we started out on our experimental work in Greece, we quickly discovered that an extension agent had to be a multipurpose agent, which he is not in the United States. He is the one educated man who goes to the village, and if you have a sick cow or a sick child or a broken piece of machinery, you ask this man from the government, and therefore he had to know much more than agriculture. He had to be a health extension agent; he had to be a machinery extension agent; he had to be a veterinarian extension agent. One had to train him for the multipurpose demands that come upon him, and the American system did not do that.

This was true in every country that one went into. You have to get going before you know where you are going and how to train a man for it. This is really, I think, the biggest contribution that the Near East Foundation made, in edging that concept in and beginning to operate only when one had discovered what the possibilities were, what the needs were, how to train for them.

* * *

Afghanistan was one of the first projects that we took on outside of the traditional Near East area itself. We were brought into Afghanistan because the International Cooperation Administration (ICA), which had been called Point Four, was operating in the country. Eisenhower had been through Afghanistan and it had been identified as a country where there was a good deal of Russian effort, and so we were invited by ICA to go into Afghanistan as a contractor and to run a program of rural development, based very largely on what we had been doing in Iran.

We had a program in an area to the south of Kabul, the Logar valley, and we were working in an attempt to launch an agricultural extension service. I went into Afghanistan two times, about a year apart, in 1958 or 1959. Henry Byroade was our Ambassador during that period, and I stayed briefly in the country, visiting work in the Logar valley, and then going south to the Helmand valley, where a great dam had been built. We were trying to assist the farmers to prepare for the transformation of their economy into an irrigation system.

I found Afghanistan a fascinating country. When God finished creating the earth, all the stones that were left over He threw into Afghanistan and made a mountain of nothing but stones. When you ride from Kabul to Qandahar in the south, you pass these enormous mountains of stone. I found the Afghanis an interesting people. I met the King at the time, and Prince Daud, who was later overthrown, as he himself overthrew the King. But my visit to the country was very brief.

One of the interesting things was the rapport that Henry Byroade had been able to establish. Byroade, one may remember, had been Ambassador in Egypt at the time of Suez, and he was out of favor with Dulles because he said to Dulles, I told you so. He was sent into exile in South Africa. In South Africa, in those days, there was nothing to do really, and since Byroade was a big game hunter, he did a lot of big game hunting, and his Embassy was replete with stuffed animals.

When he presented his credentials in Afghanistan, he was very anxious to get up into the Wakhan corridor, that part of Afghanistan which penetrates into China, and prevents the Soviet Union from having a border with India. This is sensitive country indeed. At the time of presenting his credentials, or shortly thereafter, he asked the government if he could travel in that part of Afghanistan.

The answer was that no ambassador was permitted to travel in that part of Afghanistan, that the Russian Ambassador was not permitted to travel there either, and that, very regretfully, the answer had to be no. After a pause the Prime Minister went on to say, "However, we have no objection whatsoever to a big game hunter going up there—and I may say, this is the home of the famous Marco Polo mountain sheep, one of the rarest bags a hunter can get —we would be delighted to have you do so."

So Byroade went up there, accompanied by the Prime Minister I think, and he hunted through that country. The Russian Ambassador had no cause for complaint, because he was not a big game hunter.

There were only some six or eight people on the Near East Foundation team there. What we did was to choose a series of sites in the Logar agricultural valley, pick out promising young men, without any special preparation, as agricultural extension agents, put them on the job and let them learn on the job, while we learned with them what it was that had to be done. This was always the way we attempted to start, because despite surface similarities, the agricultural problems of the farmers around Afghanistan would not be the same as those in Iran by any means.

As I recall it, this program only lasted about two years, partly because of funding in the US government and partly because the Afghan government and the American government could not fully agree on certain methods of conducting the research.

A frequent problem was, under whose auspices should a program be placed in the government? There was a tendency for a while in our US government services to gather all this kind of work under the heading of community development; there was a section in ICA in Washington headed by an able and joyous bureaucrat, Louis Miniclier, who felt that community development was going to be the golden touchstone to solve all problems. Therefore, these new programs, when they were started, often had the label "community development" and sought to bring into existence a new government body, which the host government would direct—the idea of community development being that it was multipurpose, that it involved education, sanitation, health education, agriculture and so forth.

The trouble was that in many governments the Ministry of Agriculture was the oldest and most stable ministry and it wanted to run these things—in my opinion, quite rightly. So there were frequently differences of opinion between the US government experts and the local government. Something of that sort occurred in Afghanistan. Funding was reduced and after a couple of years, although we thought results were quite promising, the project stopped because the contract was terminated.

On the way home from my last trip to Afghanistan, I was invited by the University of California to lead a seminar on rural development in southwestern Asia. One of the considerable discussions revolved around the questions: Under whose auspices should a program finally come to rest? How should we integrate new development? In the course of discussion, I cited my own observations that in many cases the Ministry of Agriculture is probably the best home, because it is usually the oldest ministry. It often has the best educated people, since agriculturists are educated abroad, and it usually gets better appropriations, and if the program is put under the Ministry of Agriculture, it is apt to survive longer.

When I got back to New York City after that trip, I was called to Washington, and talked to the people in government, and they just skinned me alive, because I had dared suggest that Agriculture was the place. It was the policy of ICA to put all these programs under community development. This undoubtedly was partly because the community development section of ICA depended for its importance upon the number of programs that it had, and here I was out torpedoing its position, as well as what it claimed were sound practices that it was trying to foster. I did not accept this at all. I got a lot of flak out of this, and the thing that really amused me—this was less than a year before I was called to the Cairo Embassy—was the moment I came back to Washington with an interest in accepting this diplomatic appointment, the attitude could not have changed more rapidly. They came right around then, but I had been skinned alive simply for suggesting that the Ministry of Agriculture was the better locus. Most of this was sincere. I do not question their motives, but there was a good deal of direction on the part of the government that was not always wise.

I came across this at almost every level. Another example:

when we went into Jordan, prior to 1956, the then director of the Point Four program in Jordan called the head of our Jordan program into his office. He said, you know, one of your chief objects here is to make me look good, and us look good. He said, you mustn't be surprised, therefore, if we take credit for what you do. That's why you're here.

This is very human and understandable, but it does lead to a kind of rigidity, and at a good many points we had problems. The reason was not only private group *versus* government, but also it is perhaps, as I have indicated earlier, the more cautious and pragmatic approach of the Foundation, admitting from the beginning that we really did not know what to do in advance, that by and large the local authorities knew pretty well what would work if we could help them to bring it about. *And* a certain attitude, almost inevitable on the part of a large technical government agency, that they did know what to do and they were going to tell other people just how to do it. So there was a built-in conflict. It was not merely government-private agency; there were two methods of approach. These programs represented money. They represented influence, prestige and positions, and there was always conflict within governments as to who could get their hands on a program and where it should come to rest.

One has to remember that, technically speaking, the Near East Foundation never had a project of its own. The project was always the project of the host government. We were there to operate it for them, and while we certainly tried to exercise influence, it was not a case of our direction. We tried to work out an initial agreement as to how a project should get under way, and in our large successful programs we were not too much beset by this. In some places, we were. I recall in Syria, for instance, there was a certain Syrian deputy who tried to latch onto the program and use it for political purposes, and made a nuisance of himself and made things very difficult for us, because when he did not get what he wanted he would cause trouble with the Syrian government.

But Syria is a case by itself. Let me digress: there is an old Egyptian proverb which says that when God created all things, He created them in pairs. Poverty said, I will go and live among the

Bedouin tribes. Health said, I will go with you. Restriction in Activity and Life said, I will live in Egypt. I will go by your side, said Contentment. Reason said, I will dwell in Syria. I will be your companion, said Rebellion. I think that this proverb is at least a hundred years old. It underscores the fact that in the eyes of its neighbors, Syria is fractious.

On the other hand, as I look back, I am impressed by the number of local government leaders who were sincerely concerned with what could be done for their people, and who, on the whole, did very well indeed.

We were never a threat to anybody; the government was a threat. An experience in Iran was very illuminating to me. We had developed, after nine or ten years, a complex of programs in the test area outside of Tehran. There was a teacher training school, a school preparing home economics workers, a group of agricultural cooperatives. There was an ongoing program in the valley, some of it financed with grants from Ford, some of it by grants from Point Four, and the Iranian government had put a lot of money into it.

Just before I left the Foundation, the time came when we were convinced that most of these projects ought to pass out of our hands as operators. They always had been, technically, Iranian government programs, but now they should come directly within the ministry, and we should withdraw from them, except if we were asked, say, to provide an adviser.

So on one of my trips to Iran I undertook to negotiate the handing-over of the Varamin valley, especially the large and very successful Varamin training school for agricultural extension workers and for rural school teachers. Much to my surprise, when I began to work through the government, I found a lack of response to the idea that they should be prepared to take over this really valuable project with a lot of money behind it. I could not quite understand it. It was not that the Iranian government was afraid of money because, by this time, our government had been involved.

Finally, when I got to the Prime Minister and had a long talk with him, he dropped an aside. So often in these things, it is the aside that counts and not the main point, and the aside was, "Of course, the US government is forcing you to do this."

I said, "Mr. Prime Minister, on the contrary, they are not entirely happy about it. It is our idea, and we're doing it because we think our contribution has been made and you're perfectly capable. . . . " At which point he picked it up as quickly as he could; the resistance had gone. It was the feeling that our government was making us turn it over to them that made them suspicious. So we were not a threat to anybody and that was quite an asset that could not be found in any government operation.

William Warne had been the director of the US government operation in Iran, and we had gotten along very well with him indeed. He was transferred to Korea, and when he got there, he requested that we come over and assist in further developing rural services of various kinds, extension and other kinds, in Korea.

We had a long debate in the Foundation about it. Traditionally, we had only operated in the Middle East and we raised money on that basis, and I think there was a good deal of feeling on our Board that this was enough. I was very strongly for it, however, not only because I felt we ought to be of service where we could, but because it seemed to me to give us an opportunity to test whether the conclusions which we had reached on the basis of our 25 or 30 years in the Middle East were really universal in their operation, or whether they reflected a peculiar outlook of Middle Eastern society and Middle East agriculture. Indeed, the method of approach we had used in the Middle East translated itself to the Korean scene, the cautious and experimental development of programs proving equally effective in community and agricultural development in Korea, and subsequently in Africa.

A call to go to Ghana was quite interesting. We did not seek it out. We had sought calls in the past, but not this one. It came from the Ghana government, and in an interesting way indeed.

Years ago, the Foundation had done one of its early projects in Cyprus, based partly upon agricultural extension work that we had done in Greece. Some of this had been written up, and if I recall correctly, had resulted in a kind of handbook on agricultural work, which British administrators in Cyprus had used after our program was over, to carry it on.

Some of these administrators, after independence in Cyprus,

came to Ghana and brought the material with them. Robert Gardiner is one of the names I remember. When Britain decided to withdraw and Ghana launched on its own independent life, there apparently was a feeling that they did not want British influence to continue under the guise of assistance. They looked around for another country, and this other country was America and the connection was already made because of these men. Therefore they approached us to know whether or not we would be interested in entering the country. We had a team who had been there perhaps nine or ten months at the time of my visit.

One of the questions that had immediately arisen then was whether this team should be an all-white team, all-black, or mixed. This was before this kind of question was a burning issue in America, but it was of great concern to us, because we did not want to err on either side. Our experience had been that while the Middle East, with its Muslim culture, had no color bar, and therefore no feeling that the nonwhite was not fully the equal of anyone else, they knew that in traditional America we felt differently. Therefore, when we sent them a nonwhite diplomat or whatever, they assumed that we felt they were second-rate in sending somebody *we* felt was second-rate, whether *they* felt so or not. Now the question was, how would this be in Africa? I went to the Phelps-Stokes Foundation and took counsel with them, and I got what I felt was a very wise answer, which proved itself in our experience.

The first answer was that probably the black man would have a more difficult time than a white man. The reason for this, said the man I talked to, was that the African assumed that the American black, because he was black, sympathized with him and understood him better than the white man. He said, that's not true. The American black man is an American. He has all the American cultural reactions. When he goes into Africa, he's going to act like an American, and when he makes a mistake, it's much more difficult for the black African to forgive him than to forgive a white man.

He said, if you recruit a team with some blacks on it, they have to be better qualified than the white man and more sensitive to this factor. Otherwise, their blackness will be a disability rather than an asset. So we did sent two or three black members of the team, the most highly qualified members in terms of education and experience. They did very well indeed.

CHAPTER 9

RETURNING TO EGYPT UNDER KENNEDY

I went to the Middle East for the Foundation every year to visit projects and deal with governments. Before I left on my trip in the winter of 1960-61, I was approached by the Salzburg American Seminar, then headed by Dexter Perkins, Professor of History at the University of Rochester, to know whether I would spend most of the month of January in Salzburg, with a team of people, lecturing on American foreign policy toward the Middle East. It was one of the seminar sections, not so much for students but for newspaper editors, government officials and others.

My most vivid memory of the seminar is the night President Kennedy was inaugurated. Perkins, a very decided New England type, had a short-wave radio. It was very cold that winter in Salzburg, and we sat in the room of an old *schloss*. It was hailing and sleeting outside, and Perkins' short-wave radio was picking up the inaugural proceedings in Washington, where it was also very stormy. The reception was not very good, but we did hear clearly his well-known statement, "Ask not what your country can do for you, but what you can do for your country." At which Perkins said,

"Nobody has talked to the American public for a long time the way this young man has."

I spent about three and a half weeks there which were quite useful because they gave me time to sit down and put together, connectedly, ideas on the Middle East as they had developed out of my various thoughts and travels. I went on to Iran, Jordan and other places where we had programs, returning home in February.

The first morning I went into the office when I got back I was told to call Washington, that there had been a number of calls for me. I promptly phoned someone in the State Department with whom I had a past connection, Jimmy Thomson.

Jimmy Thomson's father and mother were younger contemporaries of my parents; they had been missionaries in China. Jimmy was a Chinese scholar, I think at Yale. He had joined the State Department with Chester Bowles. When I got Jimmy on the telephone he said, please come to Washington, we have some business to talk over with you.

I went to Washington, surmising that with the new administration there would be some further activity in the field of technical assistance.

I saw Jimmy briefly, and he took me to see Chester Bowles; much to my astonishment Bowles wanted to know whether I would be interested in a diplomatic appointment to the area. So I stayed on in Washington and finally saw Dean Rusk, who made it a little bit more definite and mentioned Egypt. I went home to think it over and this marked the beginning of my transfer from the Near East Foundation to diplomatic work. They did not argue too strongly. They simply said, we need you. Would you be willing to come over and help us?

The offer at once raised questions in my mind, in three different directions. One was, how effective can a non-career officer be in the service? I have a great respect for the trained career American diplomat. I think we have a good service and I have known many of them in my years in the Middle East.

I took counsel with a number of my old friends, Ray Hare*

---

*Raymond A. Hare was Ambassador to Saudi Arabia, Lebanon, Egypt and Turkey, in the course of a distinguished career.

and others, asking them quite candidly whether or not a man who came from the outside really could operate. How much resentment would he meet?

A second question that I had very largely to satisfy myself on was whether one's long acquaintance with the area would be an asset or a liability. And the third was, what direction is American policy prepared to take and how could I contribute to that direction? In the case of the Middle East, and the Arab-Israeli problem, my views were fairly well-known—I had sent that cable to President Truman.

I did not know where we were going or whether or not I could be effective. If one is not reasonably in support of government policy, then one should not go. I did not conceive it as anybody's function to go in and try to throw a monkey wrench into the works.

I meditated on these three questions and discussed them with various persons, then went back and had a second talk with Dean Rusk. Really what he had to say was—and I had to discuss this later with President Kennedy—that the basic objective of the administration was to identify certain countries in which foreign relations had come to an impasse, and in these countries to make a fresh start without commitment. He named India, Japan and Egypt. There was no promise made as to what direction policy would be going, but a willingness to say, now let's start afresh and see if we can't break the log jam.

I did not think you could get any stronger affirmation from a new government, and it seemed reasonably satisfactory because it did show that one would have an opportunity to contribute in some measure to the formation of a working policy. On the basis of my mulling over these three aspects, I came to the conclusion that there possibly was something I could do.

Of course, there was the whole dimension of one's personal life. I was well ensconced in the Foundation; I had great belief in its work. I knew that the Foundation could not be without a president for too long a term. In 1960, I was 57, and one does not shift gears at that age very easily. I had to go on to earn a living, as well as to be useful.

It involved for both my wife and myself a major upheaval. We had children here. My wife was busy in New York on the staff at the Riverside church. I did not know how much of a strain it would be on both of us, to stop in mid-career. But looking it over, we both finally came to the conclusion it was a very hard thing to say no to. One accepted it not because it was a great adventure, but simply, given all the circumstances, it seemed that if a contribution could be made this way, one ought to make it.

Afterwards, I was told that I had also been under consideration for an appointment to Iran. The Ambassador who was appointed to Iran faced what might have been a difficult confirmation hearing. And had that confirmation not been made, I was told, I would have been offered that post as well. Of the two, Egypt was certainly much more fitting, and I was glad that was where I was to go.

Ray Hare was one of the most helpful to me in my decision. I have a great respect for his basic soundness. He said in the first place that it is traditional in the American foreign service to have about a third of the chiefs of mission appointed from outside the service. And he said, on the whole, it is recognized that this is good, because it prevents the service from seeming to become too parochial.

So the fact that one is appointed from outside is in itself a certain tradition. Two kinds of people are appointed from the outside. Some are appointed as straight political payoff, and usually they are sent to posts where there are not many problems. It used to be Cuba, in the old palmy days, and countries like Ireland, Australia, Switzerland. Nobody expected much of people like this.

Other outsiders are chosen not on a political basis, and some very good men have come that way. Ellsworth Bunker, for instance, was a businessman in South America. David Bruce was a businessman. And at this point, Ray said, the attitude of your staff toward you depends upon you and your ability. If you have ability, if you do the job, you get cooperation and respect. What makes bad feeling is if you loaf on the job, if you somehow feel this is an honor that has been given to you and you don't have to do anything for it. Unless you can be professional and hard-working, you will not be accepted. But if you are, then the fact that you were appointed in this way is no drawback.

I would fully subscribe to this view based on my own limited experience. I couldn't have asked for a more loyal and supportive embassy than I had in Cairo. They were good; they were professional; they received me warmly. They helped me greatly, and I never had any feeling whatever from them—perhaps I was not sensitive to it—that the manner in which I was appointed in any way affected our relationship.

It was sometime in March that the decision was made, and from then into June I was winding up affairs at the Foundation and also being given briefings in Washington. The confirmation hearings went smoothly; I had no problems. Not many members of the Foreign Relations Committee appeared, maybe three or four, but Chairman Fulbright was there. And Fulbright kept circling around the question of Israel. I did not know whether he was trying to find out whether I was too pro-Arab or not, and finally he sort of blurted out, "Well, what we don't want to do is to send a pro-Israeli to Egypt." But I had no difficulty in those hearings, of any kind.

Just before leaving, my wife and I went to the White House. She met both President and Mrs. Kennedy, and then I had a good session with the President. It was the first time I had met him. The occasion raised the question that I never have been able fully to answer, and that is, why me? I had no political connection that was in any sense influential. I never was asked whether I was a Republican or a Democrat. This was not a problem.

I had known Dean Rusk through the Council on Foreign Relations in New York. I had conducted seminars, and so had Dean. We knew each other on speaking terms, but not intimately. Chester Bowles I had never met before, and all that I know is that a task force was put together by the President to go out and recruit people, and somehow my name got into the hopper.

I am familiar with the idea that the Council on Foreign Relations was all-powerful in these matters. As a matter of fact, there is a radio program from Canada, of an extreme right-wing character, that is always condemning the Council on Foreign Relations as the secret penetration point of Communism, running the affairs of the country—the poor old sleepy Council on Foreign Relations, a lot of us elderly guys sitting around in a half stupor.

Through the work of the Foundation, I had dealt with foreign governments in the context of American interests, and I knew a number of UN ambassadors. Also, I think that my assignment was a reflection of a policy that Kennedy brought to his ambassadorial appointments. He had identified certain countries where he wanted to make a fresh start, and it was in these countries that he apparently recruited outside people.

For Japan he had Reischauer, for a very particular reason—he knew the language and had a thorough knowledge of the country. John Everton, who went to Burma, had been in those parts and, again, knew the language. The Harvard economist John Kenneth Galbraith went to India on the basis, I was told, that India was the great developing economy and Galbraith was the great economist of development. And I went to Egypt, because I had lived in Egypt for so long and was somewhat identified with it.

* * *

President Kennedy was a very human, remarkable man. When I went to see him, I had been packing trunks and other things, and whenever I do that I get a bad back and sort of wriggle when I walk. Any man with a bad back recognizes it.

When I left the President in his office in the White House, he noticed this and asked me if I had a bad back, and I said, "Yes, Mr. President, I do."

"Well," he said, "I have a bad back too. What do you do for your back?"

I told him that among my more effective remedies had been to lie on the floor and let my daughter take her shoes off and massage my back by walking on it. He asked how old my daughter was, and I told him she was a college graduate. And he replied, "Caroline's only three. She's not big enough."

I think I saw the President five times on consultation during the two years I was in Egypt. The next time I came back, I had had some health problems and had lost about 60 pounds, which made quite a difference. I had only seen the President once, and when I came back from Cairo for consultation and met him, he looked at me and said, "You've gotten thin. I hope you haven't been sick."

Perhaps he was briefed, but I do not think so—I think it was his acute observation. And I found him a very good man with whom to talk because he was not concerned with generalities. It was not, well now, how's Nasser these days? How are you getting along with Nasser? What are your problems with him? He was very specific. He knew exactly what he wanted to know and he asked specific questions about the Egyptian situation, or about President Nasser and our relationship, and he wanted specific answers. This made you feel that he had been following the situation, that he knew what he was talking about and he expected you to know what you were talking about.

He did practice personal diplomacy in a variety of ways. One was through correspondence, especially the nonwritten or spoken letter, which means a letter very carefully drafted, but one which you take to the recipient and read to him and afterwards send the text as an aide-memoire. It is, therefore, not an official letter. It is called a verbal letter.

I had a good example of how carefully this was done. One time when I was with the President—I always saw him just before I went back to Egypt—he said, "I have a verbal letter to send to President Nasser." He called one of his secretaries into the room and said, "Let's have the text." It was read to him, and he said, "This will not do at all." He said, "I've got something very direct and slightly unpleasant to say to Nasser in the first paragraph. You didn't say it. You pussyfooted about it. You have something unpleasant to say? Say it." And he said, "The second paragraph sounds like the end of a treaty. This isn't a treaty. This is a personal letter. Now, take this draft."

So he sat down in my presence, and we drafted it, making the first paragraph not unpleasant, but a very clear statement of what the problem was, and then a second paragraph—a very warm, personal greeting between people, saying in effect, I've got my problems, you've got your problems, and these are the circumstances. It was typed and given to me, and when I got back to Egypt, I delivered it to President Nasser by reading it to him.

The other thing the President did—and I do not know how widespread this was—was to communicate privately with Nasser, sometimes in the form of a message and sometimes in the form of an emissary, to inform him as to policy changes or coming events that might cause problems and embarrassment. In the summer of 1962, a decision had been reached by the American government to sell Hawk missiles to Israel, the Hawk being a defensive ground-to-air rocket, designed to protect airfields. It was very illuminating as to how this decision was reached. I was told by acquaintances in the Department of State—all in private but I believe it to be true—that when the 1962 congressional elections began to come up, several groups of people who were questioning what President Kennedy's policy toward Israel might be saw to it that campaign contributions in some very important races, especially in the Southwest, were withheld until it was clear what the Administration wanted to do about Israel. Apparently Kennedy had tense discussions on this particular theme on several occasions.

This bothered the Administration; they needed supporters in the new Congress. Therefore a review was made of the situation, and the decision was made to sell Hawk missiles to Israel. The sale could be justified from a military estimate of the situation which showed that the Israeli airfields were vulnerable. The Hawk missile was purely defensive, and therefore could be justified in policy terms of trying to prevent any obvious weakness on either the Arab or the Israeli side that might tempt the other toward some kind of preemptive strike. But that's not the reason it was done; the reason it was done was politics.

The President knew the decision would upset Nasser. I had been there only one year, we were just beginning to get along pretty well, and the President did not want to upset the applecart. What he did was to send a special emissary to Cairo, and he and I together went to see Nasser. There was no publicity given this at all; I never saw it reported in the American papers.

We told President Nasser that within the next 48 hours this announcement was going to be made, and we told him why it was going to be made. We did not say it was because of the American political situation, but we did call attention to our well-known policy of trying to prevent an imbalance. This was done not to justify it or to argue about it, but simply because the President did not want him taken by surprise, realizing it would create a political problem for him.

Nasser was on vacation in Alexandria. We spent quite a delightful afternoon looking over the Mediterranean in a cabana. His answer was, of course, you don't expect that I'm going to like this very much. But he said, "I do appreciate the fact that I know what's going to happen." The result was that, although there was a lot of flak in the newspapers, we never had any trouble with the Egyptian government about it.

That was another kind of personal touch, and it was done on a number of occasions. When we decided to return to nuclear testing, again Nasser was informed 24 or 48 hours beforehand, so he could be prepared for what was to come. By these two devices, in addition to more formal correspondence, President Kennedy did conduct a very personal type of diplomacy, at least with Egypt.

I replaced Frederick Reinhardt, who had been on post in Egypt only for a few months. He was being moved by the President to Italy, where he had been Ambassador, because he was particularly skilled both politically and linguistically, and understood Communist affairs. Italy had probably the largest Communist Party in the West and was felt to be an appropriate place for him. I think the fact that he had been posted to Egypt was indicative of a certain nervousness about Egypt felt by the Eisenhower administration, a feeling that Communist influence after the High Dam was considerable. Equally, the fact that Kennedy moved him for someone who did not have that background would probably indicate somewhat of a shift of judgment.

One must remember, at the period I went to Egypt, we were just beginning to emerge out of a deep freeze in American-Egyptian relations. The deep freeze came about primarily as the result of the 1956 nationalization of the Canal and American-Egyptian actions thereafter.

In that connection, there is an incident I have not seen reported elsewhere which was rather illuminating. It was told to me by Worth Howard, Dean of the American University in Cairo, who had been my colleague for many years and was perfectly reliable. He had known Henry Byroade, Ambassador to Egypt at the time of the High Dam fiasco, rather well, and he told me that in his opinion the strain in American-Egyptian relationships had begun with an incident connected with Byroade and Nasser at the time of the Bandung Conference (1955).

Nasser went to the Bandung Conference, and the night before he went he had dinner with Ambassador Byroade. Nasser very rarely accepted dinner invitations to any embassy, just occasionally to one of the Middle Eastern embassies. During my three years in Cairo, I never knew him to attend an embassy dinner of one of the large outside powers. He broke this rule and accepted an invitation to a private dinner with Byroade the night before he left for Bandung, apparently in order to tell Byroade rather fully how he saw the situation and what were his objectives and hopes in going there.

While he was in Bandung, the Western world—France, in particular, and Dulles, because of his attitude against the nonaligned—felt that Nasser had made an injudicious move and decided to punish him for doing so. Byroade was instructed by the State Department to join with the French and the British in not going out to the airfield to welcome Nasser when he came back, as they would ordinarily do. The result was that when Nasser came back from Bandung, the only major ambassador who met him at the airport was the Russian, and Nasser was absolutely furious. He felt that he had broken his custom, that he had told Byroade what he was going to do, and that he had been very badly compromised.

Worth Howard said that he felt this was the beginning of the tension and chill that began to affect relations between Egypt and the United States. During the early years of the Nasser regime, we had been really very friendly and had, on the whole, looked with approval at what was going on in Egypt. After the 1956 experience, both countries undertook a course of trying to hurt each other. Nasser, I think, tried to do his best to injure the American position in the rest of the Arab world and certainly, under Dulles, we hoped to do the same to Nasser. Indeed, I think that Dulles' initial decision not to participate in building the High Dam was an attempt to cut Nasser down to size.

This was the period (1957-58) of the deep freeze, and it did not work very well. Nasser found he really could not hurt us, and we found we could not hurt Nasser. The then Ambassador, Raymond Hare, had numerous conversations with Nasser in which both men agreed that something should be done about our relations, but Nasser would never make any specific suggestions or requests as to what could or should be done. Finally, through an intermediary Nasser indicated an interest in PL-480 wheat, and our relations began to move toward what eventually became a honeymoon period under Kennedy.

The thaw coincided with Dulles' departure as Secretary of State. This was about the position when I got there. We had been through a bad experience; both sides had started to try to mend their fences. Ray Hare had been replaced by Reinhardt, and the latter's departure was not only a judgment of our new Administration on the nature of the Communist threat in Egypt but was also a new start. President Kennedy made it clear to me that he wanted to make a new beginning with Egypt, to see what could be done.

The Egyptian Ambassador in Washington, Mustafa Kamil, had been very diligent in this same enterprise. In talking to me before he went to Washington, he said: "Let us put our differences in the icebox." That was literally his phrase. When I presented my credentials to Nasser, after I had waited about two weeks, the normal time, Nasser used this same phrase to me—the differences, of course, at this point being chiefly the matter of Israel and Palestine. We both agreed that neither country was going to change its attitude for the sake of the other.

So, said Nasser, using his Ambassador's phrase, let us put the thing in the icebox and try to find other mutual interests. That, indeed, became the chief concern of the Embassy and the Administration in the years that I was there.

There were still aftermaths of chilly feelings. The CIA was in some sense following Nasser's movements closely, following Nasser's family, to see where they went and what they were doing. Very early in my conversations with Nasser he complained about this, and because I was in the happy circumstance of being young and ignorant and fresh, I could say, I don't know anything about this, but I'll look into it.

On the other hand, the Egyptians were keeping a very close watch on us. We had perhaps seven or eight policemen around the residence every night, and if we had a dinner party the license of every car that came in was noted. All of this was a hangover from the period of bad relationships.

My first task when I got there was to see if we could alleviate the situation and find some positive interests of joint concern. The difficulty of developing a policy of this kind was that the United States had very few direct interests in Egypt. There were a few companies operating, Socony-Vacuum for one, no very large investment. Our concern with Nasser was almost entirely about what he could do to injure us, or to injure Western interests generally in other parts of the Middle East.

On the other hand, we did have a very great value to Nasser, because we presented the only counterpoint he had to the Russian position. Our job at the Embassy was to try to develop a series of mutual interests, when we really didn't have too much mutuality upon which to build.

* * *

The breakup of the United Arab Republic (UAR)* had several effects that were directly or peripherally important. In the first place, it shook the position of Nasser in the Arab world. He no longer had the immediate position of strength from which he could move, and to that extent his capacity to rally area influence in our favor or against us was lessened.

In the second place, we did not try to exploit the breakup. Had Dulles been Secretary, we probably would have tried to exploit it, but there was certainly no one within the current Administration who would. I felt strongly, and I think people in the Department did, that it would be a great mistake to do so, and while we

---

*The Syrian Army revolted against the United Arab Republic on September 28, 1961, and Syria resumed its sovereign status.

certainly did nothing to assist Egypt in regaining the departing province, neither did we play it up as a big thing. I think Nasser was conscious of this, and realized that we were trying to act in good faith and not try some trick to catch him off balance.

The situation was useful also because it gave me my first genuine opportunity to see Nasser at some length. When I went out, several people within the Department had suggested that I ought to try and arrange to see Nasser regularly, once a month or something of the sort. I resisted this strongly. It smacked far too much of the British adviser. There had been advisers in Egypt for 40 or 50 years, and they did the wrong things. I was perfectly sure that if I made such a suggestion, Nasser would read into it that we wanted to have some kind of an advisory capacity, which they were not prepared to accept. I did not have to resist this too strongly; that kind of relationship was not developed.

On the other hand, the breakup of the UAR gave me a perfectly legitimate reason to start to see Nasser. These were things that very much concerned him and us, and I tried to practice a fairly personal diplomatic stance, because I think that is the way we got along best—at least the way I have gotten along best—in the Middle East. The contact was useful, and Nasser was, given the situation, reasonably forthcoming in discussion. Since the breakup was followed almost immediately by the Yemen war, which gave me more reason to see Nasser, I was fortunate to be able to get into a position where we did have some mutuality of interests.

* * *

It seemed to me that we ought to make our intentions clear to Nasser. I remember reading a book by Harold Nicolson,* the British diplomat, who quotes an old hand as saying that when you're dealing with a foreign government, don't worry so much

---

Diplomacy (The actual quote is " 'Do not waste your time in trying to discover what is at the back of an Oriental's mind; there may, for all you know, be nothing at the back; concentrate all your attention upon making quite certain that he is left in no doubt whatsoever in regard to what is at the back of *your* mind.' ")

about what's on their minds, don't try to outguess them. Be perfectly sure that they know what's on your mind.

I thought that in regard to the Suez affair there had been a lack of frankness on both sides. I tried to see to it that, within the proper bounds and with caution, our legitimate points of view were brought quite clearly to Nasser's attention. I did not feel at the time that he was overly concerned with the American reaction, partly because from the very beginning our reaction was a very reasonable one.

It was an interesting experience, however. Nasser had a great deal of self-control, and it was very difficult when one went to talk to him to detect what I would call signs of nervousness. During this period, at the time of the UAR breakup, and subsequently during the Yemen war, there were persistent rumors in Egypt that Nasser feared for his life, that he had sent his family to Alexandria or even out of the country. One report had it that at the time of the breakup of the union he was sleeping in a different bedroom every night for fear he would be assassinated. This was nonsense, not true at all. In my talks with him during this period he showed no hint of hysteria or nervousness. It seemed to me that he accepted the departure of Syria quite well.

When the matter first broke, he sent Abd al-Hakim Amr, the Chief of Staff of the Army, who later committed suicide after the 1967 war, as an emissary to Syria to try to persuade the Syrians not to depart, and I have reason to believe that he and Amr had a very heated exchange after Amr arrived in Damascus. Amr insisted that the Syrians could not be brought back into the union, and Nasser insisted they ought to be. Whether that is correct I do not know, but I have good reasons for believing it. But I would say that within a couple of days Nasser had settled down and accepted the fact of the departure. Two or three days after the major events, he said: "You know, I was reluctant to enter into the union with Syria at the time I did." He said, "We had worked out, or I had worked out, a fairly reasonable timetable. I believe that we had the beginning of a nonpolitical union of one kind or another, cultural and economic. And only when these had shown promise and were really working would we lead on to the much more difficult union, political. When the Syrians came down here, there were different groups—the army, the businessmen, and the political party [Baath]. Against my better judgment, I consented to political union."

Whether that was true, I have my doubts. It was either hindsight or justification, but nevertheless these are the terms in which he put it. And he argued that it all proved his original judgment was right. Then he went on to say that the fundamental cause of the breakup was the fact that the Syrians are not Egyptians, and he thought they were, and the Egyptians are not Syrians, and they thought we were. Under those circumstances, he said, there really was not very much that could be done about it.

Within a week's time, I had gone to see the Minister of Foreign Affairs, Mahmud Fawzi, whom I had known before. Fawzi was one of the very few holdovers from the old regime, in many ways a diplomat's diplomat—smooth, well-versed in everything that had to do with diplomacy. Fawzi and I could talk to each other with a good deal of frankness, and we did. I asked him whether Egypt was developing any strategy to mend the break. Was it their policy to accept it? With the judiciousness that was typical of him, he meditated, pursed his lips, and finally he said, "Well, Mr. Badeau, you and I are both historians." In both cases this was false; he was not and I was not. He said to me, "We know, according to history, that when a union like this is broken up, it almost never occurs again. I repeat, never occurs again."

I sent this information on to the Department and I appended to it a note saying, this is as near a positive statement as Fawzi has ever given me. He was replaced later, but on the whole he was a very able man. In connection with Fawzi, it is interesting to have Nasser's judgment on him.

I used to smoke a pipe and cigars. I was having a conversation with Nasser, and I had either forgotten to bring them, or I had run out of the little cigarillos that I smoked, so I did not have any, and Nasser noticed this. He said, "What's wrong?" I said, "I've brought nothing to smoke but my pipe." And he said, "Smoke your pipe." I said, "Mr. President, our President doesn't like a pipe smoker, and I thought maybe you didn't." He said, "Oh, no. Smoke your pipe."

So I took my pipe out, and then I said, "You know, Mr. President, I think a pipe is an ideal appurtenance for an Ambassador. For instance, when I call on your Foreign Minister, if he asks me a difficult question, I can take my pipe out, knock it out, tamp the tobacco. It will take me five minutes to get it going, and when the five minutes are over I can hope to have a wise answer."

At which Nasser looked at me and said, "Tell me, has my Foreign Minister ever asked you a direct and difficult question?" Well, the answer would have been no. He was not that kind of man. Nasser knew pretty well who he was dealing with.

Nevertheless, I thought that Fawzi's guarded response was a clear indication that Egypt and Nasser had given up hope of restoring the union, at least at that time, and because this was followed so quickly by the Yemen imbroglio, attention was shifted to another direction. I may say that the general mood I found in Egypt, even among senior government officials, was on the whole one of relief. There was resentment that the bride had run off at the altar, but not much love lost. As one very senior official said to me, at last we're in a position to spend our money on ourselves instead of the Syrians. It was not as traumatic an experience as one might have expected.

The only basis on which Egypt was really prepared to seek a political union was one in which Egypt had a dominant position. This was partly due to the size of Egypt in relation to other countries, and also the fact that Egypt was more stable, more cohesive, and had begun the process of modernization much earlier, beginning with Muhammad Ali, and had for generations supplied teachers and technicians all over the area. Therefore, wherever one had a union, it was to be posited on Egyptian leadership. When they discovered that this was not acceptable, they were not prepared to pay much of a price for unity.

The question came up as to how quickly we should recognize the new government of Syria. It was a sensitive matter. Turkey and especially Iran rushed in to recognize Syria at once. Iran moved so quickly that Egypt broke off relations with that nation. In general, as in the case of Yemen, we tried to adopt a policy of being about midway—neither leading the van nor coming up in the rear guard.

If we had rushed in, it would have been a clear mark of exploitation.

Under Dulles, it seems to me, we got ourselves into a difficult position. Dulles had not liked nonalignment at all. He went on the Biblical principle that he who is not for me is against me, and that had really led nowhere. This outworn philosophy was revived, albeit in a more sophisticated form, during the Yemen affair, in opposition to those of us who sought to identify the United States in some measure with new trends in the world, not solely with the traditional forms of society and government. The White House had its own staff working on the Middle East, fortunately. Bob Komer, later our Ambassador to Turkey, was active and vigorous and kept after the State Department.

The man on the desk in Washington covering my area was Bob Strong, a career officer who had been DCM in Syria and knew his way around in the area. Phillips Talbot was Assistant Secretary of State, and while I had never known Phil before, he and my son-in-law Doak Barnett were well acquainted. I had very good support from the Department by and large, and I do not recall any query as to the possibilities of US exploitation of the UAR breakup.

There were people, especially in the CIA, who would have been so disposed. There was always a group in the CIA, and perhaps in Defense, who judged Nasser to be either a Communist or a Communist tool and who thought that the object of our policy should be to curtail him at every point. That was not the policy of the Department, and if it ever was suggested it never came to me in direct terms. I tried to forestall anything by reporting our views fully, and I was backed up on that.

* * *

One of the most interesting problems in the Embassy was how to get your opinion registered with Washington and get action on it. In the first place, you were competing with everybody. There were about a thousand coded messages a day that went into Washington, and you had to compete with 999 other messages to be read.

Also, one had to be very aware of the fact that the man on the spot has a very limited view of the situation. One is often asked, why doesn't the Department listen to the Ambassador? The reason is that the Ambassador sits under a palm tree in Cairo, and what he sees is what you see from under a palm tree in Cairo. Only as you move back into Washington, where you get people who understand the situation in England, or the situation in Saudi Arabia, do you grasp the whole impact of the problem. Furthermore, there are dimensions of military strategy and defense which you cannot know. So I never felt that the prerogative of the Ambassador and the staff in Cairo in any sense was to make policy. This could only be made by the people who had the whole horizon of interests in front of them and a flow of all the information coming in.

What you wanted was to be listened to, and you could not ask for more than to be listened to well. At the Embassy, my very good staff and I developed several devices that I think helped in this area. In the first place, if you gave it a little thought, you discovered that in each section of the government that dealt with your area, and this meant the Department of Defense, the CIA, even Agriculture, there were usually two groups of people who were concerned. The first were those who were officially concerned, and when you sent a message it was slugged for the attention of all these people. Very often, however, in the Department and elsewhere, the person who was the official recipient of the message was not really the person who ran herd on the situation. What you tried to do was to identify those people. When you had a message which was important and had some special, say, defense dimension to it, you saw to it that that man got a copy, which he might not ordinarily have received if you had left it to routine distribution. This meant that the actors, the people who were dealing with the action in the various sections, were in close touch, and that always helped.

A second thing that helped a good deal was to try to back off from the pressure of the daily flow of events, which is always difficult. You get so absorbed in the flow of events of the day that you really do not have time to take a longer view. We tried to back off every once in a while and ask ourselves—looking down the road and given what we had at the time—what major issues do we see on the horizon that might come up in the next six months? If we could identify such issues, then I would have the political staff or the appropriate section of the embassy do a series of studies. If this situation develops, what are its implications in this field and that?

These studies were drafted and sent in to the desk officer and to some others. I discovered that State Department people whether at home or abroad are very alike. We are all lazy, and if you have in your file a good study of a certain situation, and that situation arises, you are apt to turn to it, haul it out, rather than start from scratch. Furthermore, by the time something has been in your file six months, it no longer belongs to the man who wrote it—they are your files.

So we quite carefully and regularly tried to identify issues and send in the studies. Sometimes what we foresaw did not happen. Sometimes, if it did happen, what we had written was not appropriate. Sometimes it was, and when that happened there was a tendency to pull these things out, look them over; on a number of occasions we got back instructions that were at least 50 percent in our own words, words drawn out of these papers.

Another thing I found rather early on was that a message written in the atmosphere of Cairo is read in the atmosphere of Washington, and a word or a judgment that means one thing in Cairo does not mean the same thing in Washington. There were sometimes misunderstandings or failure to perceive the situation because of this factor.

To a modest extent we tried to get around that. About every three months, I would get the staff to work up what I called an atmosphere piece. What is Cairo like during Ramadan in 1961? What are the headlines in the newspaper? If you cull the columns in the newspapers, what's the single largest topic? It never is foreign policy. It may very well be the rents in Cairo. What are the stories that have gone around this month? These are very often indicative of how people think—in other words, here is the feeling. The idea was that particular messages should be read in the context of this atmosphere.

These were devices that I think were of some assistance in keeping communications flowing fairly well, and in seeing to it that we really were listened to, and being listened to is about all one can expect.

I do not believe in magazine journalism, where everybody writes a paragraph. I had one or two very good drafters, and what they would do is sit down and write a draft of the atmosphere piece. Then the people I thought important would sit down and talk it all over again, and it would be redrafted, not by a committee but by several men. Finally, what went off was basically the work of one man, but it reflected a certain group decision.

It is also important, of course, to consider the amount of reporting. One cannot expect Embassy officers to cut down on their reports unless one can get the end users in Washington to cut down what they want. A possibility though is to have the half-time attaché. I would have a half-time labor attaché, because if I had a full-time labor attaché, he would have written daily reports full-time. A number of other attachés I had half-time, because I did not know any other way to cut the reporting.

A second thing is to keep working with your staff, insofar as you have freedom to do so, as to what they report on. There is always a temptation to report on the reportable. An issue makes for a good report, so you write it; it may not really be important. The things that are hard to report are the things that ought to be reported on. So, as the reports and cables went over one's desk, one looked at them and talked to the heads of departments and tried everything possible to urge people to get out of the routine, or at least to keep it to an absolute minimum.

* * *

It has been suggested that the country team concept* of the Embassy did not appear to do very much. Early in the Kennedy Administration, the President (as others had done before him) sent out a message reinforcing the authority of the Ambassador, and

---

*That all US government agency representatives in the country are members of a single team presided over by the Ambassador. The principal manifestation of the team concept is a weekly staff meeting in which all agencies are represented.

since then this has been done again and again. I think this was done partly because, in his judgment, or at least the judgment of his advisers, the country team concept had gotten a little out of hand. In that concept one is really running things by committee, where each department has a man you sit down and talk with.

Certainly you must utilize as fully as possible all of the skill, knowledge and expertise that your staff has. They must be included, but in the end it is the Ambassador's name that goes on a telegram. If it's wrong, his is the neck that is risked, and I did not feel you could really run an Embassy by committee. So, while I tried to have the fullest consultation with everybody, we did not attack things quite in that country team aspect.

There were other ways in which we tried to get participation. One thing I did was known by the staff as "Professor Badeau's Diplomatic Seminar." Every Friday we had a staff meeting that included the chiefs of all sections and two or three steps down, so perhaps we would have 35 or 40 people. The custom was, or had been generally, to go around the table to the economic officer, the cultural officer, and so forth, each telling what had happened in his department during that week. In addition, I tried once a month to take some particular question and bring it up before the whole staff and get a reaction. For instance, after Nasser had nationalized the industry of Egypt—the start of Arab socialism—I asked Robert Ford, the Canadian Ambassador who had been stationed in Belgrade, a very able man, to come over and talk to us about what degree of Yugoslav influence he saw in Nasser's Arab Socialist program.

In this way I tried to keep the staff from being bound solely by the horizons of their immediate, limited concerns, and to find something everybody could react to, and from my standpoint I often got not only information but understanding of the attitudes of my staff on this kind of issue. The staff reaction was, I thought, positive. You had to be sure that what you presented was good, but I never felt that there was much resistance.

I had army attachés, air attachés, naval attachés, all three, and my relations with them were very good. We did try, during this period, to amalgamate the three attaché services into a single armed services attaché, but that did not work. It has not worked in general. This was something that I initiated because I discovered that these attachés were duplicating their own intelligence. Not only that, the Egyptians got a little confused. They would come to the army attaché, and he would say, that really isn't my job, you have to talk with the air attaché. I had the feeling that if we had one armed services attaché, under whom there would be assistant attachés in the three services, we could deal with the Egyptians better. But this cut into the high prerogatives of tradition and of office, and I could not do anything about it.

I did not find any resistance from the CIA. Rarely, I think, would the CIA openly resist. It had to be the other way around—what didn't you know? Before I went out, I saw Allen Dulles, who was then Director of the CIA, and had a long talk with him, and with his support and consent, very willingly given, we cut the size of the CIA staff—it seems to me that something like a quarter of the Embassy were CIA people. It was simply too much, and he agreed that the staff should be cut.

The chief of the CIA in Cairo was a man with whom I got along well, and when I first got out there I sat down and talked very frankly with him, so that I was fully informed about the various kinds of operations that were going on. There were some operations that I did not want to know about in detail, because it was a great protection, if asked by the Egyptian government, to be able to say honestly, I'm sorry, I don't know about that, but I'll find out.

But I did know what was going on. I knew all the categories, and if any new actions were instituted, they had to go through me or be discussed with me first, and every week I was briefed. I did not always agree with some of the CIA proceedings. As an example, when I got to Cairo, I found that they had a number of local informants, Egyptian or other nationalities, and some of them had been in contact with the CIA for 10 or 15 years. The Egyptians are not dumb. They catch on to this sort of thing very quickly. It would seem to me that one was not getting much out of these fellows anyhow, and one is in a vulnerable position.

I did not force that issue. Later, after I left, one of these people was picked up, and I'm sure that nobody was fooled by it. But I was not experienced at intelligence gathering, so I let the CIA carry on. There were certain things that we did get stopped. We stopped Nasser's being followed. I thought that was ridiculous.

We had a number of other operations that went on in Cairo that really had nothing to do with the Egyptian government at all, but were due to the fact either that Egypt was a natural center for concern about Africa to the south, or as a great international exchange center it was a place where defectors might turn up.

All of these things I knew about, but I did not try to run the CIA. On the other hand, as far as I know, and I think I know pretty well, they did not try any dirty tricks either.

I can say, because I have said it to the CIA itself several times, that in the three years I was with the Embassy I cannot really recall the CIA uncovering intelligence that made very much difference in our approach to policy. The time when it was really tested was when the Yemen war was at its height. I very much wanted to know, in order to deal with Nasser, how many Egyptian troops were in the country and where the Saudis were. In other words, good military information. I simply could not get it from the CIA. They said, you know, we have a lot of raw information. By the time we tell you this, it's all out of date. Well, I said, what's the use of having it? Well, the reply was, what you ask costs too much.

I found by and large that you got much better guidance if you had a man who was an expert, say an economist, who followed the public economic news that appeared in the Egyptian and foreign newspapers, who talked with the economics departments of the Egyptian government, and then said, if you put this all together, it means this. I thought on the whole you got a truer picture that way than you did by trying to put a man under the Economy Minister's bed at midnight to hear what he talked about in his sleep.

* * *

As I mentioned earlier, one of our problems was to find mutual interests with Egypt we could develop, and thus avoid some of the impasses we had reached. We did have a mutual interest to this degree: the Kennedy Administration had judged that a stable developing Egypt, even in a revolutionary pattern, was very much to our interest. One reason was, if it was not stable, it might easily fall into some kind of further revolution or *coup d'état*, which would perhaps give the Soviets already there a chance further to enhance their position, and also might have a domino effect across the Arab world. After all, in his prime, Nasser bestrode the Arab world up to a point, and if things really blew up in Egypt, there was a real chance of repercussions, so stability was to our advantage.

The other reason, it seemed to me, was that it was to our advantage to have Nasser's brand of pragmatic state socialism work, rather than have him driven in the direction of real Communist economic and political life. Nasser was not an ideologue. He was a highly pragmatic man indeed; he took some things from the Communist system and some things from the capitalist. At that time it was quite strongly represented in the Department—it was not just my idea—that this was kind of a vaccination, if you will, against a real onslaught of a worse disease.

Those two factors put together meant that our economic program did involve a mutuality of interests. Furthermore, the economic program created solid grounds for consulting with Nasser and his top aides. The chief of the aid mission would have to go and talk to the Minister of Economics, Dr. Qaisuni, for instance. For all of these reasons, the economic aid program was fairly important.

When I went to Cairo, the Administration was just beginning to consider a multiyear PL-480 food program. This had been brought about, as I recall, because there were also negotiations with Israel for a multiyear PL-480 program, and in the Administration's attempt to ameliorate Egyptian-Israeli tension, we thought we ought to move in the same way toward Nasser. So, one of the first things we had done, and I think the negotiations had been pretty well sewed up before I reached Cairo, was to negotiate a multiyear PL-480 pact, which involved something like 200 million dollars, and indeed I think it was the largest PL-480 program outside India.

This became the basis of our aid program in Egypt, because it did two things. On the one hand, it supplied direct and much needed foodstuffs, and on the other, it generated local currency, which we then loaned back to the Egyptians at very low interest rates for the development of their economy. That was the chief point of the program while I was there.

I insisted—I really insisted on this—over the initial opposition of AID that instead of having an AID mission director and an economic counselor—two posts—that they be the same man. That man was recruited: he was the economic counselor, and he was also appointed head of the AID Board. This arrangement prevented the kind of built-in rivalry that I had seen in other countries, between what I would call the old economic interests of the Embassy and a new autonomous body that wanted to make a place for itself. In Iran, I thought this rivalry was quite apparent. We did not have that kind of rivalry in Cairo, and Ed Moline, the man who held both posts and was later the Economic Counselor in Germany, was a very able man indeed.

Thus the Embassy had the full benefit in its relations with the government of anything that was developed because of the AID contacts. Otherwise, one might have had a large AID program, with other members of the Embassy having very little to do with it. What we needed was something to get us all into Egyptian offices, to give us a chance to develop a mutuality of interests.

PL-480 differed from some of the other programs because the chief element was the counterpart funds, which could be loaned back, and there were only a certain number of things that you could do with counterpart funds. I thought, on the whole, our counterpart funds were spent fairly wisely. I would not say that they resulted in the initiation of great, long-term programs that sailed on after they had dropped the pilot. I think that has rarely been true in other countries. Certainly, I would not expect it to be true in Egypt. For one thing, with all its problems, Egypt was a fairly sophisticated country, with some very able people, and it would be a great mistake to belittle their ability and come in and say, this is what you guys are going to do.

For another thing, when you only have Egyptian pounds to deal with, and do not have very many dollars, what you can do is limited. What we tried to do was to use the pound equivalents to strengthen programs already in being in Egypt, most of which lay in the field of food consumption and of agriculture.

Because of the later effect of the Yemen war, and other factors, it was not possible to do ideally what I thought would have been most wise. Egypt was in the position of not being able to grow enough food for itself, and as the thing then stood, and later developed, it would be a long time before it could, because its population was growing so fast.

The trouble with the PL-480 program is that it makes the most basic resource of the life of the country, food, a gift, and you cannot live eternally on a gift. What you have to do is to develop your own food production resources. What I would have liked to see happen was a gradual diminution of food sales to Egypt, with a corresponding increase in the kinds of help that would increase its own food production, so that you come to a point where food contribution is minimal and the rise in capacity is maximal. But this calls for very long-term planning. It calls for contracts which I do not think Congress was ready to accept, and a willingness to be steadfast and tolerant through a great many recurring political squalls. We really could not get this kind of commitment, and I was not able to focus on the increase in productive capacity as much as I would have liked.

At one time, approximately a third of all the cereal grain eaten in Egypt was supplied by the United States, and when we had a shipping strike on the East Coast, and could not use American bottoms—one of the conditions of the plan was that American bottoms be used for shipping—there were no shipments. Only a five-day supply of wheat was left in Egypt, and this could have meant starvation.

One does not rub the Egyptian nose in this, of course, although there were Congressmen who wanted to do just that. Nevertheless, the fact was there, and it had an effect. For instance, during that period there was a nonaligned economic conference in Cairo, which Nasser chaired. Nkrumah and many other Africans were present. The Department was very worried lest it be an occasion for bitter anti-American attack, and every possible pressure was put on the Embassy in order to head off any such development. They wanted to flood the country with CIA people. They wanted to send 25 or 30 people and have them running all over the place. I did not see that they could do any more than we, and we fought it and pretty well kept them out. They wanted me to make a lot of special representations to Nasser, which I did not think were wise and which I was able to head off.

As a matter of fact, the conference went very well. There was not really any anti-American feeling. The Third World countries spoke their piece about wanting more help and assistance, but that was all.

When it was over, I went to talk to Ali Sabry, one of the vice presidents and very often Nasser's alter ego. If Nasser could not see me, he would say, you ought to talk to Ali Sabry. (He was another I had known in the old days.) I told him that I thought it was a very good conference. It was well run, it was constructive, it didn't waste its energies on attacking other countries. "Yes," he said, "I thought it was good," and added, "I am sure you noted, as did we, that while this conference was on, the US Congress was voting on the PL-480 renewal bill." Egypt's leaders knew that anything which threatened the bill would not be to their advantage.

So I think PL-480 aid did form a useful political bond. I think it later turned into a liability, just as I was leaving. But it had made a genuine contribution. Whether or not it made the country turn the corner, nobody can say. I do not know where the take-off point is, and I do not think Walt Rostow knew either.

Nasser's program of socialization gave ammunition to critics of PL-480. The PL-480 agreement was for three years, and certainly we had no basis to repudiate it. PL-480 was not costing the United States anything. It was all surplus food, but there was a good deal of criticism from members of Congress about giving aid and support to Socialists, as well as to Communists, and to a firebrand. I heard this complaint from many directions.

Finally, we got together a message which helped—that is all I can say. We made a careful study, and we noted that at the time, let us say, about 18 percent of the productive capacity of Egypt had been socialized, or nationalized—it is more than that now, but this was during the first two years. We noted that in Israel, one of the happy friends of the United States, something like 30 percent was nationalized. In Nationalist China, on Formosa, about 25 percent had been nationalized. The best figure we could get from the United States was that about 29 percent of American productive capacity falls under government controls of some kind. We sent this study back and said, you will please note that Nasser has not gone as far down this road as either Israel, Taiwan or the United States, which was quite true at the time.

But those who were opposed to the regime for a variety of reasons seized upon the nationalization. What was more pressing, I think, was the feeling that since we contributed so much in terms of such a vital factor as food, we ought to get much more direct political payoff.

I remember one US Senator coming to my office in Cairo, going over all this, how much we were paying, and he asked, what are we getting for this? Well, I told him what I thought we were getting. He said, it's not enough. So I said, tell me what you think we ought to get? Oh, he said, at a minimum we ought to get peace with Israel. If no peace is made with Israel, it should be cut off.

I said, Senator, how much money would you have to pay the government of the United States to have it change its policy toward Red China? Which, of course, at that time, was our worst enemy. He said, don't be an idiot, there's not enough money in the world to make us change our policy. I said, why do you think the Egyptians are going to change their policy for greed or for money? And he kind of mumbled and grumbled, but that was the end of that.

I got more senators than congressmen as visitors; it was a very mixed bag, up and down—some very able ones indeed—Mike Mansfield, Senator George,* Hubert Humphrey, and so forth; I also got some of the others.

I cannot resist reporting what in my opinion was one of the baldest exhibitions of the US Senate at its worst. A certain Senator was to be in Cairo with his wife for 24 hours, and the Department had indicated to me what his interests were, and what his wife's interests were, and I had set up a program of things they might want to do.

―――――――――
*Walter George, then Chairman of the Foreign Relations Committee of the Senate.

One of the things that the Senator wanted to do was to see the Minister of Economics, who handled all this aid. So I arranged a meeting with Dr. Qaisuni, then Minister of Economics. Qaisuni is a very cultivated man, a British university graduate, who speaks the most beautiful English and is very able. For a long time he was a professor—a gentle and kind man.

On the way over, the Senator said to me, well now, can I talk to him in English? Sometimes something rings a bell in your head. This little bell rang and I said, well, I think Dr. Qaisuni knows English. Let us see when we get there. If necessary, I'll interpret.

When we got there, I introduced them, and Qaisuni, who is very quiet, bowed, and said, please, and then the Senator said, "I've got something to tell you." And he said, in effect, "You know, I'm one of the most important men in Congress. I sit on a great many committees and I'm going to report on this trip, and the report that I make will probably determine whether you get any more PL-480 funds or not. That's why I've come here."

I said, "Senator, you'd better let me translate that." So I said to Qaisuni—I knew him very well—"Mr. Minister, you know very well that the agreements for our food sale are negotiated between your Ambassador to Washington and the Department of State, and between your government and myself. You realize, I'm sure, that this Senator is not entirely accurate in what he just said."

At which Qaisuni smiled, and said, "Please don't apologize. We have people just like this in the Egyptian government."

All the time the Senator is sitting there—"What is he saying? What is he saying?"

Well, I said, "Senator, he's very glad to see you indeed. He's conscious of the fact that you are interested in this program and would be very glad to hear what you have to say." The Senator went on, delivered himself and left, and that was that.

If Qaisuni had not been the kind of man he was, you know, this could have made a lot of trouble. But I must say this was somewhat in keeping with all I knew about this Senator's actions. He wanted very much to see President Nasser, but the Presidency had a policy that you could not take in a request to see the President until the person was actually in the country, and since the Senator was to be in Egypt only 24 hours, we were not able to get an appointment. The Senator was furious, and as he left the airport the next morning, before flying on to Israel, he gave a press interview. He said, I don't understand why, when we give Egypt millions of pounds, I can't have an hour's talk with Nasser. I'm going to Israel. They've got time for me in Israel to talk to the President.

Generally, this Senator made an ass out of himself. He was the worst. But we did have a number of others. Senator Gruening* came out, and was also difficult, though not for the same reason. Gruening came out convinced that Nasser was a firebrand—this was after the Yemen war had broken out—and that he was upsetting the Arab world. Gruening left behind one of his staff to write a report, and that was really a very bitter attack upon Nasser and Egypt and all its works.

One has to be careful. I gave good briefings to these people, and I do not know that it ever caused me any difficulty, but I do not think they made any particular contribution. There were some very thoughtful people. I am thinking of Senator George and of Mike Mansfield, in particular, who were very concerned, wanted to know what the situation was, and talked about it at great length. This was useful to me, but I do not know that the senators had any effect upon our relations with the Egyptian government *per se*.

The difficulty is that the funds which are appropriated for tours, or junkets, are voted by Congress itself, and the State Department does not have much control. I do not know that there's too much you can do about it. Our friend, the unnamed Senator, spent about 1,300 dollars in 24 hours in Egypt, a lot of it in the bazaars. These may have been counterpart funds, but that is not really what they are there for. I would think that stricter methods of accounting and more defensible reasons for visiting a country would help, but I'm not familiar enough with the way that these things go in Washington to suggest how this could be done.

---

*Clark Gruening of Alaska.

CHAPTER 10
THE YEMEN ADVENTURE

The first thing to realize about the Yemen war is that, like so many crises in the Middle East, it came with practically no warning. Certainly, our intelligence reports did not forecast it, and as far as I know neither did the Egyptian.

A sign of how unprepared the Egyptians were is the fact that very shortly after the announcement was made of the situation—I would say within three days—I had a private inquiry from Nasser, through one of his messengers, Sami Sharaf. (He was still languishing in jail, the last I heard of him.) Sharaf asked if we had any information on Yemen that would be helpful to them. We did have, among other things, an economic report, perfectly innocuous as far as any military value was concerned, but nevertheless it had a good deal of general information. I sent it along to Nasser, who was very grateful to have it.

I was told by friends in the government that when the Yemen affair broke out, there was a good deal of debate within the Presidency as to whether and to what degree Egypt should get involved. It took about three days to reach a decision: that being done, Egypt moved fairly rapidly to involve itself.

I saw no evidence that the decision was due in any sense to Soviet pressure. In my opinion, there had to be a certain amount of Soviet compliance, because if Egypt was going to use Soviet arms in Yemen at the risk of losing them, they would have to be replaced. Unless the Egyptians were sure replacements would be forthcoming, I do not think they would have risked them; but we could see no indication of direct Soviet involvement.

Our greatest concern was that this involvement would raise problems for US policy toward Egypt. It would make it difficult to sustain the efforts of seeking to put certain questions, as I said, "in the icebox," and to exercise some kind of restraining influence on Nasser. And it also would, and did indeed, form a rallying point for all the forces in the United States who were basically anti-Nasser and anti-Egyptian, who could point to this as one more instance of Nasser's adventurism. We looked at it very largely from that viewpoint.

To a lesser degree, we knew it would cause problems between the United States and Saudi Arabia, but naturally we were not prepared to judge that aspect. It was of far greater consideration in the Department than with us. I do not mean to say that we overlooked it; we were not in a position to make judgments.

From the US government viewpoint, the Saudi question was most important. For one thing, the Saudi government at this time was not very stable. King Saud bin Abd al-Aziz, whom I had met on a number of occasions, was a nice man, but he had not inherited his father's cloak of leadership. He was not able to balance the progressive and conservative religious forces the way his father or his brother Faisal did. It was thought, and I think with a good deal of reason, that a successful overthrow of the royal family in neighboring Yemen might backfire and cause the overthrow of the royal system in Arabia.

Indeed, we were told that at one time in the early stages of the Yemen affair, Saud himself was so unsure of the loyalty of the Royal Guard that he had all the batteries taken out of the tanks stationed around his palace so that they were immobilized. I cannot give hard evidence on that, but the report reached us.

In general, there was the fear that Saudi Arabia would be tipped over, and if that were successful, perhaps a wave of attacks upon the remnants of monarchy in the Arab world. Another question was involved; our traditional interest and friendship had loomed very largely in those parts of the Arab world that remained under the old system—Jordan and Saudi Arabia in particular, and Kuwait as well—all the traditional states. The revolutionary states, Egypt, Syria and Iraq, did not involve nearly as much in the way of direct American interests. There was no oil in Egypt. There was, of course, oil in Iraq, but American interest in that oil was not nearly as great as it was down the Gulf. The natural tendency of US policy would be to support its conservative friends.

We were very much exercised about that, as were people in the State Department, and I believe President Kennedy himself. Given the Russian position in Egypt, and the attempt by the Russians to identify themselves as the supporters of change and revolution as they do in Africa today, we did not feel that it was in the United States' interest always to come out as the supporter of what looked to be collapsing regimes. The problem was, how could you support old, conservative regimes in Arabia and yet recognize the revolutionary movement in Yemen and give it—if not backing—at least sympathy, so that you at best would be neutral. How to accomplish that really was the center of our Yemen policy as regards American interests during this affair.

We were much blamed by certain powers that be in the United States. I was personally very much blamed by a group of Congressmen, who felt that the recognition of Yemen and other revolutionary governments had been our responsibility, arguing that we had hoodwinked the Department. Nobody hoodwinks the Department; nobody hoodwinked President Kennedy. But certainly we made this a chief part of our presentation.

At the same time we were conscious of the fact that nobody sitting under the Cairo palms saw the whole picture; all we could do was to say, from the standpoint of the situation, as it affects our position in Egypt, and as we see Egypt's relation to the Arab world, we think this is the policy to pursue, although we fully recognize that there are other concerns. Not least among these was British policy, because the British were still in Aden Colony, in what is now called South Yemen. The Governor of the Colony was not in any sense sympathetic toward the revolution in Yemen. I was personally very conscious of the difficulty that had arisen during the Suez Canal crisis because of a lack of clear communication or understanding between the British and the Americans about who was doing what.

So, as soon as the Yemen crisis broke out, I made it a matter of personal concern to keep very closely in touch with the British Ambassador, not that we were necessarily always agreeing with each other, but in order to be completely sure that we knew what our governments were doing. The British Ambassador was a very able man, Sir Harold Beeley. He was not an Arabist, but he was an excellent diplomat and he had served in other parts of the Arab world. He was very approachable and he and I saw a lot of each other. I went to such an extent at times that I drafted a message on what I thought US policy might be and showed it to him before I sent it.

I do not know whether the State Department thought this proper or not. As a matter of fact, I do not think I ever told them. But on several occasions I went over, discussed the matter and showed him the draft of the message, sufficiently paraphrased so that the code could not be broken. In substance, he and I agreed on the necessity of both Great Britain and the United States not allowing themselves to become merely the supporters of the kings.

I thought Beeley's comment on the British problem was very interesting. He pointed out that at times in the past the trouble was that the Colonial Office took one attitude and the Foreign Office took another. The Colonial Office was substantially backing the outlook of the Governor of Aden, which meant allowing Aden to be used as a refuge, and as a base perhaps for royalist attempts to cross the border into Yemen. The Foreign Office, like ourselves, looked at this as a much more complex issue and also was in the process of trying to restore the British position in Egypt.

Beeley said the trouble with the Colonial Office was that there were too many Arab "experts" in it, and the trouble with Arab experts is that they never learn anything. They think because something worked in 1880, it's going to work in 1970, and they are absolutely wrong. I would say I agree with him—an expert is sometimes defined as a man who has stopped thinking because he knows the answer.

His number two man in the Embassy, who later became head of the Middle East section in the Foreign Office and then Ambassador to Kuwait, was Geoffrey Arthur, an able Arabist who knew Arab affairs as well as I did.

So Beeley and I tried to prevent our countries from getting into the adamant position of supporting what really were unsupportable regimes, particularly in Yemen. You could argue the merits of the regime in Saudi Arabia, but I do not see how anybody who knew the facts of Yemen could argue on behalf of the Imamate. Yemen had always been a loosely held territory. The Imam represented a small, elite religious group that used its religious position as a basis for power and dominated the majority. He was completely unenlightened; he used to bury gold sovereigns in tin cans as a way of keeping spare cash. The country was ruled with absolute autocracy. I was told that a citizen could not change his residence from one major city to another without getting the Imam's permission to do so.

We got soundings from the Egyptians at once, first on the matter of recognition, and in some ways it was the recognition question, at least at the early stages, that formed the center of our policy consideration. Were the military successes of the revolution such that we could apply the normal criteria of recognition, one of which is general control of the territory, accepted by the populace?

It was very difficult to get good information, Egyptian or American, on this question. The Yemen was a wild place. The CIA could not tell us very much about it. Nasser used to show me his maps of actions that took place. I had no means of knowing, of course, whether they were genuine, although I think on the whole they were. The rural warfare of the tribal groups left the Egyptians in a difficult position. The Egyptians are not fighters of that kind and, while they did not make too bad a military showing, these roving tribesmen that popped back and forth across the border and took sanctuary in Saudi Arabia were never controlled well.

When you had come that far, you had the further question of the point at which American recognition should come. Shall we be a bellwether of general recognition from the West? Shall we be a reluctant tail-ender and come last? Shall we come someplace in the middle? In addition to all that, how can we use the strong Egyptian desire for us to recognize and thereby legitimize the revolution issue to put some pressure on Egypt?

These questions were all debated, especially the latter. The real basis of American policy in Egypt, lacking any strong interest of our own, was the hope that by observing the situation in Egypt we could restrain Nasser from being a disruptive influence all over the Arab world, particularly the parts of it where we had great interests. Here was a prime case. Could we restrain him? It was around these questions that most of our policy discussions revolved.

There was quite a strong group within certain sections of CIA that had long been convinced, at least since the Suez Canal and the High Dam incident, that, wittingly or unwittingly, Egypt was a pawn of Russia, and the Yemen affair therefore was essentially a Soviet attempt to get down into the peninsula, adjacent to the oil fields. Then you had those who saw the issue not so much in Soviet terms as in terms of Nasser's imposition of Egyptian leadership and Egyptian empire. A good deal of this appeared in the popular American press: he was driving all the way to the Gulf.

The Shah of Iran aided and abetted this fear, using it, in my opinion, somewhat artificially, as a ploy to try to get more airplanes out of the United States, because he saw the Egyptians down there right across from his territory and they were going to fly over and bomb him. So he said. I did not really believe this on Mondays, Wednesdays and Fridays. I thought on Tuesdays, Thursdays and Saturdays that he knew better.

How all this was to be judged was really essential to the definition of our policy. As we looked at it in Egypt, it did not seem that either explanation was really justifiable. I have long been convinced that Nasser was very pragmatic in his development of foreign policy. I did not see much evidence of a master plan. There have been attempts to detect a master plan in Nasser's *Philosophy of the Revolution*, but only by people who have never read it. If you read it, you do not find very much in there to forecast what later happened under Nasser.

Some have made much out of the three circles of Egyptian influence discussed in *Philosophy of the Revolution*, but the interesting thing is that in these circles of influence, Egypt was not part of the Arab circle. It lay near to the Arab circle, but the fact is that the concept of the three circles was not invented by Nasser. If I remember correctly, you can find it in the secondary schoolbooks which taught Middle East geography before World War II. I think Nasser was saying something he heard his teacher say when he was a child, or when he was in military college.

I do not think Nasser really wrote very much of that book. He may have talked to somebody about it. It has often been asserted that Haikal* did most of the writing, but the trouble with that theory is that Haikal would like very much to have one believe it— he is a very vain man. I never saw proof one way or the other.

You could not really look at Nasser's actions as part of a master plan at all. This didn't mean it was not dangerous. Judgments taken on the spot, for pragmatic reasons, may not be as well considered as master plans are. I had had a previous indication from Nasser that such a tendency was strong in the Egyptian government. Slightly before the Yemen affair, there was a move by Iraq to grab Kuwait, with consequent tension in the Arab world. I went to talk to Nasser about it, and I asked him what he thought was the reason for the Iraqi action, and he countered by asking, what do you people say?

I said, we think that probably part of this is generated by the fact that the nationalization of oil in Iraq was not as financially successful as Qasim† thought it would be. There was a lot of confusion. Here was rich Kuwait right down on the southern border, and it was quite possible that Qasim was trying to recoup his economic position—undo some of his mistakes in the oil takeover by going down and grabbing Kuwait.

"Yes," Nasser said, "you are right, that is what people say, but I don't think that is ultimately what the reason was." When I inquired, and this is almost a literal quotation, he said, "I think that one morning Qasim was in the men's room and he met his

---

*Muhammad Hasanayn Haikal was at that time editor of *Al-Ahram*, the leading Cairo daily.

†Abd al-Karim Qasim overthrew the Hashimite regime in Iraq in July 1958. He was killed in a takeover by Col. Abd al-Salam Arif in February 1963.

Chief of Staff, and one man said to the other, 'Why don't we take Kuwait?' Then the other man said, '*Wallahi, billahi, tallahi*' (that's a good idea, let's do it)." Nasser said, "That's the way we sometimes reach decisions." He *was* a very pragmatic man.

Curiously enough, at a slightly later period, there was information that came out of our intelligence service which showed a certain justification of this theory. As I recall, we had reason to believe that, under the old regime in Iraq, a position paper on the Iraqi claims to Kuwait had been prepared. The Iraqi claims on Kuwait were very old—the Qasim regime simply picked them up. After the new regime came in, all the paper and studies in the Foreign Office had been mixed up. Gradually, after several years, officials began to straighten out the paperwork, and one day this study of Iraqi claims floated up and on to Qasim's desk. Qasim looked at it and acted on it.

There is sure to be much more to it than that, but nevertheless I think there was a pragmatic element there, and certainly in the Egyptian case in Yemen, as well.

It seems to me that these pragmatic choices were derived from two or three sources. In the first instance, the breakup of the United Arab Republic had greatly damaged Nasser's position, the more so because it was Syria that left Egypt rather than Egypt leaving Syria. This was bitterly resented as a slur on Egyptian leadership and Egyptian authority, and Yemen was really the first chance that Nasser had to retrieve that reputation. People said, now he's finished. He couldn't even hold on to Syria. What could he hold on to? Therefore a sharp and quick affirmative reaction in Yemen seemed to us to be the natural outgrowth of the Syrian situation.

A second reason was that, as a result of the Syrian affair, Nasser announced what he called a new foreign policy, the policy of *wahdat al-hadaf*—the unity of goals. What he said in effect was, you cannot unite with another Arab country unless that country shares your ultimate revolutionary outlook. What had happened in Syria, as he saw it, was that it did not share that outlook and this broke up the union. Therefore, if union was to move forward, it would have to do so by amalgamation between revolutionary countries.

Here was a little country that had the same *hadaf* as Egypt. The new regime was very much patterned on the Egyptian revolution, and I think Nasser saw in this a genuine basis for further expansion, remembering, of course, that Yemen had been related to the United Arab Republic, not in the same organic way as Syria but as a third, distant member of the union. Remembering also that Egypt had a long history of supplying Yemen with teachers, and of other relationships, I thought that the decision was a pragmatic judgment that involved the revolutionary objectives of the regime.

We began to see this not simply in Nasser's own language. I talked with a good many people throughout the government and with others who followed the government line. I talked with the Minister of Education, whom I knew well. He was American-educated, a very modern and good man. While deploring all of the problems the Yemen involvement had brought, he said: What can we do? Here's a little backward country. It has a revolution. It wants to follow the path that we have taken. How can we turn our back on it? That attitude I found very widespread at the beginning throughout the Egyptian public, and I think to a very large degree there was genuineness in it.

Perhaps there is a third reason that, while not necessarily one of the activating causes, quickly appeared. Certainly Nasser made the Yemen adventure into an opportunity to give his forces field experience and to discover how far he had been able to rebuild a new and more modern army after the 1956 debacle. He frankly told me that he spent a lot of time and money building an army. "I don't know who the good officers are. If I send them to Yemen, then I'll find out." And he said, "Our policy is to rotate all our units in Yemen; out of this we'll really know what kind of leadership we have."

I felt that all of those factors put together probably amply explained what Nasser was after, and while it is possible that he might have gone on to invade Saudi Arabia to seize the oil fields, one saw no evidence of such a plan at the time. I do not think it was in his mind.

The US Congress was not directly involved in making policy on the Yemen issue, but it was involved in renewal of the PL-480 food agreement and things of that kind. Kennedy had his problems with Congress, and he was sensitive to congressional reaction, but I do not recall that much of the opposition came from that source. There was some determined opposition in the Department of Defense, in which there was a judgment that Nasser was a Communist and a troublemaker, and a judgment that the Saudis had a longstanding military arrangement with the United States which should continue. There was one CIA man in particular, the head of one of the sections, who was absolutely convinced that Nasser was a Communist stooge. I felt this was nonsense, but a case could be made for it, and he did.

We were very much helped in this period by our Ambassador in Saudi Arabia, who at that time was Pete Hart. It was not that Pete always agreed with our estimate, but he is a very thoughtful and able man. He knew Nasser; he had been the number two man in Egypt after the Suez Canal affair, and it was while Pete was there that Egyptian-American relations began to mend. He understood our situation, and had won a great deal of confidence from the Saudi government. While he urged various considerations in regard to Saudi sensibilities, he did not stand in strong opposition to us in Cairo. What we had was a three-cornered discussion between Riyadh, Cairo and Washington as to what might be done, and the final judgment was made to grant recognition.

When that judgment was made, we had to allay the fear on the part of the Saudis that a revolutionary government in Yemen would attack them forthwith and overthrow the regime, and an equal fear of many in Aden Colony that Yemen would turn on them. Yemen, even under the Imamate, had laid claim to Aden for a long time.

I had to make it clear to the Egyptians that if we recognized the regime in Yemen, they would have to undertake self-restraint and not focus any belligerent intentions on any of Yemen's neighbors. This led to quite long and difficult negotiations with Egypt insisting publicly that it did not control the Yemen government, that it was helping them as Russia and Cuba are helping Africa today, and thus that it could not speak for the Yemen government. Yet everybody knew that, in fact, they could pretty well control what was going on there. We had to find a formula that would meet this objection and yet would give us a basis for saying to the Saudis and to the Adenites, this is why we recognize this regime.

A good deal of the time I dealt with Ali Sabry, who was one of Nasser's chief instruments. We finally suggested that Sallal* in Yemen make a statement on the nonbelligerent intent of the revolution, to the effect that it was not aimed at any of the neighboring states. At the same time the Egyptian government would make a statement saying that it noted with gratification that the Yemeni statement had been made and would support it.

I came back the next day, and Ali said he had written a statement that the Egyptian government was prepared to make. It was awful. None of these revolutionary people knew very much about the niceties of diplomatic procedure, and what he produced was a beginning statement to the effect that we wanted, and then about two pages of the most vicious propaganda.

I said to Ali, "This won't do at all. It's all right if you want to make a propaganda statement, but don't put it in an official government proclamation. Why don't you make the proclamation of what has to be said and then give a press interview afterwards? In a press interview, you can say anything about the Saudis or anybody else you want to, but it's not an official document." Somewhat to my surprise, he bought this, and finally said, well, why don't you write a statement?

So the Embassy prepared the kind of statement we felt would do the job. I took it to Ali Sabry the next day, and to save face he shifted around a few commas and changed a couple of words. But he accepted it, and the announcement was made, both by Sallal and by Egypt. Recognition was accomplished.

We arranged with some of our European allies that they would extend recognition to Yemen before we did. As I recall it, the Germans were among the earliest. Russia and her satellites had rushed in immediately. We tried to time it just about in the

*Abdallah Sallal overthrew the royal regime of Imam Badr in September 1962. He was deposed as President in November 1967.

middle, neither too early nor too late. With that, we were in a position to take the second step of our plan—to get a cease-fire agreement.

The part of the CIA that really processed intelligence as such was almost entirely nonpolitical. We had no trouble there. There was another section of CIA which had more to do with strategic estimates, based upon intelligence, and it was in that department that one found a very strong contrary viewpoint. How it was represented in Washington I do not know; I was not there. It was represented very strongly out in the field. From time to time, we would get echoes, through telegrams and such. I feel that one individual was certainly doing the best he could to have his voice heard. I think he was genuinely concerned and therefore tried to direct policy; he did not get very far.

In many ways this was the first major Middle East crisis that the Kennedy Administration faced. There was no major Arab-Israeli clash. The Syrian affair had been a crisis in that it involved the split-up of the union, but it did not affect any American interests. Here one had what at the outset looked as though it might be the beginning of a widespread wave of instability throughout the area, adjacent to the oil fields, and therefore it affected US interests to a much higher degree than anything else that could happen.

For the first time, moreover, it also challenged the Administration to demonstrate that its policy approach, in contrast to the old Dulles hard line, was working. Dulles had had no taste for the Third World or for neutrals, as the Suez Canal affair had shown. The question was, can we get along with countries that don't follow our pattern? Can you get along without using military force? Kennedy continued to practice personal diplomacy; the Administration, I think, hoped that it could talk the contestants into settling the problem.

That is why, after recognition had finally been accomplished, the Administration—Kennedy—immediately turned to the next stage, which was to get a disengagement and move on. He sent out a special emissary, Ambassador Ellsworth Bunker, later Ambassador to Vietnam, and negotiator of the Panama Canal Treaties. He is an absolutely superb negotiator, and it was an education and a delight to watch Bunker work. He came out accompanied by Department of State officer Talcott Seelye, who later became our Ambassador in Tunisia and Syria.

From the very beginning, the United States sought to reassure Saudi Arabia that it would not allow the regime to be overthrown. The Saudis made a number of requests for assistance of various kinds. What we did, as I recall, was to send an aircraft training mission there. We had a number of planes which were there ostensibly to train the Saudis in the use of aircraft. (When we consider the recent AWACS sale, it is well to remember that it stands in the line of a longstanding aspect of American policy.) These American planes were flying all around Saudi Arabia, and it was hoped that this fact would keep the Egyptians from being tempted to cross the border, bomb Saudi Arabia and bring about wholesale war.

The King of Saudi Arabia had given refuge to the Imam and to some of his tribal followers. They would dash in, raid Yemen and go back to their Saudi sanctuary; the Egyptians took a dim view of this practice and wanted to go across the border and bomb these places so that they could not be used as refuge. We foresaw a messy situation if a bombing raid from the Egyptians were to run into a US plane training a Saudi pilot and a plane were shot down.

We were concerned to prevent this kind of untoward accident, and a good deal of my effort during this period was spent in keeping in touch with the Egyptians, following closely the news of their raids, calling the situation to their attention and warning them that everything would be spoiled if they and we ran into unplanned confrontation of this kind. Obviously the way to avoid it was to get a disengagement agreement.

We had hoped that the United Nations might do this. Investigations were made about UN activity and placing a UN team in the area, but it was slow—the Russians held a veto. So while UN deliberations went on, we took the initiative and sent Bunker and Seelye out to shuttle back and forth and try to bring about agreement.

An agreement was finally reached. Its wording was satisfactory to the Saudis; Bunker came over to Cairo, and he and I went out together with the agreement to see Nasser. I remember with great clarity the evening spent with him. It was just Bunker and I, and Bunker, as I have mentioned, was a very able and persuasive negotiator. We went over the agreement; one of its clauses was that the Egyptians should withdraw from Yemen as expeditiously as possible. Nasser's English was pretty good. Despite claims to the contrary from Haikal—Haikal didn't like me—I did all my business with Nasser in English, with the exception of a word or two. And this phrase, "expeditiously as possible," bothered Nasser. He did not know what it meant, and he never had a translator present.

By great good fortune I knew the Arabic word, or I knew an Arabic word for expeditious, which came from an interesting source. In the Egyptian Army there is a department which is called, really, in Arabic, the Department of Expediting Things—the department that sees that everybody else does their job. *Yallah*—get on with it. I explained this to Nasser and said it really meant, as soon as it possibly could be done, *asra ma yakun*. He understood this and agreed to it.

Bunker was not satisfied. He said, "You know, Mr. President, I have to be able to go back and say you actually withdrew some forces." So he and Nasser argued about what forces should be withdrawn, with Bunker emphasizing that he did not expect any large withdrawal, given the military situation. He finally said, "Mr. President, won't you give me just half a company? Just half a company? It really isn't anything, half a company." Nasser, smiling somewhat, agreed. Whether they ever withdrew or not, I do not know. But with that the agreement was signed.

The trouble was that, having signed the agreement, we were really unable to police it properly. Both the Saudis and the Egyptians said, if we have this agreement, we have to get observers in place right away. We can't always control our troops—and I think this was probably much more true on the Saudi side than on the Egyptian side.

Therefore the plan was to send in a UN force, but the United Nations moved as slowly as cold molasses. The Russians could block it; they tried to, at various points. We, in Cairo, urged very strongly that there be an American observer team. Both the Saudis and the Egyptians wanted it, and we had military missions in Iran and Turkey and other places. We could have put a hundred observers in there within a week's time. Had that been done, it is possible that this agreement would have taken effect.

But we could not do it. As I recall, it was some time around April 1963 that the agreement was finally initialed, and it was not until July that the UN force arrived on the spot. During that period, up to July, quite a lot happened. For one thing, Saud was not able to control the flow of arms and money to the royalists, which he had promised to cut off. Pete Hart hinted, as I recall it, that there was too much money being made out of this by members of the elite in Saudi Arabia and that, probably without the King's knowledge, they simply kept on pumping stuff into the pipeline.

Another thing was that during this period the Egyptian military efforts looked a little better. The Imam was not doing too well. He could always be troublesome, but he had not won any big victories. By the time July came, the Egyptians felt they were in a much stronger position than in April, when they really were in very bad shape, and they were not, therefore, particularly anxious to comply with the agreement and could always fall back on the fact that the Saudis were not complying with it.

Thus, while this disengagement agreement was drawn up, and formed a basis on which I could continue to go to Nasser and urge him to do certain things, especially to keep his airplanes out of the area, it did not actually bring about a disengagement. It was not until the 1967 war, some five years later, that the matter was wound up, and then by necessity and Saudi diplomacy, not by US diplomacy.

I have not observed many negotiators, but it seemed to me that Bunker's ability lay in the fact that he was thoroughly conversant with every aspect of the situation. He was not a Middle East expert; it would not have been surprising if he had failed to remember or to grasp some point or other, but he had at his fingertips a wide and complete knowledge of what the situation actually was. He was undoubtedly supported in this area by Talcott Seelye, a very able man, who I am sure supplied a great deal of information, but be that as it may, when he got into the negotiating situation, he knew what he was talking about.

Also, Bunker had the ability to be firm without being irritating. There are different ways of saying no. Someone said that a certain American president had the great gift of being able to say no in such a way that when you left the room you were really glad he had done it. I cannot quite say that of Bunker, but he did have great firmness. You saw the hand beneath the glove, yet never in an unpleasant way.

Thirdly, he used a great deal of personal as opposed to official argumentative presentation. Whether this was his usual style or whether it was Seelye's support, he understood that the Arabs are a personal people, and given the institution of the *wasit* (mediator/middleman) in Arab culture, there is a person-to-person situation. He could say to Nasser, "Mr. President, I've got to have something in my hand to go back with. You can give me this," rather than arguing on the higher level of disembodied Egyptian-US interest. He could do this charmingly but very, very firmly.

Not too long before, Queen Farah of Iran had given birth to the first male heir of the Shah, and one may remember that the story went around that, after the birth was over, she came to and asked, was it a boy or a girl. "It's a boy." And she said, "I did it. I did it." Bunker remembered this comment. He said, "We did it. We did it."

This combination of thorough knowledge, firmness, and personal rapport was in this case very effective. As for Nasser, he was not negotiating in quite the same sense. He was a good listener, first of all, and not only in a negotiating situation. Whenever you had something to say, he was likely to hear you out. He listened to Chester Bowles once for something like five hours, which is pretty good.

Nasser did not speak in long, argumentative retorts. He tended to think about a situation and state his own position fairly simply. I think he was a good negotiator; on the other hand, I would not say that, within the context of our relationship, negotiation was the chief instrument on which he relied.

He was very quiet and rather succinct when I dealt with him, and we dealt in English when we were actually negotiating. When we met on the Yemen question, I think Nasser sensed that we were as anxious not to have a rupture with Egypt as Egypt was anxious to have us recognize the Yemen, and at no point in the negotiations did I ever see him overly eager. Overly importunate—that was not his stance at all. One was very clearly dealing with a man who felt himself in command of his own situation. He would discuss the matter, but he wouldn't come crawling. I think this was very hard for many Americans to understand; they felt that, given our position, our power, Nasser ought to just come crawling. He never did and never would.

By the time I left as Ambassador—and I was only there three years—there wasn't much war spirit in the Egyptians. I do not think they were ever deeply impressed by this adventure. Egypt has a very strongly marked personality of its own. Whatever Nasser's plans may have been, the average Egyptian has not, in general, been an expansionist, and there were aspects of the Yemen war that chilled the public. I remember having someone from the Embassy attend the funeral of one of the first officers killed in Yemen, a Copt. He was buried from the Cathedral, in Heliopolis, and the coffin, against popular custom, was closed. It was closed because the corpse was headless; the Yemenis cut off heads. This sort of information began to get back to Cairo, painting an increasingly bloody picture of Yemenis as totally wild men.

By and large there was not any feeling of fraternity. The Yemenis were regarded as *badawiyin* (bedouins), and the Egyptian looked down his nose at them. The story went around Cairo that Sallal sent a telegram to the Egyptian government saying, now that the war is succeeding the greatest need of revolutionary Yemen is education. Please send us 500 schoolteachers. The next week came another telegram saying, the greatest need in revolutionary Yemen is still education. Please send us 20,000 schoolbooks. The third week there was another telegram saying, the greatest need in revolutionary Yemen remains education. Please send us 50,000 students at once.

CHAPTER 11

LEADERSHIP UNDER THE EGYPTIAN REVOLUTION

My views of Egyptian officialdom were drawn from highly selective contacts. I did not think it was necessary for the Chief of Mission to know everybody, and what we tried to do was to identify the various people in government with whom we had reason to be in contact, and then assign officers in the Embassy to communicate with them. I developed my own circle of people that I dealt with personally because of my role as Ambassador.

In the first instance there was Nasser, and I stress that because to an unusual degree I was able to take things directly to Nasser. During my years as Ambassador, I saw him officially at his residence on business something like 36 times, which was certainly more than any of the other envoys in Cairo at the time. I almost always saw him alone. If it were a question that required some particular expertise, he would occasionally have someone there, but that would be the exception rather than the rule—perhaps three times in all. Nasser's English was good but very deliberate, and I would not have been surprised had he had an interpreter with him.

He spoke slowly and usually followed without too much difficulty what was said.

I kept to English as far as possible. Some people said I ought to use a great deal of Arabic. Professor Philip Hitti* thought it would be a great thing to present my credentials in Arabic, but I felt that was a bad idea and I did not do it. For one thing, while I know good conversational Arabic, I am not good enough in Arabic to talk diplomacy. In diplomacy you had better be pretty sure what you say, and that takes a highly skilled linguist in diplomatic language.

A second reason was that in Egypt, which had long had connections with Europe, where French was widely spoken, and where English under the occupation became the second language, there is real internationalism at the upper level of culture. The foreigner who rushes in and speaks Arabic will give the impression that he does not think Egyptians are sufficiently sophisticated to cope with English. Unless you speak flawlessly, I think Arabic would be resented, and so I left it up to them. They could always get an interpreter, which is the common thing to do.

A third reason was that Nasser would sometimes have someone else there who would speak in Arabic. I could listen to what was being said without saying anything myself.

So for all these years, I used English, and if Nasser did not understand a word, he would sometimes ask me, what is that in Arabic? And if I knew it, which was not always the case, I would use it. If I was in the Foreign Ministry and met a lower-level official who did not speak English, I could chat with him in Arabic, but then I was not really doing diplomatic business.

The Soviet Ambassador once complained to Nasser that I was seeing him much more than he was. Nasser's answer, according to the Soviet Ambassador himself, was, "You know, Badeau and I are both Orientalists, and you're not an Orientalist. We like to talk about Oriental things." Well, true or not. . . .

So, whereas many of the other ambassadors had to do a great deal of business with others, on all the really important matters, such as the Yemen, I dealt with Nasser directly. It was either at

*Professor of Arabic studies at Princeton University.

Nasser's initiative or at my own. I mentioned that the Department was very anxious that I try to set up regular meetings with Nasser, but this I would not do. Our frequent meetings were partly the result of circumstances. Almost immediately we had the serious question of the breakup with Syria, and Nasser wanted to know what the Americans thought. Then there was the long Yemen affair, and by the time that came along, I think I had established my *bona fides* with the government.

Either Nasser called me or I called him; I could tell the Presidency what it was I wanted, and I would either see Nasser or I would be put onto one of the people I have mentioned, or at times Nasser told me, "Go and see so-and-so. I'm going to be busy; I can't handle it." It was on a mutual basis that we did this.

Around Nasser there were the vice presidents, a number of them, and during the years that I was there they occupied different roles. When I first went out, they were really supra-cabinet ministers, each being responsible for some particular activity of government. Later on, in 1962 or 1963, there was an attempt to broaden the base of government a little. A Presidential Council was established, made up of the vice presidents, who at least in theory were to constitute an executive body taking the load off Nasser's shoulders. I do not think that worked very well. They had different approaches.

The vice president that I dealt with most was Zakaria Muhyi al-Din, who held a number of different posts. On occasion, he was Minister of the Interior, but always he was in charge of internal security and intelligence. I did quite a lot of business with him, because anything that really had to do with internal questions concerning the positions of Americans in the country or anybody else, Zakaria was the man to see, and I saw him, I suppose, most often next to Nasser, perhaps more.

He was a very quiet man. He was one of the young officers of the Nasser type, but quite unlike Nasser. With Nasser one felt the force of leadership at once, but not with Zakaria. He talked very little and listened a great deal, but he was always a help to me. He had the reputation of being the pro-Western member of the cabinet, and when he was brought in as Prime Minister in 1965, there was a tendency in Egypt and in the Western press to say, now Egypt is turning toward the West.

I never felt that was true. I do not think he was primarily an ideologue. He was primarily a shrewd, good operator, and he believed that relations with the West were essential for the political and economic well-being of Egypt, and therefore he tried to keep those relations in good order, but not just because he was pro-Western. Rather it was because he was pro-Egyptian.

On a number of occasions, he sounded a cautionary vote within the councils of government. If I was correctly informed, he was one of those most strongly opposed to the Yemen adventure. He simply felt it was beyond Egypt's capacity to carry off. He had a good reputation in Egypt, partly, as I say, because he was considered pro-Western, partly because he was known to stand for moderation.

One occasion in particular was the case of the French espionage trial. After 1956, France had no direct diplomatic relations with Egypt. They did have a commission in Cairo that was to take care of the disposition of sequestered French property, and deal with commercial matters between the two countries. This commission, which was quasi-diplomatic, was housed in a villa near the Embassy—maybe a hundred feet away. In the course of checking our Embassy for security, we intercepted the broadcast of conversations that were going on in the French mission. The only explanation was that the Egyptians had a secret microphone in there and were picking up those conversations.

When I satisfied myself that this was true, I called on the chief of the French mission and told him about it. He laughed at me and said, the Egyptians aren't that smart. But within two or three days after I had sounded this caution, the Egyptians swooped down on them, arrested the whole group and accused them of espionage. I think they were jailed, and there were preparations for a trial.

This affair was none of our direct concern, and yet anything that tended to present the Egyptian government in a bad light would be picked up in the United States by those who were opposed to the Administration's policy. My only interest was really to find out what they had on these people, what they were up to—and I did not trust the French either.

The matter was sharpened because a former member of our government, Ernest Gross, came to Cairo. He had served with our mission at the United Nations, and as Assistant Secretary in the State Department; he was an international lawyer. There was a French woman in the Cairo group who, I think, only happened to be there at the time. In any case, she was picked up, and the family had sent Ernie Gross out to see what could be done to release her. Gross came to the Embassy to see what I could do.

Of course, I had to tell him she was not an American national, and officially I could not do anything, but I said, "Zakaria Muhyi al-Din handles these matters, and I'll introduce you to him." I took him over to Zakaria and said, "Mr. Gross is an extremely reputable and well-known man, and I will be grateful for anything that legally can be done to further the mission he has come on." Zakaria never replied to me, but ultimately the woman was released.

I later found out that the brouhaha about the French mission involved a struggle for power between Zakaria Muhyi al-Din's security forces and another section of the government also involved in security. They got hold of the tapes, which were in French, and the trouble was—President Nasser told me this when it was all over—that they hadn't interpreted the tapes quite correctly. It was rapid colloquial French, and they had missed a couple of things. I think the French were put out of the country, but nothing untoward happened.

That's the kind of thing one would go to Zakaria Muhyi al-Din about. I went to him on another matter, which relates to the matter of using Arabic. The Italian Ambassador came to see me because for about six months Zakaria had held an Italian subject incommunicado, accused of espionage, and the Ambassador had been unable to see or communicate with him. Several journalists were coming out from Italy, and the Ambassador was afraid if they got on to this story, they would splash it all over the newspapers in Italy and make a lot of trouble. So he came to ask whether there was anything I could do about it. Of course, I had to say that since he was not an American national, there was nothing officially I could do about it, but I would see whether I could pass any word on.

So I went over to see Zakaria. I usually went over to his house in Dokki. It must have been around five o'clock in the afternoon. I explained the case to him, and he said of course the man is not an American. I said, no, he's not an American, and I'm not trying to make representations. My only concern is that if you get a nasty article in the Italian newspapers, it will certainly be picked up in the American newspapers. If it is picked up in American newspapers, some American politician will make a speech about it, I'll get a message from the State Department and I'll have to answer it.

I said, "If you have the evidence, why don't you try him and hang him? If he's a spy, you have a perfect right to do that. If you don't have any evidence on him and *are* holding him, let him go. What difference does it make? This is my only concern."

He smiled an enigmatic, quiet smile, and said, "I think I know all about that case." We were speaking English. He said, "As a matter of fact, I think that case has been disposed of, just before you came this afternoon."

He picked up the telephone, called the prison and got the warden. He said, in effect, in good colloquial Arabic, "You know that damn Dago you've got there? Well, the American Ambassador is here asking about him, and I don't want any trouble. I want him out. O-U-T, out. By six o'clock. *Yallah*, get on with it."

He hung up and said to me in English, "Just as I thought. He was released this afternoon."

Muhyi al-Din knew perfectly well that I had understood what he said. This was his way of telling me that he had taken action without having to admit officially that I had any right to have brought it about. That was Muhyi al-Din. I found him helpful and I think he was one of the steadier influences around the . . . around the throne, I was going to say. Yes, let's call it the throne.

* * *

I find it difficult to make a judgment on the charge that Egyptian intelligence was ham-handed, clumsy, and inefficient.

(The French had said, "Nonsense, the Egyptians are not up to it.") After all, when it comes to starting rumors and collecting rumors, no one can beat the Easterner on his own soil, and therefore in the sense of collecting intelligence, I think the Egyptians did pretty well. The trouble was, in my opinion, that there were too many political motives mixed in. To a much greater degree than the CIA, they tended to get operational intelligence and reporting intelligence mixed up. And when they tried to pull something off, it did not seem to me to be well done. But in terms of straight intelligence, in knowing what was going on, I think they did reasonably well. Zakaria was certainly one of the principal figures in that.

I never was able to make a judgment on how good Egyptian intelligence was during the Yemen war, even though Nasser eventually talked quite freely about what he knew. On one or two occasions, I had intelligence that Nasser did not have and that I took to him. The chief instance had to do with the trouble between Morocco and Algeria in the border war around 1963. Nasser was deep in the Yemen war, and I got intelligence that the Cubans were *en route* to or had landed in Algeria. As I recall it, we had the name of a vessel that was carrying in some military advisers, something of the sort. I knew this was going to make trouble, and I told Nasser so; I said we have this intelligence, and you know perfectly well, considering your connections with Algeria, if this happens it's going to look as though Russia is using you in Yemen and using the Cubans in Algeria. That made him very angry indeed.

I have reason to know that almost immediately after I had seen him, he got in touch with Ben Bella and raised an awful ruckus, complaining that Cuban troops were being brought in without his knowledge.

Zakaria Muhyi al-Din and Nasser seemed to me to be the central figures, but I never saw or heard of any indication of personal ambition on Zakaria Muhyi al-Din's part. Baghdadi* had disappeared by the time I got there. I was told by a source in the

---

*Abdul Latif Baghdadi was one of the original Free Officers and took a prominent role in early revolutionary governments.

Egyptian government that during the 1956 Suez affair, there was a meeting of the high command of the Free Officers Council. The matter looked very grave indeed, with France and England coming into it, and the consensus was that Egypt would have to give in. Nasser stood up and said, "Look. You can give in if you want to. I don't intend to." He started to walk out of the room, and Zakaria Muhyi al-Din and Baghdadi accompanied him out of the room, as if to say what is good enough for him is good enough for us. It was this that swung Egypt around. That may be an apocryphal story, but it was believed in Egypt, and it certainly identifies Zakaria with that group.

Another of the vice presidents I saw a fair amount of was Anwar al-Sadat. I did not see him as much as I did Zakaria, because the latter had a continuing responsibility, and Sadat tended to be shifted around from one thing to another. Often he was used as Nasser's troubleshooter, but after the National Assembly was reestablished, he became Speaker of the Assembly and in that capacity I had occasion to see him. Also, when the Yemen affair was at its height, he and Abd al-Hakim Amr were used as intermediaries, or *wasit*s, to go to Yemen and try to iron things out. So in connection with our Yemen diplomacy I often had occasion to see Sadat.

Sadat was very different from Zakaria Muhyi al-Din. He was much more positive, much more outgoing, much more aggressive really; Zakaria was not that way at all, although I do not mean he was timid.

One's reaction to Sadat was different; he was what I would call an active village leader. He was a peasant, he had determination, he had strength, he liked to talk very directly. He wore tight yellow shoes that buttoned up the side—a very sharp dresser. You could talk straight to him and he would answer straight back, too. Once, when things were really bad in Yemen, I was afraid that some of the Egyptian planes that were helping the Yemenis would fly up into Saudi territory and run afoul of some of our ambushes there. I went to Sadat to warn them, and he bridled. He said, you're giving me an ultimatum.

I said, no, Mr. Vice President, I'm not giving you an

ultimatum. I'm simply saying that certain causes bring about certain effects, and if you know what the effect is, don't establish the cause. He said, what do you mean? I debated a little bit. I didn't know if it was wise or not, but I said, well, it's not an ultimatum if a boy says to a girl before he takes her to bed, look, you might get a baby out of this. That's cause and effect.

He looked at me for a moment and burst out laughing. He said, *Mafhum*. Understood. Understood.

You could deal with him very directly, but one did not see under these circumstances the characteristics that came out in his leadership later. He either was not displaying them in the situation wherein I knew him, or they lay dormant because they were not being called upon.

I would say Sadat was less polished than others in the leadership; some of those people were very smooth indeed. Zakaria was a correct army officer, very quiet, and he rarely said or did anything amiss. There was a certain impetuosity, perhaps, in Sadat. He, of course, had been a revolutionary youth with Nasser. They had got into trouble, thrown bombs and so forth. When he went down to Yemen to try and iron out matters, and Abd al-Hakim Amr went with him, it was Abd al-Hakim Amr who was the greater success. But Sadat was not regarded as a buffoon; he was less polished and somewhat more of a typical Egyptian political product.

After 1967, we maintained a diplomatic mission in Egypt under the aegis of the Spanish Embassy. This office was headed by the then chief political officer, named Don Bergus.* Don and Sadat worked out a relationship at least as close as I had with Nasser. Sadat became great friends with Don Bergus and his wife, and Don told me that they were able, as I had been with Nasser, to talk about things on a very personal basis and to anticipate situations. I did not have that relationship with him, because I did not have the need for it. I only went to see Sadat if Nasser told me to.

The third vice president was Abd al-Hakim Amr, the Chief of Staff of the Army and Nasser's designated successor. As I recall it, I

---

*Donald Bergus was later Ambassador to the Sudan.

only called on him twice. In each case, I think it had something to do with military decisions. I called on him once at the time of the Cuban crisis. I had with me photographs of the missile sites that we had taken. Copies had been given to Nasser, and I think Nasser told me to take them to Amr as Chief of the Army, so he could see them.

He was monosyllabic. He had the reputation of being a drug user, a *hashshash*, and his eyes had that peculiar pupil intensity which is the mark of a user of hashish. I do not want to slander the dead, but he had this reputation, and he was very lethargic when I saw him.

Incidentally, not that it is important to history, but there was one interesting sidelight on him. The life story of Christine Keeler—all about the notorious affair with the British minister Profumo—began to come out serially in a Cairo paper. It appeared for two weeks, then stopped, and then came out again. People in the government whom I knew said that Amr had stopped publication because he had an Algerian girlfriend, and he did not want attention paid to extracurricular activities. This was very rare in the Nasser group; they were quite puritanical, and most of them were free from popular gossip of this kind, but not Amr.

On the next level, there were people who did not hold either cabinet or vice-presidential rank at that time, but whom Nasser used in a special capacity and to whom he sent me. The first of these was Ali Sabry (who became Prime Minister in 1969). Ali Sabry was one of three brothers—Ali, Zulficar and a third one. They had come from an old regime family, quite wealthy, and lived at Maadi, the upper-class suburb to the south of Cairo. When I was at the American University I knew the three Sabry boys.

Ali Sabry was not one of the leading members of the officers' movement, but he had been an anti-British revolutionary. They put Ali in jail; he had served his time as a patriot, as it were, and sometime early in the revolutionary movement he was drawn into the Revolutionary Council.

During the Yemen affair, Nasser used him as something of an alter ego. He said to me, "You can't always see me. I'm busy. But if you can't see me, you can always see Ali Sabry." I saw Ali Sabry often at that time, and if what I had to say to him was of sufficient interest, Nasser would call me and I would see him afterward. I think the last time I talked to him was about the recognition of Yemen by the United States.

In a certain sense, he stood with Zakaria Muhyi al-Din rather than with Sadat. He was a polished man of the Egyptian upper classes. I do not know the extent of his education, but he spoke excellent French, excellent English, and had a fundamental grasp of diplomatic procedure. He was always very quiet, listened, smiled, answered, but there was none of the direct back-and-forth that one had with Sadat.

He had the reputation of being pro-Communist, pro-Russian, the counterpart of Zakaria Muhyi al-Din, and, as in the case of Zakaria, I don't think this was deserved. Ali Sabry was not a Communist, although popularly believed to be. I was interested to learn from the British Ambassador that in their files they felt they had evidence to show he was not a Communist, although they would classify him as pro-Communist.

It seemed to me that just as Zakaria had judged that a good Western connection was essential for Egypt, so Ali Sabry had judged that a good Russian connection was essential for Egypt. I think there were two other factors that pushed him in the direction of being more partial both to China and to the Soviet than to the Western world. One was the fact that, as a practitioner of politics, he believed in power, and he was very much impressed by Chinese power and by Russian power. He made a visit to China while I was there and came back talking quite glowingly about what he felt was the military capacity of China, and I think his judgment of the power potential of the Soviets was a factor in giving him a reputation as a pro-Communist.

One thing he was—bitterly anti-British. I never saw this in Zakaria. I assume Zakaria was a patriotic man, but, after all, Ali Sabry had been put in jail as a young man. He went back to the days of anti-British riots. He hated the British, and while I didn't have any indication that he hated Americans, we were, after all, British allies and tarred with the same brush.

I think also that Nasser deliberately played this up, because it meant that he could put in Zakaria Muhyi al-Din at one time, and everybody would say, ah, they're turning West. If he put in Ali Sabry, they'd say, ah, they're going back to the Commies. That was useful to him, but it was quite clear that Nasser was in command and that Ali Sabry could not go beyond the limits that Nasser set. To this extent, he had less discretion and less authority than Zakaria did, who was one of the original group and closer to Nasser.

Robert Komer, later head of the CORDS program in Vietnam and then Ambassador to Turkey, more or less ran the Middle East section of the White House staff. Bob felt that Ali Sabry lied to me. I did not feel that. I think sometimes he was not telling the whole truth, but there is a difference between not telling the whole truth and deliberately lying. I think Nasser had given him very specific orders as to how to act and react, and I know that everything I told Sabry went at once to Nasser. He did not have things in his own hands at all. He was one of the group, after Nasser's death, that was involved in the bid for power against Anwar al-Sadat, and finally finished up in jail.

His brother, Zulficar, who was much less well-known, was the number two man in the Foreign Office when I went to Egypt. For a while I saw more of him than I did of the Foreign Minister. I had a lot of business there, because everything that went personally to the President also went officially to the Foreign Office.

He was a very difficult man to get along with. For one thing, he had a stomach ulcer, and when his ulcer was bad he was impossible. It was not his fault but, nevertheless, when you went in to see him he looked as though he had just finished sucking a dill pickle. You knew he was having a bad time.

The second thing was that he was absolutely furious about the Palestine question, and for the first six months, every time I went to see him, no matter what the subject was, I would have to sit for 15 minutes and be lectured about US policy in Palestine. This gradually wore off, but I think myself it was a deliberate tactic that was being put on, and it was not a pleasant way to get things done.

The third thing—he was really anti-American. I think his anti-Americanism stemmed in part from the same things that affected his brother Ali's general attitude toward the West, but also from more personal matters. As a young man, I was told, he was a great sportsman and an amateur boxer. He finally ran away from home, from this well-to-do *ancien régime* family, to the United States, intending to make a career as a pugilist. In his first fight in the United States, he was knocked out by an American, and that ended his career. From then on he was anti-American.

Interviews with him were always very unsatisfactory, although you usually got done what had to be done, if you could go through these various hazards and hurdles. His policy, when I first got there, was one of trying to get the maximum benefit out of the United States by waving the Soviet Union over our head. In other words, if you can't do this, we'll go to the Soviet Union, and after listening for about three months, I got fed up and I told him, then go to the Soviet Union. What's the difference?

I am terribly Eastern in using stories to illustrate things, and I did so in one case when I had a long and very unpleasant meeting with Zulficar. I had known him before, so we had a personal relationship. I said, "Zulficar, this conversation reminds me of one of the earliest things I saw when I came out to the Middle East." He said, "What was that?" I said, "We lived in Mosul and we went out to tea one day in one of the Mosul houses, and there was a family living there, a widow with a 13-year-old boy, who was a *shaytan* (devil). He was in trouble all the time. In the middle of the courtyard, there was a well, and if he couldn't get what he wanted out of his mother, he'd run, screaming, 'I'll throw myself into the well.'

"We were there one day for tea and he put on a tantrum. His uncle was there, and without a word his uncle took him by the collar and plumped him in the well, saying 'If you want to go in the well, there you are.' "

Zulficar looked at me, and he never again mentioned going to the Russians. He got the idea.

Nasser recognized the difficulties apparently, because around the middle of the Yemen affair or a little earlier, there was a reorganization of the Foreign Office. Zulficar was removed and put on the Presidential staff at the Heliopolis Palace Hotel, and nobody ever heard of him again. He didn't deal with the public at all, and I think it was recognized that he had his drawbacks.

There was a third character that Nasser put me on to, who had no standing whatever in the government. His name was Sami Sharaf, one of the "young officers." Sharaf also landed in jail, as a conspirator against Sadat. Sami Sharaf was, to use the American expression, a "dirty tricks" operator. He knew what was going on and he was involved in espionage and in propaganda, and Nasser would sometimes send him to me if he wanted to send a personal message. I must have seen Sami Sharaf 10-20 times.

At one time, Nasser indicated that a considerable sum of money as a loan would be useful; I have forgotten what the project was. He sent Sami Sharaf out to ask me whether I thought this could be done—that was the sort of role he played. Also, during the period when the Iranians and the Egyptians were bombarding each other with anti-Egyptian and anti-Persian propaganda, Sami Sharaf was the man through whom I worked to try to get that abated. He was a very odd character with all the mannerisms which you associate with a serpentine personality, and activity.

When the Egyptians finally began to mend their relations with the rest of the Arab world in the fall of 1963, I was bothered by the propaganda that was going out over the clandestine radio station, *Sawt al-Umma al-Arabiyya* (Voice of the Arab Nation). It was beaming propaganda to the surrounding Arab world and elsewhere. Whereas Egyptian government propaganda was fairly restrained, this was of the most vicious character. In one broadcast, it claimed King Saud had been castrated. That kind of thing was making a lot of trouble. Finally, I got some of our people to come in from outside and run coordinates and find out just where the broadcasts were coming from. I found that back of the Citadel, on one of the hills up there, there was a transmitting station. I sent a message to Sami Sharaf that I would like to talk to him, and we went over the situation. I think I told him, "I have to deal with all these things. What are you trying to do—what's got into you?" He looked at me blandly and said, "*Sawt al-Umma al-Arabiyya*? There's no such Egyptian station." And I said, "Sami. Come off it. It's the third spur to the right of the Muhammad Ali mosque, up on the Muqattam Hills." He looked at me and said, "I'm sorry. I never heard of it."

It so happened, I think it was the next day, I had an

appointment to see President Nasser, and the first thing he said to me was, "I understand that Sami Sharaf told you that he didn't know where the *Sawt al-Umma al-Arabiyya* station was." I said, "That's right, Mr. President." He said, "I scolded him. I told him that since you knew, he never should have denied it."

This kind of thing was very unsatisfactory, because it was like dropping a pebble into a well of feathers: one never heard anything land. Nevertheless, Sami too reported directly to Nasser, and things I would not have said to Nasser, I could say to him. I dealt with him quite a lot, and I was somewhat relieved when he was out of the government.

Two others with whom I dealt should be mentioned. One was the Minister of Economics, Abd al-Munim Qaisuni. I had a great deal to do with him, because our food contribution and general aid program was one of our chief diplomatic contacts with the Egyptians. He was in and out of government frequently thereafter.

Qaisuni had been a Professor of Economics in the Egyptian University. British-trained—I think Cambridge—and therefore impeccable in his classical economic stance and in his English, which he spoke most beautifully. He also was quiet and helpful. I negotiated programs with him and we developed, as I tried to do with a number of others, the practice of always presenting an idea unofficially to see what the response would be, so that we would save ourselves from being turned down. I did not want to have the Egyptian government come to me and ask me something to which I would have to say no.

Qaisuni would come to me and say, this is the situation. If I asked you this, what would you say, how could we change it? This would involve quite a good deal of work. His first assistant had a doctorate in economics from, I think, the University of Iowa. Together these two really ran the economic program of Egypt.

Nasser's estimate was interesting. Qaisuni was a professional and extremely able economist. Yet Nasser, it seems to me, never really quite trusted him. Perhaps trust is not the word. Nasser said to me one day, "The trouble with Qaisuni and his kind is that they're always telling me what I can't do economically. I don't want to know what I can't do. I want to know what I can do." His idea was to say, now this is what has to be done, *yallah*, go make a plan, do it, and Qaisuni was too good an economist to agree. But there is no doubt that he engendered a great deal of confidence among Americans and one reason why we could sustain our Food for Peace Program as long as we did was because of the respectability and authority which he gave it. Qaisuni really was a symbol of an interesting type of man who began to come into the government after the formation of responsible cabinet government, early in 1964.

As you look over the roster of military officers, you see, one by one, that they tended to fall by the wayside. Take Kamal al-Din Husayn, Minister of Education. The trouble was, Kamal al-Din Husayn tried to administer education the way you would administer an army. At eight o'clock in the morning, get out the machine guns and shoot. As the revolution progressed and the economic and social rearrangement of the country became more and more complex, it took more than loyalty and simple army experience to run the country.

Those army officers who had ability outside the strictly military field stayed on. The others faded into retirement. In their place there began to come people like Qaisuni. He was followed by a great many other people who were not army officers but technicians. Sayyid Marei, for example, I knew well. His niece had been one of my students. He was Minister of Agriculture, a thoroughly competent technician, who had been in and out of the revolutionary government ever since 1952. More and more of the technician type entered the government, and Qaisuni was sort of grandfather of that group.

Another man I dealt with was the Governor of Cairo, Salah Dessouqi. He was very reminiscent of Nasser—looked like him, acted like him. He was a great fencer, a great hunter. He liked to come to the United States, to visit friends in Texas, and to go shooting there. He had pearl-handled revolvers. He was a thoroughly nice and an able man. He ran the government of Cairo, the most important post in Egypt below the national level.

Dessouqi was very interested in foreign affairs and subscribed to the American quarterly, *Foreign Affairs*. He discussed foreign policy in his speeches and Nasser got a little tired of it—it was not the Governor of Cairo's duty. In addition, Dessouqi was always entertaining foreign dignitaries. Willy Brandt came from Germany, when he was not yet Chancellor. A large dinner was given by the Governor, which my wife and I attended, at which Dessouqi gave a foreign policy speech, and then introduced Willy Brandt. This involvement in foreign affairs, plus some infighting within the military, resulted in his removal. Those who didn't like him talked to Nasser and finally finished him off. He was sent abroad as Egypt's representative to some UN body.

I am particularly beholden to Dessouqi for helping me complete the diplomatic maneuver by which I got out of Cairo. After President Kennedy had been assassinated, I came to the conclusion that my service in Egypt would probably be terminated. I was at the age where I either had to spend the rest of my life in diplomacy, or I had to go back to my profession. As a personal appointee I was not even sure that I had that option, and when I got a nice offer from Columbia University I wanted to take it. I told the Department and the President, and while my decision was accepted, they kept putting off giving me permission to tell Nasser.

I was very anxious to tell Nasser. One thing Nasser could do—he could keep his mouth shut. Our relations with Egypt were beginning to cool at that time, and I was sure my resignation would be interpreted in some way as either a change of policy or disagreement with policy on my part, which was not at all the case. If I could go to Nasser quietly and tell him the circumstances, I knew that that would help. So I asked the Department, and the Department kept saying no. A resigned ambassador is a useless ambassador.

We came close to May 15, with the opening of the High Dam and Khrushchev as the guest of honor. I was certain that if my resignation were announced after Khrushchev had been there, Egypt would say, America's mad at us for inviting Khrushchev. This was not the case at all; we did not care if Khrushchev came.

Again I tried to get the Department to unfreeze this matter, but it got mixed up in a lot of administrative detail. One morning I called on Salah Dessouqi; I had been at his house a lot. After chatting for a while, he said, "Well, what can I do for you, Mr. Badeau?"

"Well," I said, "Governor Dessouqi, you can ask me a question, providing you will assure me that you will not give my answer to anybody until I tell you to."

He said, "All right, I'll do it. What do you want me to ask you?"

I said, "Please ask me, what do you expect to be doing next year at this time?"

He looked at me and said, "What *do* you expect to be doing next year at this time?"

I replied, "Well, since you asked me, I expect to be teaching at Columbia University."

Then I went back to the Embassy and sent a cable to the Department. I said—and it was all true, but it was not the whole truth—"In a courtesy call at the governorate of Cairo this morning, Governor Dessouqi asked me what I expected to be doing next year. It is possible that he may have heard rumors that may have been circulating in Washington. In line with our agreed procedure, as I have made clear before, I believe it is wrong not to answer truthfully such a direct question. And so I told him that my resignation was pending and he has agreed not to say anything about this until I give him permission. In view of this, I again request permission to see Nasser."

Within six hours I got permission to see Nasser, and I got the word to him before Khrushchev reached Cairo, which was the important thing. I was very beholden to Dessouqi for doing this for me.

* * *

Nasser put on a very good facade; he was in control of himself. I never saw him act rudely to any of his inferiors, he was always very courteous, and I got along well with him, but whether this was a particular mark of friendship, it would be difficult to say. I think it was to Nasser's advantage in his American relations to be pleasant.

I tried to work out certain understandings with him. I said to him one day, "Mr. President, I'm sure you realize that as an Ambassador, I am duty-bound to report to my government on conversations and, of course, anything you say goes back to my government. If you want to discuss something unofficially with me that involves something important, tell me first what the subject is: I will tell you whether at that moment I feel I have to report it or not, if it's not leading to any activity. If it isn't, we'll discuss it and I'll lay it aside. If it is, I'll tell you, then you can decide whether or not you will tell me."

Whether that brought out anything, I cannot say. On a number of occasions, especially in the Yemen affair, when I did not think it was necessary to report to Washington on every last bullet that had been fired, I thought it was useful. In general, my stance was one in which I did not try any tricks—I do not think it works diplomatically. I tried to be honest and as straightforward as possible. How straightforward was Nasser? I think reasonably so. He was after all a head of state. I have no way of knowing what things went around me or behind my back, but I certainly did develop a rapport with him, so that I knew how to approach a subject, what to say and when to listen. I found that Nasser had stock responses that were predictable; out they would come, and one recognized them for what they were.

I would hesitate, therefore, to say that the relationship was one of personal friendship, but it was certainly one of good rapport. After I came home, I corresponded with him for some time, and when I traveled to Egypt while at Columbia, Nasser always received me and I had good talks with him. I think I did have more than simply an official relationship, and I would put it entirely on that basis.

* * *

I think that Dulles' policy with the Suez Canal was clumsily handled. The trouble with the Dulles diplomacy was that there were perfectly good reasons for *not* financing the High Dam. It had all been discussed, known in Cairo, printed in the newspapers, and all one had to say was, these things are real and until they are cleared up, we can't go for it. I think that Nasser would have understood that it was not the kind of refusal that slapped him in the face.

I hesitate to say that this is a peculiar characteristic of either the Egyptian or the Arab, but, in general, this matter of avoiding confrontation, unless you mean it, is important. One thing I discovered with Nasser was that you did much better when you went to see him if you had some real information. Let me illustrate.

Just after Johnson became President, Nasser made a speech attacking the Wheelus Air Base in Libya. It was the first time he had ever made such an attack, and I naturally had messages from the Department to go and talk to Nasser about it. Nasser was a military man and understood military considerations. So I went back to the Department and said, before I go to see Nasser, I need to know what is the military importance of Wheelus Air Base? If I go in and tell Nasser it's important to us for this and that reason, and when you attack it, you're attacking our security establishment, I think he will understand although he won't like it. But if I go in and wring my hands and point my finger, I won't get any place.

The Department did not tell me, so I went to the Department of Defense, and they did not tell me, and finally I drafted a series of ten questions that I sent to the Department, and they still did not tell me. Because the fact is, the base was not a military necessity. So I went in to see Nasser. I had a very feeble time because I did not have anything in my hand; I felt in dealing with Nasser—this was true in the Yemen case—you did much better not threatening, "tit for tat," but simply going in and saying, this is the situation, this is the way we're going to react if you do that, and I think when that was done, you got results.

I have mentioned Kennedy's diplomacy in informing Nasser about a sale of Hawk missiles to the Israelis. We went to him and said, "We're going to sell these missiles. There are reasons for it." He said, "I don't like this, but I appreciate knowing." That, it seemed to me, was the way one did best with dealing with Nasser.

* * *

When I went to Egypt, Muhammad Hasanayn Haikal in many ways was in his heyday, and it continued that way during the period I was there. Every Friday in *Al-Ahram* his article appeared, and it was always a matter of interest in the Embassy to dissect it and frequently send a message back to the United States about it.

I had not been in Egypt long when I got a kind of private message from Haikal, a suggestion that he would be glad to have me call on him any time I cared to do so. By the same route that the message reached me, I sent back a reply saying that I was calling on all the principal newspaper editors and that when his turn came I would call on him.

My reply irked Haikal somewhat, because he had the reputation of being something of an alter ego to Nasser, at least a journalistic alter ego, and Harold Beeley, the British Ambassador, had made a great deal of use of him. He frequently attended Beeley's parties, and Beeley felt he had a good pipeline to the administration, which I think he did, and Haikal was covetous of having that same position with the American Embassy. So when I did not respond immediately, he was somewhat peeved, and I think his peeve continued for a very long time.

I did ask the Chief of the Political Section, Don Bergus, to cultivate Haikal, which he did, very successfully, because Don was a good Arabist and a very ingratiating person in the right way. I did not see Haikal very much, partly because I had my own direct contacts and partly because I was not prepared to give him the accolade of greatness that he was seeking.

It is a little hard to know what the inner relationship between Haikal and Nasser was. They had been friends and Haikal played upon this friendship, and in my opinion considerably magnified it.

On the other hand, Haikal was a very clever journalistic writer. He had style and verve, and there is a certain flavor in good Arabic writing which is unique. Apparently he was the kind of man to whom Nasser could outline an idea and say, go write it down, and he did, and Nasser liked the way he wrote. Consequently, many of Nasser's speeches were written by Haikal. This, I was told by a friend in the Foreign Office, was a problem because neither Nasser nor Haikal cleared these speeches with the Foreign Office before they were given—or at least not long enough before they were given so that comments could be made. Consequently, the Foreign Office frequently felt shut out of what it regarded as important foreign policy considerations, because Haikal had prepared the text, Nasser had delivered it, and then a copy was sent around in a kind of "Oh, by the way, I gave a speech yesterday" way to the Foreign Office.

As I go back in my mind over these Friday *Al-Ahram* articles, which were in many ways Haikal's *pièces de résistance*, I am not impressed by their profundity. He was, in my opinion, an adroit rather than a profound analyst of affairs. Indeed, he was kind of a maker of instant history. Dredge up a situation and he could almost always find a historical precedent, which he would sometimes belabor at length.

It was quite wrong, in my opinion—and we came to this decision in the Embassy—to feel that this kind of connection really represented the considered mind of the central government or of Nasser himself. I had that confirmed on one occasion. At the time of the Cuban missile crisis, when there was a great interest in this in Egypt, Haikal came out with a long Friday article, with a very extended and careful analysis of the similarities between the Cuban missile crisis and the 1956 Suez Canal crisis, done at great length and apparently with a great deal of historical background.

The day after the article appeared, I had occasion to see President Nasser, and he asked me whether I had read the article. I said, yes, I had read it, and he wanted to know what I thought of it. I replied, well, I was not really impressed by it; it didn't seem to me that the parallel was very exact. Nasser, smiling, declared: "I thought it was nonsense. I told Haikal so." He said, "There's no parallel between the Cuban case and the case here."

It seemed to me that this conversation provided a clear indication of the fact that this was not the voice of Nasser speaking through the press, it was simply Haikal, and I came to the conclusion that a good deal of Haikal's writing was in this vein. Whether or not Nasser checked the articles at times, I have no way of knowing, but I think it would be quite incorrect to read Haikal's writings as the voice of Nasser.

Of course, his most successful identification with Nasser was undoubtedly his authorship of *Philosophy of the Revolution*, which does sound Nasser-ish; but it reads as though Haikal wrote it, which he almost certainly did.

Haikal was not terribly popular with many members of the Nasser government, partly because of the innate jealousy of people in power, and partly because he sometimes overplayed his relationship to Nasser and tried to trade on it, which was irritating. Once in a while he got taken down. He was often made use of by Harold Beeley, a very adroit man indeed. I think it was after the Cuban missile crisis that I was at dinner at the British Embassy and Haikal was there, in his Jimmy Reston mood, with his Scotch tweed jacket and his pipe, pontificating on American diplomacy and the Cuban missile crisis, and he ended up by saying that on the whole he thought Kennedy had done quite well in handling the crisis. He said, of course, Kennedy is really a very young man, and as he gets more experience in government, he perhaps would not act quite so abruptly, but on the whole he did very well for a young man.

At which Beeley said, "Well, Haikal, of course you realize that Kennedy is one year older than President Nasser." At which Haikal blushed and shut up for the rest of the evening. It seems to me that, after Nasser's death, his unsuccessful attempts to play an influential role in the succeeding year made it quite clear there was a good deal of opposition to him.

* * *

When Mahmud Fawzi, who was Foreign Minister when I arrived, retired, he was replaced by Mahmud Riad, an army officer. While not one of the original Revolutionary Council, he was part of the group movement. After Riad came into office, I did more business with the Foreign Office. Still, the decisions were those that one usually talked over with Nasser, but I saw Riad more and got along well with him, and the people who followed me in Cairo likewise found that association with Riad was very helpful indeed. With Riad the Foreign Office played a somewhat more important role.

Nasser always tended to be more comfortable with people he knew personally. Fawzi was a fine man and everyone recognized this. But he was the old-fashioned diplomat—in striped pants, if you will—and I don't think Nasser really was prepared to commit things to his hands to the degree he was with his own people. I think it was true of his economic policies too, that the people who ran the various government organizations, who moved in his circle, were the people who really got along with him, because he knew them and trusted them, and to him loyalty was a very high attribute.

I think it a mistake to think of "Nasserism" simply as one individual. There was a composite "Nasser" at the center, which for a long time was composed of about four people, with Nasser the predominant influence but with this group acting together. The next circle tended to come and go according to conditions and abilities. When Baghdadi retired from government, that inner circle somewhat broke up. Zakaria Muhyi al-Din continued to be part of it, and one or two others, but by the time the government was returned to a quasiparliamentary basis with a prime minister, a further degree of institutionalization had taken place, and the personal role of Nasser had altered somewhat, although it was still the central factor.

I simply do not know whether Nasser tended to set people against each other. I never saw evidence of it, but I think it could be deduced.

* * *

By the time I left Egypt in the early summer of 1964, it was quite apparent to me that we were going to enter upon a period of more strained relationships. One has to remember that this was true on the whole in regard to all Nasser's foreign relations. They tended to go up and down with many countries, so one should not assume this was unique to Egyptian-American relations. Nevertheless, it does have to be looked at in the American context, and I think there were several factors that ended the relationship we tried to establish.

First of all, it finally became evident that we did not have strong enough common interests with Egypt to sustain a long and mutually profitable relationship. We tried very hard to establish such interests, and we had some success. But the amount of American investment in Egypt was small. And the strategic position of Egypt did not primarily concern us at the time. About the only thing we had in Egypt was the conviction that although many Americans thought Nasser was bad, a chaotic Egypt or a Communist Egypt would be much worse, and therefore to support the economy and to prevent it from going to an extreme was in our interest. That is a negative kind of common interest to share.

The situation was made more difficult because when we moved to our real interest in Egypt, which was Egypt's relationship with the Middle East, we were, in fact, in opposition to Egyptian policies even though we tried very hard not to be. And I think for a time Nasser tried also not to be in opposition to us. We were interested in stability and we did not want the applecart shaken. We were conscious of the invitation that disorder gives to the Soviet and other radical forces to come in. Our hard interests, like oil and strategic positions, were in other parts of the Middle East, which we did not want disturbed; when we dealt with these areas, we wanted quiet, peace and the *status quo*.

These were not Nasser's objectives. I do not believe that Nasser was building a world empire. There were those who thought so, but I did not. He was a revolutionary, and he was highly pragmatic. I think the adulation that came to him after 1956 quite understandably went to his head, and the many calls to modernize that came from parts of the Arab world or parties within the Arab world struck a responsive chord. Therefore he was not particularly concerned with the maintenance of any *status quo*, especially of the kind that he had abolished in Egypt. Consequently, when he moved out into the Middle East, he was a disturbing influence.

One can argue that perhaps in the long run, looking down history, he was a good disturbing influence to the extent that he was bringing about inevitable changes, and it was better to have them brought about in this way than to have them brought about by irresponsible internal revolution. But, try as we might, we found that Nasser's foreign position and our foreign position were always clashing with each other.

The classic example was the Yemen war. Many in the Administration, not President Kennedy particularly, but many others, certainly in Congress, saw this as a direct attack upon the whole structure of the Arabian peninsula. It not only brought Egypt into conflict in foreign policy, but made it appear that by supporting Nasser's economy at home, we were simply furthering an influence which was against our best interest. So it was very hard to maintain even the limited amount of common interest that we had in supporting the economy and internal stability, in view of this continuous external trouble. Every time one tried to get an aid program for Egypt or something that would be useful in making a connection with Nasser that might perhaps restrain him, one was constantly running into criticism at home, generated by this latent opposition that lay in our foreign policy.

One of the things that I wanted very much to do—and President Kennedy was very interested in this—was to get Nasser to come to this country. I had a feeling that if he could come to the United States and talk to Kennedy personally, Kennedy could tell him some things that nobody else could tell him. I could not tell him, but Kennedy could. I think, too, that he would have seen our combination of private enterprise and a certain degree of government control, which would have made America more comprehensible to him.

The trouble was that Nasser's foreign adventures were continually throwing a monkey wrench into prospects for the visit. I had it all laid out, and then the Yemen war reached its height, and in the light of this difficulty and the opposition in Congress, Kennedy said, "I just can't afford to have him come, we'll have trouble." So we dropped it.

A second factor in this was that our chief instrument of diplomatic relations lay in our aid program, and the largest component was the PL-480 Food Program. As I mentioned, I think at one time something like a third of all of Egypt's grain resources were coming from the PL-480 program. While this was a very large contribution to Egypt, it put us in a very undesirable diplomatic position, for two reasons. First, there were those in the United States, in Congress, to a lesser degree in the State Department, certainly the CIA, who argued that Egypt was so dependent upon us that we could use the food to force them to do anything we wanted. One was always under pressure to get concessions from Nasser under the threat of withdrawing the PL-480 program. This was a great misconception and made it very hard to sustain a steady relationship, and in the end it made it very hard to get renewals of the aid that we wanted. People always said, we gave all this, what did we get from it? I think we got a lot from it, but not what they expected.

Second, it is really bad for one country to be dependent on another country for its food, because if anything happens to disturb the relationship, if food is diminished, then the sending country is open to the accusation that it is using the lives of human beings and empty bellies as an instrument of diplomatic pressure.

After I left, in the prelude to the breakdown that came just before 1967, it was not possible to renew the PL-480 long-term program—not, as I understand it, because of our relationship with Egypt, but because there were so many enemies of PL-480 that President Johnson was unwilling to renew such a controversial program. Egypt did not understand this at all.

During the years I was there, I repeatedly suggested that what we ought to do was to plan with Egypt an agreed program reducing our food aid, gradually, year after year. And as we reduced our food aid, give other kinds of economic assistance that would increase the Egyptians' capacity to grow food for themselves, so that by X date they would no longer be dependent on us to such a degree. It was not possible to do that.

Nasser felt very vulnerable because of his relationship to the United States. In the summer of 1963, when the differences between Syria and Egypt were at their height, I had occasion to see Nasser, who asked me if I was still listening to broadcasts around the area. I said yes. He mentioned Radio Damascus and said, "They're continually saying that I'm going soft on Israel because I depend upon American wheat." He commented, "Imagine anybody saying that Nasser is soft on Israel." He was obviously upset about this constant theme of Syrian and other propaganda; it made him very vulnerable.

It seems to me that the heavy reliance upon PL-480 as our

chief instrument made for better relations in the short run. It was not calculated, however, to lay the base for a mutually profitable relationship.

Another factor was the Israeli problem. When I arrived, as I mentioned earlier, the idea had been put forth by the Egyptian Ambassador to Washington, and then by Nasser himself when I presented my credentials, that we would put this question in the icebox. We would agree to disagree on it. We were not going to commit them, they were not going to commit us, and we could go on to something positive. This everyone tried to do, with the exception of Zulficar Sabry, who was determined I was not going to forget it. But by and large, during the years I was in Cairo, we did not have very much difficulty over this issue, even when we sold Hawk missiles to Israel.

Again it was a good short-term ploy, but the Israeli dispute was not going to go away, and sooner or later, in one form or another, it would have to come back. And when it did, it could not help but place fresh demands and strains upon US-Egyptian relationships.

It began to come back in the winter of 1963-1964, in a number of ways. For one thing, Israeli diversion of water from the upper Jordan into the coastal plain heated up the whole Israeli question, which had been rather quiescent, and the Arab world saw it as new evidence of Israeli aggressiveness. There is a peculiar feeling about water in the Arab world. In a dry land it is indeed the "water of life," and this move was taken as a sign that Israel was going to be more aggressive.

At about this same time, and largely using the necessity for Arab consultation occasioned by the problem of the diversion, Egypt and Nasser began to shift from a policy of being concerned chiefly for relations with the other revolutionary states—Syria and Algeria and, to a lesser extent, Yemen and Iraq—to a policy aimed at reestablishing relations with the whole Arab world. After the breakup with Syria, Nasser said he had to have a policy of unity of aims, and only those countries that shared the revolutionary aims could really be partners of Egypt. When this policy resulted in a rather thorough isolation of Egypt from affairs in the Arab world, he began to shift over to *wahdat al-amal*, "unity of work." Essentially it meant that no matter what your aim is, or your form of government, or your political philosophy, if you are working for the good of the Arab world you can be a friend of Egypt. In pursuing this policy, Nasser was to a degree re-entering the Arab world and, as a result, felt fresh pressures in regard to the Israeli question.

Moreover, Kennedy had died in November, and while Kennedy had done some things, notably the Hawk missile sale, which Nasser did not like, he was not really fixed in the Egyptian mind as being a strong pro-Zionist. It was remembered that he had made a very strong speech in favor of Algerian independence, and while that had nothing to do with Israel it was a somewhat pro-Arab speech. And his method of personal diplomacy—for instance, informing Nasser beforehand that he was going to sell Hawk missiles—seemed to betoken a sensitivity to the Egyptian outlook, which assisted in keeping the Arab-Israeli dispute at low key.

President Lyndon Johnson did not have the kind of interest in the Middle East that Kennedy had. Also, he appeared to the Arabs to be a much more political figure. I am not sure that he was, but he appeared to be, and it was said that he had Zionist connections. Undoubtedly he had; I think every American politician has. It began to appear, however, that the fresh start that Kennedy had given the US-Egyptian relationship, in bypassing the Arab-Israeli dispute, was probably on the way out.

At this time, also, the Vietnam War was heating up and was beginning to absorb everybody's attention, including that of the State Department.

At about the time I left, the Egyptian Ambassador went in to see Secretary of State Rusk about some problem, and I understood the Secretary lost his temper, if one can imagine him doing that, and said rather curtly, "Look, you know, we don't have time to fool around with this Arab thing. We've got a war on over in Asia." This mood was becoming very strong indeed; it affected the financial picture, it affected the tensions and I do not think that Johnson had the additional interest in the Middle East to withstand it. I am not sure Kennedy could have withstood it either.

Egypt's position between the great powers was one of pendular oscillation. A country like Switzerland or Tibet can be neutral by simply not dealing with anybody, but a country in the middle of affairs cannot. What Nasser did was to perform a kind of oscillation between the centers of power.

When the contract for the High Dam was signed with the Russians, and for some years thereafter, he swung very far in the Russian direction—so far that there were many who thought he could never get loose. Then when we came in with our very large PL-480 and diplomatic efforts, he did not shake off the Russian connection, but he certainly did move in our direction.

It seemed to me that by the winter of 1963-1964, the pendulum had swung so far toward the United States that Nasser would have to correct it. The trouble is, we are not a calm-minded people. The Russians take these oscillations much better than we do. As things cooled off somewhat, one had to expect a mounting degree of American reaction, which did not make it easy to maintain the relationship at all.

Putting all those things together, I felt when I left that we had had a very good interlude, we had done some positive things. I think that we restrained ourselves on a number of occasions, and that our influence in the Yemen war was good, although we did not settle it; it settled itself. Nevertheless, I do not think that we had discovered a basis for a long, continued, tranquil, mutually helpful relationship. I think it was not really discoverable.

CHAPTER 12

POSTSCRIPT IN AMERICA

I left Egypt in June of 1964. Andy Cordier had been in Egypt; I think it was in the winter of 1963-64, after he had left the United Nations, where he was Assistant to the Secretary General, and had been called to head the School of International Affairs at Columbia University. I entertained him when he came out to Egypt.

After he returned to the United States in the spring, I had an offer from Columbia to head its Middle East Institute, and after thinking it over decided to accept it, so when I left Cairo, it was to return home to go to this position in the fall.

I was there from 1964 to 1971; in 1971 I turned 68, and had to retire. I then went to Georgetown University in Washington, DC, and taught three years. My seventy-first birthday came in the third year. They had a seventy-year retirement rule, so I had to retire. Of course, I did not have a tenured appointment at Georgetown; I was a visiting lecturer in Middle East history. At Columbia, I had both a tenured professorship and an administrative position in the Middle East Institute.

I never really had taught in the field of Middle Eastern studies at all. Years ago, my teaching was in the field of philosophy, and while I had done a great deal of lecturing on the Middle East and a certain amount of writing, I had not taught, and I was not a professional Orientalist by any means, although I had done graduate work in the field of Arab philosophy.

I went to Columbia University much as I went to the Embassy in Cairo, quite naïve and new to the experience, and I learned a good deal, both hard and pleasant, at Columbia.

Cordier was a great developer and organizer, and on coming to Columbia he had succeeded in getting some substantial sums of money to develop area studies. Much of it came from the Ford Foundation, and with this he was able to develop and expand the area programs, which had started at Columbia during or after the Second World War. I do not know how far they had developed in that time, but he certainly picked them up and put them together into a major program. As I remember, there were eight or ten of these programs.

The format was that of an institute—not a department of academic studies, but a program of academic studies. It was to be interdisciplinary. Columbia had long had a Department of Middle East Languages and Literature. My old friend, Arthur Jeffery, had gone there as the shining light in Arabic, and provided foundation for traditional scholarly research. To this were added people interested in the Middle East, from the fields of political science, economics, geography and so on, who were bonded together in an institute which was attached to the School of International Affairs. The school provided a two-year program ending with an M.A., from which one could go on to the Ph.D.

I came to Columbia without academic preparation in the field. Since I had never taught Middle East affairs, my view of the field was one that had very largely grown out of my own somewhat pragmatic experience in the Middle East, and what I thought people needed to know.

One of the great values, it seemed to me, in the institute approach at this point was the fact that it did make the Middle East a subject of concern and of interest. The Departments of Semitic and of Middle East Studies have almost always found their center of attention in the medieval period. I do not know whether that is because the medieval period is really great, or whether because, as one of my colleagues said at Columbia, "I much prefer to study the medieval period because there are no problems there. They're all dead and gone and I'm not part of them. The moment I study the modern Middle East, I'm beset by problems."

Be that as it may, there are a good many judgments that grew out of medieval studies that do not apply to the modern day at all. I often think of my friend, Arthur Jeffery, a really great scholar. Jeffery was a fine Islamicist. He would fulminate against the modern Muslim—that isn't Islam at all he would say. I would say, Jeff, if you ask any Presbyterian what Calvin said in his *Institutes*, he'll tell you he never heard of it, but for that you're not going to read him out of church, are you? That idea, that nothing has happened that is worth studying since the beginning of the nineteenth century, seemed to me to receive a very healthy counterbalance in considering the Middle East as a current scene.

Second to that was certainly the concept of an interdisciplinary approach, in which one tried to buttress and supplement one's own major tool of research.

The trouble, though, it seemed to me, is that this is much more easily done on paper than it is in fact. It is easy to end up by producing students who are somewhat like *Time* magazine. They know a great deal about a great many things, but they really do not have the organizing discipline to put it together. I do not think we ever really solved that problem. We had students who did not have a sufficient tool of discipline by which they could go to the necessary depths in any one direction.

Future employment in government and business was not stressed as much as one might have thought it to be. More of our students expected to teach than anything else, and to do research, and for students like this my advice always was that they should first of all develop a strong discipline of their own, and secondly, that the discipline should not be confined to the Middle East. The Middle East, or any geographic area, should at the beginning be a supplement to a basic discipline.

For instance, if you get a really good grounding in, say, nineteenth and twentieth century European history, with a good strong development in the modern Middle East, then you can go out and teach. There are many colleges that want somebody to teach history, and you can then add to it courses in your specialty.

That perhaps is too much of a career-minded comment, but I did find the students who did this, on the whole, found it was a little easier to get a place than the people who had concentrated, for example, on "the antecedents of the *Mahdi* and his movement," and knew nothing else.

Also one of the problems was that in developing these disciplines outside of the field of traditional Middle East studies, the various academic departments, such as the Political Science Department and particularly the Economics Department, really were not convinced that area studies were pertinent to their theoretical structure.

We were very fortunate in having one of the best economists in the field, Charles Issawi, now at Princeton, in Middle East economics. But when my son-in-law, Doak Barnett, who was in the East Asian Institute, tried to get the Department of Economics to support an economist on East Asian affairs, he was told, frankly, there is no such thing as East Asian economics. There's no such thing as East Asian mathematics. There's no such thing as East Asian chemistry. How can you have such a thing as East Asian economics? You just have an economist. He does not have to know anything about China or about Chinese economics.

In general, this was the background one found, perhaps a little less in political science, but still there. It seems they were under the delusion that their discipline was a kind of exact mathematical science, which could be practiced without regard to the area on which it was focused, and it was therefore hard to get from the various cooperating disciplines the support in development of an area-oriented program in their field.

We struggled valiantly. I had some fine colleagues and we did get ahead, but we got ahead because we fought the battle. This was further made difficult by the feeling that all these institutes were bidders for money that could have gone to a disciplinary department, such as economics. That was not true, because the money was not intended for those purposes. So, between these various factors it was difficult to make the multi-disciplinary approach as fruitful as it ought to be.

Then there was a particular problem that I think everybody was aware of, and that is how to bring traditional departments of Middle East studies into fruitful correlation with a program, or views of the modern world.

On one hand, you simply have to know the background. One must know the history. If I were to choose one discipline that seemed to me central, I would choose history with a corollary of the language, if necessary, to handle it. There are others, as well.

One found good people in Islamics, but they were not able to build the bridges that would take what they knew of their world and make it available to the kind of world that we wanted to study, and I found that on the whole the people in the Middle East Department, with some exceptions, either were disinclined to do this or really did not see the necessity of it.

Let me give an example—the breakup of the Syrian-Egyptian union in 1961. It was a perfectly modern phenomenon and a very important one in the history of Egypt and Syria, but Syria and Egypt had been united at least twice before this, back to the Middle Ages. They have been married and divorced a number of times.

A good Middle East historian ought to be able to tell the modern student whether that was purely accidental or whether there is something in government and in the people that has always made it difficult to maintain unions.

If one knew that, and then looked at the 1961 breakup, one would get a better comprehension. I could not find anybody in the Department of Middle East Languages and Literature that had thought about the possibility, or really cared about it very much.

Dr. Joseph Schacht, our great expert in Islamic law, was a highly lucid writer and a profound man, but one got almost nothing out of him that had any relationship to the modern day. All of his interests lay in the definition and analysis of medieval *sharia* law. When one wanted to raise the question, what does the effect of centuries of speaking of the legal system in terms of the *sharia* law do to the emergence of a modern jurisprudence in the independent state today—this was not his concern, Ibn Battuta* had never talked about that. We were never able to solve that, although I had some very good friends in the Middle East Department.

I did not know it at the time, but there had apparently been a good deal of friction between the Middle East Department and the Institute, and I was brought in in the hope that some of this could be cured, and I got along very well with everybody. But nobody had ever told me about the situation and I was somewhat put out that I had not been warned. It was indeed a very great problem and I am not sure that it ever has been completely solved.

When I went to Columbia, I was very much enamoured of the institute approach in its attempt to give a multi-disciplinary approach to the Middle East, and recognized the value of what was being done—at least, its objectives. But as I dealt with it, it seemed to me that however laudable its object was, a good deal of the actual inter-disciplinary experience was thin, and it sometimes resulted in producing people who really had no basic discipline of their own, or who made mistakes in applying other disciplines, because they knew so much of their own and so little of others that they took the other discipline in terms of their own. I am not quite sure how you get over that. If you had enough money and enough time, I think it could be done. I do not think we're nearly as insistent now upon the whole—I may be wrong on that, because I am out of touch with things.

I do not think a year or two at a Middle Eastern university does one much good before one is a fairly mature student.

I do think we are doing better than we used to in getting Middle Eastern scholars to come to this country. Some years ago, when I went up to Harvard to have a look at it, I was very interested to hear Harvard say rather contemptuously that they did not have Middle East scholars come to Harvard because none of them really met the Harvard standard of teaching. It seemed to me that they were missing the whole point. The reason why one got a Middle Eastern scholar was not only because he was a scholar, but because

*A 14th century North African theologian and traveler whose *Travels in Asia and Africa* is one of the world's great travel classics.

he presented a subject as only a Middle Easterner could. And what you learn about a disembodied subject, as seen and heard by a person living in the area.

For instance, I got the Minister of Education, after he retired in Egypt, to come to the United States, and the principal course he gave was on Arab socialism. I think one could argue very sharply as to the merits of that course as a pure analytical exercise, but what was important was to hear a former member of the Egyptian cabinet. He was present when Arab socialism was born, and he was sent out by the Nasser cabinet to sell Arab socialism up and down the Nile, to tell students what he thought Arab socialism was. I did not particularly agree with his analysis, but he was in a position to understand this particular aspect of revolutionary Egypt.

* * *

As I look back on my life in and with the Middle East, I realize how difficult it would be to repeat that experience today. For one thing, there is seldom the motivation which existed in my generation for young people to go to a foreign area with the expectation of spending their lives there. When we boarded the little American freighter, the *Clontarf*, in August of 1928, and headed for Beirut and ultimately for Mosul in Iraq, it was with the belief, and indeed the desire, that we were going to establish a new and lifelong residence for ourselves. This being so, we knew we would have to learn the language, become part of the community, and identify ourselves as completely as we could with the life of what was a new country for us.

That would be difficult to do today. Few of the activities which take Americans into the Middle East expect of them a lifelong residence in the area. And the ease of travel, by which one can fly home for a weekend and be back on Monday morning, makes most Americans peripatetic or intermittent in their life in a foreign land. The result is that while they might become deeply knowledgeable about and interested in the country in which they happen to be serving, there is always the background of feeling that their stay there is temporary—that they are passing guests in the country rather than permanent residents in its life. And this, I believe, may have a profound effect upon understanding the area and responding to its life and its people.

Another reason why it would be difficult to repeat the experience is because the institutions in which Americans found a base for lifelong commitment have very largely vanished. The missionary movement has greatly altered. It is no longer composed largely of foreigners going to a country but rather of indigenous people, or in many cases, of Asiatic Christians who serve in nearby countries. As in the case of other types of work, stays are sometimes brief and it seemed to me that after the war, my American mission friends in Cairo were either just coming back from America or just returning. Moreover, with the attainment of full independence by Middle East countries, the essentially foreign enterprises have had to alter their position and as far as possible become part of, or identified with, some truly indigenous movement.

In a different sense, this same process has gone on in the world of American education, whose institutions in the past played such an important role in service to the Middle East. While Robert College in Istanbul, the American University of Beirut, the American University in Cairo, have played great roles in the past, I think it would be impossible to launch them afresh under current conditions. In them also the purely foreign staff has shrunk, the staff of indigenous scholars has grown, and more and more, it seems to me, the American in the educational institutions is one who comes and goes rather than stays permanently.

When I went to the American University in Cairo, again it was with the expectation of long service, and when as Dean and as President I recruited new American staff, it was with the understanding that they would spend a major part of their career in the area. Moreover, we then required that new staff members, unless they were on a short three-year term, learn the Arabic language, at least enough to be at home in the country. And I think there is no American institution in the Middle East today that has any such requirement.

So it is with other institutions, like technical assistance, which I served in the Near East Foundation. Only perhaps in the area of diplomacy has the essential character of the institution remained unchanged, and of course diplomacy is generally not a place where one seeks for a long continued residence in one particular country or region. The consequence of all these things is that too often the American is really a pilgrim and a stranger, bringing his knowledge to the Middle East for a few years and then going back, either for professional enrichment or to seek a new career in the United States. This may indeed bring Eastern life and Western life together more frequently, as both Middle Easterners and Americans travel back and forth. But on the other hand, it does not lead to that long process of acclimatization by which one, although a foreigner, learns to be at home and concerned, and very often identified deeply, with the life of the community in which he lives.

Behind this factor is the more basic one of the general change of the position between West and East, Western culture and Eastern culture. When I first went to the Middle East, the area was really just beginning its process of modernization, and anything which came from abroad in the field of the professions or sciences or education, and those who brought it, enjoyed a special reputation in the community, and often their service or acquaintance was eagerly sought. After 50 years, the Middle East no longer has this attitude. It has developed with a rapidity that is most remarkable. It has developed its own institutions, its own technical proficiency, and the glamour has worn off a great deal of Western life. Indeed, I think in recent years there has been a genuine resurgence of the desire to retain historic values and institutions in the Middle East and in the Islamic world, and to find some way of using them to replace institutions and ideas which formerly came from the West. So it seems to me that on almost all counts the long experience in the area, which it was my good fortune to have, would be very difficult to come by today.

One of the most rewarding aspects of my years in the area has been the diverse roles I have been called on to play. I began as a missionary, passed on to higher education at the American University in Cairo, then entered the field of administering technical assistance in the Near East Foundation, had a term of diplomacy at the Embassy in Cairo, and then tried to carry this knowledge back to the United States in the field of scholarship and teaching at Columbia University. This diversity of occupation did not come from any restlessness on my part, or because I grew disinterested or disillusioned with any one. Rather, one seemed with a certain naturalness to grow out of the other. Opportunities came, doors opened, and it seemed clear to me that I ought to enter them. The result has been that I have known the Middle East from many different angles, and when I returned to Columbia to teach, I found that this fact greatly enriched my own understanding of events—which I hope was useful in helping students see the area in the round, if that is an appropriate phrase. Each one of these occupations made a special contribution to my own life, and also furnished me with a particular instrument which was useful in understanding and serving in the area.

Let me here say something about my beginnings as a missionary. This is a time when the missionary movement has undergone profound change and a profound questioning on the part of a great many people. Its ultimate motivation within personal judgment and personal commitment is not something that can be measured by entirely rational argument. My concern here is neither to defend nor criticize the impetus which through the decades—indeed through the centuries—has sent out missionaries from one faith into the lands of another faith.

It ought to be pointed out, I think, that all of the great, so-called universal world religions have been and remain deeply missionary. Buddhism, Christianity, and certainly Islam have all had a permanent missionary dimension to their activity, none more than Islam. I remember years ago being out with a colleague of mine from the American University in Cairo, in one of the older quarters of the city. My friend stopped to chat with a little girl, perhaps ten years old, who was playing along the side of a house, and after saying a few words to her in Arabic, the child looked up and said to him, "*Khawaga*," which is the Arabic word for foreigner, "You're a *Nasrani* (a Christian), aren't you?" And he said, yes. And then she said most solemnly, "God willing, you will become a Muslim."

So the fact of bearing witness to a faith was not strange to

Islam nor strange in the world today. Indeed, almost every ideological commitment has carried with it a certain missionary spirit. There is something of the missionary spirit in the American devotion to the spread of democracy throughout the world. And I would say myself that science is deeply imbued with the missionary spirit in which it feels that only by spreading its techniques can advancement be brought to mankind.

Very often this missionary spirit takes forms and institutes programs which are difficult to defend. Far too often it has been insensitive to the devotion of the people among whom it moves, disinterested in their spiritual aspirations, uncomprehending of their formulation of values and of faith. This I may say is not only true of the religious missionary; it's true of the political missionary also. US policies in some South American countries are not very shining examples of what the zeal for a democratic world ought to lead to.

But at its best, the missionary enterprise formed a unique meeting ground where the spiritual view and values of the Christian world and of a non-Christian world could view each other with sympathy and with a shared concern. It is no accident that some of the earliest and finest scholarship in the Middle East came from missionaries. And in my own day there were still notable contributions made by people like Dr. Charles Adams, whose study of the Muslim reformer, Muhammad Abduh, showed a sympathetic comprehension of the problems through which the Muslim intellectual was passing in the last generation. My own beginning in the Middle East as a missionary led to a profound appreciation for this spiritual dimension of Eastern life, and whatever my occupation, I never ceased to be interested by its intellectual formulation and moved by its spiritual concerns and aspirations, moved, I hope, with sympathy and understanding.

Now, I think this experience does not often come outside of the field of perhaps somewhat professional religious work. To be sure, there are armies of Islamicists in universities who study every aspect of Islamic faith, Islamic intellectual endeavor. But all too often these are only really intellectual exercises. Some of my Islamic colleagues at Columbia seemed to me to be somewhat like Lord

Palmerston, the foreign secretary of Great Britain in the early part of the 19th century, who was fascinated by and widely read in Scottish Calvinist theology. But for him it was only an intellectual exercise. It had no relationship whatever to the life he or anybody else lived day by day. So while the Islamicist studied intellectually the intellectual phenomenon of religion, such study, it seems to me, seldom led to the sympathetic attempt to understand what it was people were seeking and how they formulated the world as they saw it.

Certainly I have found it of enormous value to me through my life to have this facet of Middle Eastern life constantly present. When I was active at the Council on Foreign Relations in New York, I would insist, in any seminar on a Middle East political problem, that some consideration be given to the religious situation. Usually I was voted down by my colleagues, who believed that religion was moribund in the area, growing weaker and weaker, and really need not be considered as an active political or social force.

Of course, the events of recent years have proved how illusory was this judgment, beginning perhaps with the Muslim Brotherhood in the 1930s, and passing on to the Khomeini revolution and the other movements that have sprung up. There is a resurgence of religious restlessness that needs to be understood with sympathy and concern because it is a restlessness we share also within our own Christian world.

So I feel that having begun as a missionary, far from being a liability, was a constant asset in keeping before me this important, ubiquitous aspect of Middle East life.

Finally, let me say a word about the general view of the changes that have come about in the area. I have always been interested in the broad frame within which human action takes place. Its details are of course important and must be mastered, but left to themselves they become bewildering and confusing. The trees take over the forest.

The years I was associated with the Middle East were years of constant turmoil and crises, beginning with the massacres in Iraq in 1932 and reaching down through all the other alarms and excursions that have filled the region. Many reasons are given for this history of instability and in a sense all are valid, for the situation in the area is exceedingly complex and cannot easily be dismissed in one or two root causes. But, as I look back to the Middle East into which I came in 1928 and which I left in 1964, it seems to me that one needs to find a sense of new order replacing the Ottoman Empire which collapsed at the end of World War I. To be sure, by the time World War I broke out, the Ottoman Empire was moribund and large sections of the Arab world had semi-autonomy. And yet the Ottoman Empire, then some 300 years old, did provide a general framework of society, of identity, of administration, and above all, of Muslim political life within whose parameters the Middle East, and especially the Arab lands, had maintained a certain stability.

Travel from part to part, from Cairo to Jerusalem, to Beirut, to Damascus, to Bagdad, to Jiddah was free without let or hindrance—no passports to be gotten, no border guards to stop people, no customs to pay. A legal system was universal throughout the area, and even in its dissolution the Ottoman state had provided a framework which gave a certain sense of unity to the area.

Now, with that disappearance, the Middle Eastern states—the Arab world—that is, the ex-Ottoman territories, were left naked to the entrance of a new order and ever since have been struggling to find how to relate themselves to each other and how to develop their own identity and statehood.

What happened of course is that the victorious Allied powers in a sense tried to supersede the Ottoman Empire, imposing a solution on the area. Had this been imposed by a single force, say Great Britain or France, it might have had a measure of success, but France and Britain were in competition, and thus the area was divided, which it never had been under the Ottomans. Moreover, Ottoman dominions were carved up into the states of Syria, Jordan, Palestine, Iraq and Lebanon without much regard either to historic factors or natural boundaries, and certainly not to the wishes of the people. And therefore, the states which emerged began with a certain artificial character which has been difficult for them to overcome. All of this might have worked out—patiently and with the years—but certainly the creation of the state of Israel introduced an element of instability into the post-war adjustment that has yet to be exorcized.

I say an element of instability because Israel has presented an insoluble problem to the Arab world. On one hand, these countries have been unable to accept it, for understandable reasons of history and identity. On the other hand, it is quite beyond the ability of any single Arab state—perhaps of all of them put together—to really come to terms with a constructive solution. Consequently, there has been a long, continued frustration that intermittently operates at the heart of the emerging life of Arab states. And, in my opinion, until this problem is laid to rest finally, it will be difficult, indeed impossible, for the Arab world to find itself fully and to build its new role in the world of today.

INDEX

Abd al-Hadi: & *Classical Arabic Made Easy*, p. 20
Abd al-Krim al-Rifi: incident of, 108-110
Abd al-Rahman, Shaykh, 27, 28
Abduh, Muhammad: Muslim reformer, 256
Abdullah, Amir: as tribal chief, 43
Abi, Shaykh: as Yazidi leader, 29
Al-Adab fi al-Din (Ghazali), 45
Adams, Charles: as Islamicist, 256
Aden, 201, 208
Agency for International Development (AID), 193
al-Ahram: Haikal articles, 236-237
Ajil, Shaykh: as Shammar ruler, 23
Akhbar al-Yawm, 56
Ambassadorship, see Chapters 9, 10, 11 (see also "Kennedy", "Nasser-Badeau relationship"): communicating with Washington, 185-188; Congressional visitors, 196-198; modus operandi, 188-191; as non-career appointment, 170-174; resignation problems, 232-233

American Club in Cairo, 116
American Export Line, 13, 93
American Girls College, 123
American Locomotive Works, 5
American University in Cairo (AUC), 53-59, 71-75, 85-86, 122-128: Abd al-Krim Incident, 109-110; & Egyptian government, 123-127; & Faruq, 117-121; a forum for public debate, 51, 127, 129; & Israeli question, 117- 126; journalism, 58, 19, 123; post World War II period, 106-107, 122-128; Public Service, Division of, 51, 53, 123, 127; relations with US government, 108-110, 126; students at, 53-55, 105, 117
Amin, Ahmad: in Ministry of Awqaf, 92
Amin, Ali: as journalist, 56
Amin, Mustafa: as journalist, 56, 57
Amr, Abd al-Hakim: as Army Chief of Staff, 182; as Vice-President, 224, 225; Yemen War, 223
Anabasis, 10
Arab Academy, 88

Arab League, 90, 113, 114
Arabic: at AUC, 54, 92; Badeau study of, 8, 19, 20, 21, 45; requirements today, 253; use in diplomacy, 97, 212, 217, 221
Arabism: under Nasser, 113, 114
Architecture, Islamic, 74-83 (see also "Cresswell", "Architecture, Mosques,")
Architecture, Mosques: Barquq, 81; Ibn Tulun, 78-79-81; Muayyad, 80; Muhammad Ali, 82; Muhammad al-Nasir, 77, 78, 80; Seth, 25, 26; Sultan Hasan, 80, 81; Qait Bey, 78, 79, 80; Qalaun, 77, 80
Arthur, Geoffrey: as British diplomat, 203
Assyrian Protestant Church, 19
Assyrians, 21 (see also "Mosul", "Shimun, Mar"): Assyrian Levies, 25, 31; & Iraqi nationalism, 24; massacre at Filfil, 33, 35; political aspirations, 30, 31, 33, 34; religious identity, 19, 22, 30; revolt of 1932, 20, 34
Athos II, S. S., 103
Atiya, Aziz, 46
"atmosphere piece", 187 (see also "Ambassadorship")
al-Azhar, 103, 127: in Egyptian educational system, 49, 91, 92, 123; as political force, 65, 67, 70, 112
Azzam, Abd al-Rahman: of Arab League, 43

Badeau, Mary Lyle Stothoff (mother), 3, 7, 10
Baghdad: Assyrian community, 34; Badeau mission work in, 38-44; contrast with Cairo, 48-49; history, 76-77
Baghdadi, Abdul Latif, 239: & Egyptian intelligence, 222
Balfour Declaration, 112
Bandung Conference: & Egyptian-American "chill", 178
Barnett, A. Doak, 185, 249
Beeley, Sir Harold, 202: & Haikal, 236, 238
Beirut; in 1928, 15, 16
Bergus, Donald, 236: & Sadat, 224
Ben Bella, 222
Birth control clinics (Egypt), 131
"Black Saturday", 132 (see also Egyptian Revolution): role of various political forces in, 133-134
Bowles, Chester, 173, 214
Boy Scout movement: in Egypt, 69; in Iraq, 39
Brandt, Willy: visit to Egypt, 232
Breasted, James, 131
Brinton, Judge Jasper Y., 125
Bruce, David: as non-career ambassador, 172
Bunker, Ellsworth: as non-career ambassador, 172; Yemen War negotiations, 210, 211, 212-214
Byroade, Ambassador Henry: in Afghanistan, 161-162; Nasser incident, 178

B

Badeau, Charles Stothoff (father), 3, 4, 10
Badeau, Margaret Louise Hathaway, 6, 7, 8, 9, 13, 15, 24

C

Caffrey, Jefferson: as Ambassador, 108-110, 143
Cairo: contrast with Baghdad in 1936, 48-49; history of, 76-83

Calverly, E. E.: as Arabist, 45, 46
Cantine, James, 17, 20, 26, 27, 28
Carpenter, George, 5
Central Intelligence Agency (CIA), 94: as information source, 191, 203; & Nasser, 179, 185; & US Embassy, 190, 191, 210
Chamberlain, Dr.: & Dutch Reformed Church, 10
"charter of technical assistance", 147
Christian Syriac Nestorians, see "Nestorians"
Classical Arabic Made Easy, (Abd al-Hadi), 20
Cleland, Wendell, 51, 53, 96, 97, 130 (see also AUC)
Clontarf, S.S., 13, 16
Columbia University, 73, 90: Badeau professor at, 246; Badeau philosophy student at, 44-47; Middle East studies at, 247-251
Communism: & Egypt, 146, 177, 192, 226
Congregational Church: mission work in Mosul, 19, 21; & Near East Relief, 147
Congress, US: & PL-480, 194-197, 207-208; & Yemen War, 201, 241; visitors to Cairo, 196-198
Coptic Church of Egypt: & Ethiopia, 101
Copts: & Egyptian Revolution, 135, 136, 137
Cordier, Andrew, 246, 247
Council on Foreign Relations, 173, 257
Counterpart funds, 192-193, 198 (see also PL-480)
"country team concept", 188 (see also "Ambassadorship")
Creswell, K. A. C., 73-76
Ctesiphon, 30

Cuban Missile Crisis: Haikal on, 237, 238
"cultural blindness", 97
Cultural nationalism: in Egypt, 86-90; in Middle East, 259
Cumberland, Harriet (Mrs. Roger), 17, 34, 35
Cumberland, Roger, 18, 34 (see also "Kurds"): murder of, 17, 35
Cyprus: & NEF, 166

D

Davis, Elmer, 95, 96, 97 (see also OWI)
Dawn of Conscience (Breasted), 131
"deep freeze" period in U.S.-Egyptian relations, 177-179
Deir ez-Zor, 17
Demonstration High School: Cairo, 90
Dessouqi, Salah: Governor of Cairo, 231; in foreign affairs, 231-232; role in Badeau resignation, 232-233
Destouris: Egyptian political party, 65
Dimashqiya, Nadim: as Lebanese ambassador to Egypt, 87
Dulles, Allen, 190
Dulles, John Foster, 178, 179, 185, 210, 234
Dutch Reformed Church, 10; family roots in, 4, 7; in Middle East, 8, 20

E

Eden, Anthony, 113
Education, Egypt (see also "Egyp-

tian University" and "Students"): post World War II, 122-126, 231; pre-World War II, 54, 64, 84-92, 107, 122

Egypt, see Chapters 4, 5, 6, 7, 9, 10, 11 (see also "AUC", "al-Azhar", "Cairo", "Communism", "Copts", "Education", "Egyptian Revolution", "Faruq", "Great Britain", "High Dam", "Intelligence", "Italians", "Israel", "Land reform", "Muslim Brotherhood", "Nasser", "Nasser's Aides", "Nasser's foreign policy", Nasser's Vice Presidents", "PL-480", "Political parties", "Political situation", "Political stability", "Radio", "Social reform", "Soviet Union", "Treaty of 1936", "UAR", "US-Egyptian relations", "Yemen War", "Youth organizations")

"Egypt in search of political community", 65

Egyptian Revolution, 100 (see Chapter 7): land reform, 141-42; social change, 137, 138, 141; social reform, 129-131; US role in, 136, 143

Egyptian Society for Social Work, 130

Egyptian University, The, 49, 50, 54, 74, 91, 105, 117, 125 (see also "Education, Egypt" and "Students")

Ethiopia: crisis of 1936, 63; & Egypt, 100, 101

"Evacuation Before Negotiation", 110

"Evacuation with blood", 104

Evacuation Day incident, 110-111

Everton, John: as non-career ambassador, 174

Ewart, Miss: AUC benefactor, 52-53

F

Faisal I, King of Iraq, 31, 33, 40, 43: death of, 34,42; leadership style, 41

The Faith of Islam (Sell), 13

Farida, Queen, 61, 66

Faruq, King, 49 (see also "Political situation in Egypt"): accession to Throne, 61-66; Badeau relations with, 117, 121; end of monarchy, 132, 134, 135; loss of popularity, 67, 100, 102

Fawzi, Mahmud: as Minister of Foreign Affairs, 183-84, 238-239

Filfil, Massacre at, 33, 35 (see also "Assyrians")

Food for Peace, 231

Ford Foundation, 17: & Near East Foundation, 159, 165

Ford, Robert: as Canadian Ambassador to Egypt, 189

Foreign Service of USA: effectiveness of non-career officers, 170-174

France: cultural influence, 86-91; French espionage trial 219-220; Abd al-Krim incident 108-110

French espionage trial, Case of the, 219-220

French Law School, Cairo, 125

Fuad, King, 49, 58, 60, 61

Fulbright, Senator William, 173

G

Galbraith, John Kenneth: as non-career ambassador, 174

Gardiner, Robert: & Near East Foundation, 167

General Electric Company: & Schenectady, NY, 4, 5, 6

George, Senator Walter, 196

Georgetown University: Badeau professor at, 246
German Officers' Club, Libya, 97, 98
German Reformed Church: in Middle East, 7, 8, 20
Gezira Sporting Club: Faruq at, 120
Ghana: & Near East Foundation, 166-168
al-Ghazali: Islamic philosopher, 45, 46
Ghazi I, King, 33, 41
Ghorbal, Shafiq: & Egyptian radio, 89, 90
Gianiclis: & AUC, 50, 117
Gibb, Sir Hamilton: & Arab Academy, 88
Great Britain: & Egypt, 60-66, 99-104, 110-113; in Egypt under Nasser, 110-113; & Iraq, 17-19, 21, 31, 32, 40, 41, 44; Yemen War, 201-203
Greece: & Near East Foundation, 148, 150, 160
Green Shirts, 69, 71
Griffis, Stanton: as ambassador to Egypt, 116, 117
Gross, Ernest: & French espionage trial, 220
Gruening, Senator Clark, 198

H

Haikal, Muhammad Hasanayn: 212, 236, 237: *Philosophy of the Revolution,* 205, 238
Hanim, Lady Surma, 30 (see also "Assyrians")
Harding, President Warren, 62
Hare, Ambassador Raymond A., 170, 172: negotiations with Nasser, 179
Hart, Ambassador Parker T., 208: & Yemen War, 213
Hawk missile sale, 243, 244: informing Nasser of, 176, 177, 235
al-Haydari, Daud: in Iraqi cabinet, 39
High Dam, 177, 178, 232-233, 234, 245
Hitti, Philip, 217
Hog Island freighters, 13, 14
Howard, Worth, 177, 178
Howell, J. Morton: as first US Minister to Egypt, 62-64
Hulugu: as Mongol invader, 77
Hume, David, 13
Humphrey, Senator Hubert, 196
Husayn, Ahmad: as Minister for Social Affairs, 53, 130
Husayn, Kamal al-Din: as Minister of Education, 231
Husayn, Taha, 53, 85, 87, 89, 92: as Minister of Education, 86
Husayni, Fuad: as AUC student, 117
Hussein, King, 41

I

Ibn Battuta, 251
Ibn Sina, 89
Ignatius, Mar (Saint): as Patriarch of Antioch, 27-28
Ikhwan, 131 (see also "Muslim Brotherhood")
Intelligence, Egyptian, 6, 218, 221-222
Iran, 97 (see also "Shah of Iran"): & Near East Foundation, 148, 157, 158, 159, 165, 166; political situation in, 153-156; & Yemen War, 204

Islam, 60, 80-83, 84, 250, 256 (see also "Missionary scholars", "Muslim Brotherhood"): Badeau studies of, 12, 13, 20, 45-46; charity in, 128; & Christianity, 14, 25, 26, 255; history, 78, 79; resurgence of, 254, 257

Islam: Belief and Institutions, footnote, 20

Iraq, (see Chapters 2 and 3 and also see "Baghdad", "Faisal, King", "Mosul"): Badeau travels in, 33, 39, 43; Kuwait affair, 205-206; nationalism, 24, 25; religious minorities, 32

Israel: Hawk missile sale, 176; PL-480, 192; ramifications of founding of, 112-113, 258-259; & US-Egyptian relations, 179, 243

Issawi, Charles, 249

Istiqlal: Egyptian political party, 65, 105

Italians in Egypt: Egyptian attitude toward, 71

Italy, 100, 220

J

Jacobite Church, see "Syrian Orthodox Church"

Jeffery, Arthur: as Islamicist, 71-73, 203, 247, 248

Jerusalem: in 1934, 43-44

Johnson, President Lyndon: interest in Middle East, 244; & PL-480, 242

Jones, Stanley, 6

Jordan, 43: & Near East Foundation, 157, 164

Journal of the Royal Asiatic Society, 35

K

"kalaks" (rafts), 23-24

Kamil, Mustafa: as Egyptian Ambassador to US, 179

Katabasis, 10

Kennedy, President John F. (see also Chapter 9): Badeau conversations with, 173-175; personal diplomacy with Nasser, 175-177, 210

Khalfallah, Mohammad: as Dean at University at Alexandria, 89-90

Khruschev, Premier Nikita: at opening of High Dam, 232-233

Kilearn, Lord, see "Lampson, Miles"

Komer, Robert: in Kennedy administration, 185, 227

Korea: & Near East Foundation, 166

Kurdistan: 18, 34, 36, 37

Kurds, (see also "Cumberland, Roger"): in Mosul, 21; political aspiration of, 25, 31, 32, 35, 36, 37

Kuwait: Iraqi threat to, 205-206

L

Lammens, Henri: as Islamicist, 20

Lampson, Sir Miles: as British ambassador to Egypt, 102

Land reform, Egypt, 140-141

Landis, James M.: at Harvard Law School, 62

Lawrence, T. E., 31

League of Nations: & Egypt, 104; & Iraq, 31, 32

Lindenhurst, NY: Badeau teacher in, 7, 9

Lloyd, Lord: as British High Commissioner in Egypt, 63, 102

M

MacDonald, Ramsay, 31
Madhkur, Ibrahim Bayyumi, 89: & education, 88
Mahir, Ahmad, 104: assassination of 110, 132
Mahir, Ali, 70
Making of the Modern Mind (Randall), 45
Maniel Village project, 130
Mansfield, Senator Mike, 196
al-Maraghi, Muhammad Mustafa: as Rector of al-Azhar, 65, 70
"Mardinli" Christians: in Mosul, 20, 22, 24, 25, 26
Marei, Sayyid: as Minister of Agriculture, 231
Middlebush, N.J.: family roots in, 3,7
Middle East: changing role of US institutions, 253, 254; general view of changes in, 257-259
Middle East studies: academic tradition of, 60, 248-252, 256-257
Miniclier, Louis: in ICA, 162
al-Misri, Aziz Ali: as Chief of Staff, 99
Missionary institutions, see "Congregational Church", "Dutch Reformed Church", "German Reformed Church", "Presbyterian Church", "Reformed Church in America", "United Mission in Mesopotamia"
Missionary movement, 5, 6, 14, 90: changes in, 251-256; in Middle East, 7, 8, 19, 20, 126
Missionary scholars, 256 (see also "Adams", "Calverly", "Cantine", "Carpenter", "Jeffrey", "Sell", "Van Dyke", "Zwemer"
Moline, Edwin G.: in AID, 193

Morocco-Algeria Border War, 222
Mosque of Seth riots, 25, 26
Mosul, 18-37: Badeau arrival in, 16, 17; minority inhabitants of, see "Assyrians", "Kurds", "Mardinli Christians", "Shammar bedoin", "Yazidis"
Mott, John R., 6
Muhyi al-Din, Zakaria, 142, 227, 239: Vice-President, 218-223
Muslim Brotherhood: 70, 112, 116, 257: Israel, 113, & labor unrest, 140; & "Black Saturday", 133; & social reform, 131

N

Naguib, Muhammad, 136, 142: contrast with Nasser, 143, 144
Nahhas, Mustafa, 134: as Prime Minister, 69, 100, 103; & Wafd, 68, 101
Nasser, Gamal Abd al, 6, 70, 88, 137, 142, 143 (see Chapters 9, 10, 11): Arabism of, 113, 114; & Communism, 71, 192, 208; contrast with Naguib, 143, 144; negotiating style, 214, 215; *Philosophy of the Revolution,* 204, 205, 238; position in Arab world, 180; pragmatism of, 204, 206, 240
Nasser-Badeau relationship: frequency of interviews, 216, 218; language used, 217; nature of, 233-234; style of, 235
Nasser's aides, see "Sabry, Ali", "Sabry, Zulficar", "Sharaf, Sami"
Nasser's foreign policy, 240-242 (see also Chapters 10 & 11, "Nasser", "Yemen"): "pendular oscillation", 245; "three circles of Egyp-

tian influence", 204, 205; "wahdat al-amal" (unity of work), 244; "wahdat-al-hadaf" (unity of goals), 206-207, 243

Nasser's Vice Presidents, 718-725 (see also "Amr", "Muhyi al-Din", "al-Sadat")

"Nasserism", 239

The Natural History of Religion (Hume), 13

Near East Christian Council: 1934 Conference, 42

Near East Foundation (NEF), see Chapter 8: country programs in Afghanistan 160-163; Cyprus 166, Ghana 166-168, Greece 148, 150, 160, Iran 157-159, 165, 166, Jordan 157, 164, Korea 166, Syria, 157, 164; & ICA, 160-163; philosophy of technical assistance 157-164; & Point Four, 157-59, 165; recruitment 148-149, 160, 167-168; relations with host governments 149, 159, 162

Near East Relief, 147

Nestorians, 22, 30 (see also "Assyrians", "Mar Shimun")

New Brunswick, NJ: Badeau childhood 3,4,7

New Brunswick Theological Seminary: Badeau student at, 7, 13; curriculum 8-10, 12

Nicolson, Harold: on diplomacy, 181

Nuqrashi Pasha: & AUC-Israel affair, 115

O

Obeid, Makram: as Copt in Wafd, 131, 139

Office of War Information (OWI): Badeau in, 94-97

Officers Club movement, 136, 137, 138, 143 (see Chapter 7)

Order of the Nile: Badeau recipient of, 120, 145; Watson recipient of, 120

Ottoman Empire, 258

P

Palace incident of 1942, 100-103

Palestine, (see also "Israel"): Palestine question, 70, 112, 128, 227; students at AUC, 54, 58, 113, 117

Palmerston, Lord, 257

Patriarch of Antioch, see "Ignatius, Mar"

Pensions: in Egypt, 129-130

People's Republic of China: Ali Sabry's interest in, 226

"period of strained relations": 1964-1967, 239-245

Perkins, Dexter, 169, 170

Personal diplomacy, see "Kennedy": "verbal letter", 175

Phelps-Stokes Foundation: & Near East Foundation, 167

Philosophy of the Revolution, 205: authorship of, 204, 238

PL-480, 179, 207, 208: diplomatic consequences of, 241, 242, 243; program in Egypt, 192-193

Plato, 47

Point Four, 108, 157, 158

Political parties, Egyptian, see "Destouris", "Istiqlal", "Saadists", "Wafd"

Political situation in Egypt: see Chapters 7 & 11 (also see "Political parties", "Political stability"): "Black Saturday", 132-134; in the Monarchy, 58, 60-62, 64-71; post

WW II period, 104-107, 110-114, 122; WW II, 99-102, 103
Political stability, tradition of in Egypt, 135, 141, 142, 184
Presbyterian Church: in Middle East, 7, 8, 20
"Professor Badeau's Diplomatic Seminar", 189 (see also "Ambassadorship")
Propaganda: Egyptian, 229, 230; US, 95-97
"Putting differences in the icebox", 179, 200, 243

Q

Qabbani, Ismail: as educator, 90, 138
Qaisuni, Abd al-Munim: as Minister of Economics, 192, 197, 230, 231
Qasim, Abd al-Karim: & Iraq-Kuwait affair, 205, 206

R

Radio, Egyptian, 89, 90, 92: propaganda, 229, 230
Randall, John: at Columbia, 45-47
Reformed Church in America, 13
Reinhardt, Ambassador Frederick, 76, 177, 179
Reischauer, Edwin O.: as non-career ambassador, 174
The Republic (Plato), 47
Riad, Mahmud: as Foreign Minister, 128
al-Rifai, Samir: of Jordan, 43
al-Rihani, Najib: Lebanese playwright, 57
Rockefeller, John D. Jr., 50

Rostow, Walter, 157
Rusk, Dean, 170, 171, 173, 244

S

Saadists, 65, 105
Sabry, Ali, 195: Nasser aide, 209, 225, 226, 227
Sabry, Zulficar: Nasser aide, 225, 227, 228, 243
al-Sadat, Anwar, 142, 227: as Vice-President, 223-224
Safran, Nadav: "Egypt in search of political community", 65
Sallal, Abdullah: of Yemen, 209, 215
Salzburg American Seminar, 169, 170
Saud bin Abd al-Aziz, King, 200, 213
Saudi Arabia, 200 (see Chapter 10)
"Sawt al-Umma al-Arabiyya" (Voice of the Arab Nation): Egyptian radio, 229, 230
al-Sayyid, Lutfi: & AUC, 53
Schacht, Joseph, 60, 250, 251
Schenectady, NY, 26: Union College, 3, 4, 5, 6, 7; wife's home, 6, 8
Second Reformed Church, Schenectady, 9
Seelye, Talcott: Yemen War negotiations, 211, 213, 214
Sell, Edward, 13, 14
Serag el-Din, Fuad: & "Black Saturday", 134; & Wafd, 102, 135
Shah of Iran, 152-156, 204
Shammar Bedouin, 23
Sharaf, Sami: Nasser aide, 199, 229
Sharawi, Huda: Egyptian feminist, 128
Shaykh Abi, Shrine of, 29-30

Shimun, Mar (Saint Simon), 30, 32, 34 (see also "Assyrians")
Sidqi Pasha: as Prime Minister, 58, 110
Smith, Mr.: family friend, 4
Social reform under Nasser, 131: Land reform, 140-141; Maniel Village, 130; pensions, 129-30
Soviet Union: & Egypt, 192, 201, 254; & Yemen War, 200, 204, 209
Spenser, Lyle: & AUC, 59
Standard Grammar (Wright), 20
Stark, Freya, 19
Steinmetz, Charles P., 5
Strong, Robert, Ambassador, 36, 185
Student Volunteer Movement, 6
Students, in Egypt (see also "American University in Cairo"): Evacuation Day, 110, 111; unrest of, 104, 105, 106, 117
Suez Canal, 53, 66, 177, 223, 234, 237
Syria, 32, 242: & Near East Foundation, 157, 164, 165; & UAR breakup, 182-185, 206, 207, 210
Syrian Protestant College, 7
Syrian Orthodox Church, 27-28

T

Talbot, Phillips, 185
Technical assistance, 163 (see also "Ford Foundation", "ICA", "Near East Foundation"): origin of, 147
Thabet, Karim: & Faruq, 67
Thomson, James C., Jr., 170
"three circles of Egyptian influence,", 204-205

Treaty of 1936, 68, 100, 104, 107, 114, 122
Truman, President Harry S., 114, 115, 127, 147
Tuck, Ambassador Pinkney, 114
Turkey, 95: & Egypt, 82, 83, 86; & Iraq, 21, 22, 24, 36, 37

U

Union College, 26: Badeau engineering student at, 3-8
Union Theological Seminary: Badeau studies at, 44-47, 94
United Arab Republic: breakup of, 180-184, 206, 210
United Mission to Mesopotamia, 19, 20
United Nations: Egypt, 104; Israel, 115; Yemen War, 211, 212, 213
University of Alexandria, 89
Urabi Pasha incident, 101
Urumiyeh, Lake, 19
US-Egyptian relations, see "Congress", "Hawk missile sale", "High Dam", "Howell", "Israel", "Kennedy", "Nasser's foreign policy", "Palestine", "PL-480", "Suez Canal", "Truman", "Johnson", "Wheelus Air Base": anti-Americanism, 146, 227; "deep freeze period", 1957-58, 177-79; Egyptian Revolution, 136, 143; "mutuality of interests", 191-192; "period of strained relations" 1964-67, 239, 245; "putting differences in the icebox", 179, 200, 243; Yemen War, 201, 203, 207, 208, 210-215
USSR, see "Soviet Union"

V

Van Dyke, Cornelius, 7
"Verbal letter": in Kennedy personal diplomacy, 175

W

Wafd, 103, 105, 127: & Blue Shirts, 69; in pre-WW II period, 50, 53, 61, 65, 70; & social service, 131; & Throne, 67, 101, 102
"wahdat al-amal" (unity of work), see "Nasser's Foreign Policy"
"wahdat al-hadaf" (unity of goals), see "Nasser's Foreign Policy"
Warne, William: in Iran, 166
Watson, Charles, 15, 42, 44, 48-53, 59, 86, 93, 102, 103, 106, 107, 120 (see also "American University in Cairo")
Well Zam Zam, 30
Wheelus Air Base: & Nasser, 235
Willoughby, James: as missionary, 19
Women, 17, 19, 78, 85, 86, 128; services for, 131
Women and the New East (Woodsmall), 17
Woodsmall, Ruth, 17
Wright, William, 20

X

Xenophon, 10

Y

Yazidis, 22 (see also "Mosul"): persecution of, 24; religion, 23, 24, 29, 30
Yemen, see "Yemen War": & UAR, 207
Yemen War, see Chapter 10: British policy, 201-203; & Saudi Arabia, 200, 208, 211, 212, 213; UN role, 211-213; US negotiations in, 208, 210-215; US views of, 201, 203, 207, 208, 210
YMCA, 5, 6, 17
Young Men of Muhammad, 69
Youth, (see also "Students"): Badeau interest in, 40, 44; organizations, 5, 6, 17, 69, 71
Youth Organizations in Egypt: Blue Shirts, 69, 71; Boy Scouts, 69; Green Shirts, 69, 71; Young Men of Muhammad, 69

Z

Zionism: & US policy, 115
Zwemer, Samuel M.: as missionary, 7, 14, 26